THE
EMPOWERMENT
MANUAL

THE EMPOWERMENT MANUAL

THE EMPOWERMENT MANUAL

ISBN: 978-0-9961389-1-8

The authors of this book do not dispense medical advice or prescribe the use of any technique as a form of treatment for physical or medical problems without the advice of a physician, either directly, or indirectly. If the reader chooses to use any of the information in this book, the author and publisher assume no responsibility for their actions.

Ordering information: Quantity Sales. Special discounts are available on quantity purchases by corporations, associations, and others. For details, contact the Special Sales Department at Visionary Insight Press.

Visionary Insight Press,
822 Westchester Place,
Charleston, IL 61920

Visionary Insight Press, the Visionary Insight Press logo and its individual parts are trademarks of Visionary Insight Press.

Compiled by: Lisa Hardwick
Editor-At-Large: Chelle Thompson

Back cover photo credit: Anthony Mendonca, Sara Rogers, Jase White, Dan Skaramuca – Contempo Studio, Shelly Rose Photography, Kaitlin Lampley, Duygu Ozen of Moments Photography Studio, Melissa Corter, Roxyanne Young San Diego Portrait Photographer www.roxyanneyoung. com, Matthew Davis, Best LA Headshots – Adam Southard, Susan Sabo Photography, Long Beach, California, The Photography Room, Annie Bee's Photography, Kelly Burgoyne Photography, www.kellyburgoyne.com, Kim Coffman Photography, Little Field Photography, Thomas Amador, Maggie Mayper – Magpie Photography, Patrick Jones Studios, Sydney, Chris Walsh, John Kelly Photography, Paula Moore, Shanna Paxton Photography, Kendal Vaughan, Nicole Ryan Photography, Aaron Collado, Prasad Naik, Nicholas Pappagallo Photography & Workshops, Tammy Tate, Shannon Ridge Photography.

Table of Contents

Foreword

by Lisa Hardwick

These inspirational teachers come from various areas of the globe, therefore, you may see some words spelled in their own language — such as *realise* and realize, *colour* and color, *learnt* and learned, or *organise* and organize — and the publisher, Visionary Insight Press, chose to honor each individual's language spelling etiquette.

The publisher not only respected the author's spelling preferences, they honored so much more … for this book was designed to have an abundance of diversity to appeal and assist a multitude of views, belief systems and experiences, as they relate to the topic. My suggestion is to take what feels good to you and lovingly release what may not.

Would you like to know why some of the chapters might resonate differently to you? Allow me to share — because it is vitally important! Are you ready? Okay!

The *reason* is because what feels good to *you* was written by one of the members of *your* tribe … and you've been searching for each other. It's incredible when you find one of your own. Feel free to reach out and connect with your newly-found friend. You will find their contact information at the end of their biography and I know they will be delighted to hear from you!

One common denominator the chapters *do* have is sharing kind, loving, and heart-centered stories, presentations and mini workshops of Empowerment with the intention to assist you and/or your clients.

- Everyone loving everyone.
- Everyone putting out their energy so their "tribe" may find them.
- Everyone accepting and honoring another person's path … even though it may, indeed, be quite inconsistent with their own.

Some of the authors share their own uniquely-created Empowerment workshops they use to facilitate their own retreats and/or events. Other authors share personal stories of Empowerment with strategies to inspire you. I'm certain, without a doubt, your life will be catapulted to the next level toward your own Empowerment when you take the time to find the chapters that best resonate with you ... for when you do, you will know you have been divinely connected to one of your own.

~ Lisa Hardwick
www.lisahardwick.com

Vandana Mendonca

VANDANA MENDONCA is a highly skilled and intuitive Holistic Wellness Specialist and Trainer. She is a firm believer in the body's inherent ability to heal itself. Her unique approach addresses the *Whole: Mind, Body & Spirit,* and the connection that influences the condition. Her role in this process is one of Therapist, Mentor and Wellness Coach. She is passionate about a practical application of spirituality in everyday life.

Her holistic journey began with hands-on healing and now combines with energy healing therapies under the guidance of the Angelic realm. Her forté is connecting with Angels.

Vandana.mendonca@yahoo.com,
www.facebook.com/Vandanahealthnharmony

Potential Me

With every role or title we attain in our lifetime, we take on the responsibility that comes along with it. Parents feel responsible and assume that their actions are for the wellbeing of their child. Rightly so, but how does the child feel about it?

Teachers take on the role of imparting knowledge, the way they feel is best, to guide and educate students. But does this singular style of imparting knowledge get the best out of, or appeal to, the individuality of each and every student?

Doctors with their knowledge diagnose and offer a prognosis of how patients must carry out the healing journey. Is the prognosis merely control of symptoms or does it address the root cause of the imbalance in each patient? Does this prescribed course of action leave room for patients to be influential in their own healing process?

The financial consultant, physical trainer, nutritionist, therapist, spouse or partner all have a role in our lives that may or may not influence us in the best possible manner. Yes, expertise in a particular profession gives one the benefit of greater knowledge within that field, but does that mean the *I know more than you do* formula works best all of the time? Is it possible that our body, mind, and soul really know what is or what is not good for us and, therefore, the course of action best suited to tap into the *power* within ourselves?

Are we so conditioned to giving our power away from the time of our birth until our passing? The newborn cries to be fed at odd times, but we take it upon ourselves to train or condition the baby to set a pattern of day and night, that is convenient for us as parents or caregivers, in the belief that structure is an essential part of welfare. Of course structure has its place and our physical form essentially needs the structure so that we can feel a tangible connection to our existence. Perhaps so, but does our soul or inner spirit long for freedom or the opportunity to drift away and explore an existence without boundaries? Yet, can we have one without the other?

The balance between structure and inner-freedom provides a pathway to enjoy harmony of both the physical and the spiritual energy within, thereby eliminating the otherwise stifling influence of structure alone. A good example would be indulging in a much-treasured hobby where the needs of the inner spirit are fulfilled within the structure of doing what we love. When we *feed our soul*, our physical existence revels in a greater sense of purpose, accomplishment and fulfillment.

Looking back on my life I would have to admit that I did not know the meaning, and therefore, realize the value of the words *feed your soul*. I happily carried out my role as a daughter, wife and mother. Enriching as it was I could feel an inexplicable void in my life. In that state of blissful ignorance I immersed myself even deeper in these familiar roles. However, my soul fought for my attention in a different manner. At the age of 29, I developed an autoimmune condition that took me by surprise and would set me on a completely different path in my life's journey. I say it took me by surprise because I had always looked after my body with a healthy lifestyle. The next five years were spent on doctors and prescribed medication that did very little to improve my general condition. Physically I felt weak, but something deep inside kept telling me that I had to find the cure naturally. I needed a new set of answers to the many questions about my health and the ways of self-healing. I needed a new thought process and a new guide.

It is written "*Seek and Ye Shall Find,*" so I asked and the Universe opened various doors for me. I plunged into my physical healing journey with self-help books and guidance from various key people. I sought the expertise of a nutritionist, a kinesiologist, and most importantly as it would turn out, a homeopath. Well, not really a homeopath per se, but a physician with an integrated holistic approach. While each one guided me to the best of their ability, and with gratitude to them all, I owe my true healing to my India-based physician, Dr. V. Pathak. While he treated me on a physical level in his own unique way, he made me realize just how much my soul needed attention.

He said to me, and I quote "*You have a lot of positive energy within you. If you only direct that energy inward, you will do yourself more harm than good. As you direct that energy to heal and empower others, you will heal too.*" His words were quite a revelation for me and in total contrast to the messages I had been receiving from other doctors who kept insisting that I had to live with this autoimmune condition, with a dependency on medication, for the rest of my life. Once again, in total contrast to how I felt previously, weak and powerless, I now felt strong, empowered, in charge of my own life and of my own healing process. This was the defining moment which sowed the seeds of thought within me that I could empower others to have faith in their own strength of *mind, body, and spirit*. But first I had to take charge of my own situation and so I embarked on the journey of becoming a Holistic Therapist.

The last 10 years have been an extremely gratifying journey of healing myself and contributing to the healing process in others. Holism is an ongoing journey. Today I acknowledge and work with the *many layers of the self; mind, body, spirit, emotions, the sub-conscious and the ego/personality,* the part that best expresses us. We are blessed with this inherent ability to empower ourselves when we acknowledge the layers we are made up of, both individually and collectively, as a complete energy system unique to each one of us. When energy flows smoothly through these layers, we are empowered and in harmony with the universe.

As an individual I have made *feed my soul* my daily mantra to keep me empowered and in balance in all spheres of my life. It could be a simple yoga class, an extended day of meditation or perhaps sharing my passion through the written word.

As parents, my husband and I have encouraged our children to negotiate and not feel coerced into making a decision. We believe that negotiation is a way for them to trust their inner spirit and to perceive value on more than one level, thus to feel empowered with the pleasurable responsibility and the accountability of their own choices.

As a Holistic Therapist my personal goal is to help and empower my clients with tools that they identify with and can implement for themselves easily enough. Yes, it is so much easier to simply let someone else take charge and absorb the responsibility of projecting healing, but I want them to have faith in their inherent ability to heal on all levels and to be influential in their healing process. I believe it is also important to plant the seed of thought that could serve as an inspiration, just as much as it did for me when I needed it most.

It is my great pleasure to share with you one of the many self-empowering exercises I use in my practice:

Connecting With Your Inner Spirit

☙ **Close your eyes, inhale deeply and exhale slowly.**
- It is time to perceive yourself as pure energy. Just for now, in your mind, release yourself from all roles and attachments one by one.
- Tell yourself, *"I am not a spouse, parent, child or sibling, employee or employer. I detach from all physical expectations and obligations at this moment in time. I am pure energy."*

☙ **Take a few minutes to feel your body de-link from these attachments.**

☙ **You may perhaps perceive your energy as a light, a color or shape, even a sound.**

- Feel yourself floating and drifting freely. As you start to enjoy this sense of freedom, take a moment to ask your energy:
  - *What are you in pursuit of?*
  - *What are you seeking?*

- Do you hear, feel, sense or visualize a response being given to you?
  - This is your inner spirit or higher-self communicating with you.
  - If you need more answers, ask more questions.

- This connection will help you appreciate the need to walk in-synch with your inner spirit.

- See, sense or feel your inner spirit glow brightly with this acknowledgement.

- Holding the essence of your inner spirit, gently reconnect with your physical self.

- Slowly, in your mind's eye, recreate the space where you began this exercise.

- Take a deep, slow breath and gently open your eyes.

- Go boldly where you have not gone before. Fulfill your inner spirit.

NOTE: Most of our needs, desires and challenges spring from our earthly roles and titles. At times we need to detach from these roles to connect with our inner spirit. Do not feel discouraged if you are unable to detach initially. It will get easier with practise. This exercise is just a starting point to help us take small steps toward living an everyday structured existence in harmony with our inner spirit. In time, the essence of your inner spirit exudes in everything you do.

I have learned that to fulfill my inner spirit I do not have to experience a profound message or have an epiphany of epic proportions. Nor do I have to take on a planet-saving crusade. It could well be, but not limited to, the need to laugh some more, sing, dance or give hugs. Small steps lead to new beginnings and every day offers a new beginning.

Bruce Lee, the founder of Jeet Kune Do, famously repeated J.W. von Goethe's words, *"Knowing is not enough, we must apply. Willing is not enough, we must do!"* My journey has truly helped me discover the essence of these words.

Now that you know what, it is time to identify and commit to doing. Here are a few suggestions that have been useful to me on my journey:

🌜 **Make a list of what *feeds your soul*.**
Commit a time to doing so, whether it is daily, weekly, monthly or even annually.
- *e.g. If giving back to the community or volunteering is your dream, but your full-time job, family, or financial limitations seem like a deterrent, dedicate a day or week doing some volunteer work during your vacation. You could also pray and send positive energy to the various institutions that care for the under-privileged. Positive intentions filled with love go a long, long way.*

🌜 **Identify your talent and strengths.**
Do not be afraid to do so. You will be pleasantly surprised to know how they support your inner spirit's desire. Once you identify them, build on them. Find little ways to use your talents in your everyday life.
- *e.g. If art feeds your soul, keep a sketch book handy. Doodle, draw, paint your thoughts. Don't just write, sketch little love notes for those close to you.*

🌜 **Ground and center yourself in the present moment, giving gratitude every day.**
- *e.g. All it takes is a few minutes every day to appreciate yourself and to give gratitude through prayer, meditation or simple intention. This act of love brings with it a tremendous power that will nurture your talents and inner desires.*

🌜 **Keep a journal to help you identify progress and just how much of a difference it has made in your life. Be honest with yourself.**
I have to admit that getting to where I am now hasn't been easy. Truth be told, it hardly ever is. Life is filled with challenges enough without health being added to this list. Yet through it all, I rediscovered myself. I found what made me strong and I realized firsthand that the human spirit is far stronger than we can ever imagine. I know now, that when we are connected with our inner spirit we are open and receptive to the messages, and the universe is ever giving.

As I continue to enjoy the realization of my growing potential I know I am not alone in this. Neither are you, unless you choose to be.

With love and gratitude to all.

"Live without living, die without dying,

Nothing changing, not even trying.

Untapped potential, don't know how,

Power within, opportunity now.

Inner Spirit, introspection,

Feed my Soul, resurrection."

~ AA MENDONCA

To the incredible amalgamation of the physical power and the inner spirit existing within all creation. To mum, my angel of everlasting love, joy and strength. My soul-mate Tony, who inspires and supports my dreams. My lovely sons and best friends, Shiva and Arya; free-spirited and individual.

Thank you to all the beautiful souls who have honoured and nurtured my inner spirit. Love and gratitude to my dear soul friend Tonia Browne for believing in me. Thank you Lisa Hardwick and VIP for making me a part of this wonderful family. To my meditation mentor Edward Mendonca, Dr. Pathak, my teachers, guides and friends on my journey of self-discovery.

For my late father, thank you, Dad, for instilling in me honour and integrity. Mum, for your unconditional love. My protective brother, and my loving sister who along with their families complete my life.

~ Vandana Mendonca

Meg Davies

MEG DAVIES is an author, workshop teacher, coach, and founder of Demanding Joy. Her true passion is helping others to demand their own joy in order to live happier, healthier, more successful lives.

She is also passionate about her husband, their two beautiful, brilliant children, and their silly little bulldog. Meg lives in a noisy, crazy, funny, love-filled old house in Omaha, Nebraska.

meg@demandingjoy.com
www.demandingjoy.com

My Inner Perfectionist Tried to Kill Me

I had a really nice life. I was the classic over-achiever with a wonderful, loving husband, two beautiful, healthy children, a successful career, and a lovely home filled with lovely things. I was active in the community, well-networked, and upwardly mobile. I had done all the things I was supposed to do to have the perfect life. So I couldn't figure out why I felt so overwhelmed, so exhausted, so depleted, and so depressed.

Behind the facade of our happy upper-middle class life, I was falling apart. I was very overweight and struggling with what I now know were severe endocrine and metabolic imbalances. I had been on one diet or another my entire adult life — some of them extreme and even dangerous, but nothing worked. My weight was out of my control. I was bone tired and in pain most of the time. And it was getting worse. My back hurt, my feet hurt, my knees hurt. I got migraines. Worst of all was the fatigue. I could sleep ten hours at a time and still wake up exhausted. It was all I could do just to drag my ass through each day in a heavy grey fog. I had maxed out my antidepressant dosage and that didn't seem to help either.

I went to work each day on auto pilot. Despite my lovely title and salary, I didn't feel any passion, or any emotion whatsoever, for the work I did. I was up to my eyeballs in bureaucracy. I felt voiceless and ineffective, but I had obligations and people to feed, so I wasn't going to quit, right?

To make matters even worse, I never said 'no' to anything. I was the queen of over-commitment. I joined non-profit boards, school committees, and extra projects whenever anyone asked me to. I knew I didn't have the time or the energy, or even the interest to do most of these things, but they asked me, so I said 'yes'. I could just juggle faster. It didn't occur to me that I was over-giving because I didn't believe that I deserved to give myself a break. I thought that sacrificing my time and energy was just something I was supposed to do.

I was working impossibly hard to manage all of the demands on me. I was so deep into a state of resentment and burnout that I wanted desperately to just go to bed and stay there. Indefinitely. But there was far too much to do. I actually fantasized about getting a bad case of the flu, because then I would have the justification to stay home by myself and rest for a day or two. I equated illness with vacation. How messed up is that?

I expected that I should be the perfect wife, the perfect mom, the perfect employee, the perfect woman, but I knew that I was failing at all of it. And as my health declined, I believed that my multitudinous inadequacies were literally going to kill me — and I knew that it was all my own stupid, fat fault.

And then, a seed of hope was planted. My company sent me to a leadership seminar. Rather than the management training I expected, the seminar turned out to be a women's circle group, run by a brilliant woman who has been both a friend and mentor to me. The big turning point for me was a simple journal exercise. We were instructed to write the mean things we think about ourselves. Easy peasy. We all went to a quiet spot to write "I'm fat. I'm dumb. I'm not good enough," etc. No big surprises — we all know what we don't like about ourselves. But then we were put into pairs and instructed to say to another person's face the mean things that we said to ourselves. "YOU are fat. YOU are dumb. YOU are not good enough." It was agony. It felt completely awful to treat someone else the way I treated myself. Light bulb moment. I had never slowed down enough to examine my own thoughts and I was really shocked to learn what a mean and nasty place my head was. Self-defeating thoughts were such an ingrained habit for me that I wasn't consciously aware of them. I realized that I was treating myself with the kind of disrespect and abusiveness that I would never dream of showing anyone else. Discovering my inner mean girl was so startling to me that I committed to finding a way to shut her up. I learned that I needed to demand joy ... from myself.

From that moment forward, I spent a lot of time and energy tuning in to my own thoughts, and reframing them. I learned to compliment myself, to be grateful, and to cut myself some slack for being imperfect. In fact, I eliminated the word 'perfect' from my vocabulary altogether. I adopted the mantra "good enough is good enough." It was slow-going and frustrating, and for awhile, I thought that I was just hard-wired to be negative and mean to myself. But like anything, the more you practice, the better you get at something, and I slowly learned to treat myself as a friend. And just like that, my journey from self-hatred to self-nurturing had begun.

I started to do nice things for myself, like using fun colored pens, listening to music, and picking fresh flowers. I started keeping a gratitude journal to remind myself of my good fortune, rather than dwelling on the negative. I looked in the mirror every morning and said to myself, "I love you and I am proud of you." After the first hundred times or so, that stopped feeling weird and just felt great. I reconnected with friends, who reminded me of the vibrant, lovable person that I am. I purged commitments that I didn't value. My family noticed the changes in my demeanor and were extremely supportive. I learned that they were not demanding sacrifices from me at all — my sacrifices were self-imposed.

Changes I made in my thoughts led to changes in my words, which led to more changes in my behavior. I began to get regular massage and acupuncture treatments. I spent quite a bit of time with books by Louise Hay, Mike Dooley, Geneen Roth, Cheryl Richardson and others. I learned the perils of perfectionism and self-criticism. And sure enough, I got healthier.

The more I felt worthy of help, the more help I got, and the happier and healthier I became. The upward spiral of my life, the "Meg Renaissance," had begun. I found that the more positive changes I made, the better I felt and the more I wanted for myself. I had laid the groundwork for change, and now I wanted to go big. Over the next two years, because I learned to love myself, I was able to lose more than 100 pounds and make major strides in cleaning up my diet and my health. I changed my physical appearance too. I got my teeth straightened and grew out my wild curly hair. I took a meditation class. I took a tap dancing class. I started to smile again. I had actually forgotten how.

And then came the Big Kahuna of changes. After earning an MBA and spending fifteen years in the financial services industry, I mustered up the courage to ask for a severance package and quit my stable, high-paying job to start my own business — the business of joy. I have finally picked a major and am following my dreams. I am present and so much more deeply connected with my friends and family. And I am happier and healthier than I have ever been. I know life probably still has some curveballs in store for me, but now I am confident in my ability to overcome them and thrive.

 Through my own journey and training, I have found a passion for helping others out of the darkness of perfectionism and self-criticism. Here are some of the basics that I teach my clients to help them to have their own personal renaissance:

1. Gratitude

The foundation for joy is gratitude—an extremely powerful tool for changing the way you think about yourself and about the world. What you spend your attention on will grow. Focusing your attention on what sucks will increase the suck. Spending a lot of time thinking about cellulite and poverty? You're just ordering up more cellulite and poverty. So let's flip it around. Rather than what you don't like, what do you want to create more of? What's good? Wherever you are right now, look around you. What are you grateful for in this moment? For example, are you in a place you like? Are you near someone you love? Did you have a good meal today? Can you see or hear something beautiful where you are right now? Changing your thought patterns from negative, complaining and lacking to thoughts of gratitude for your health, your loved ones, your home, your work, your nail polish, whatever—leads to higher levels of happiness, lower levels of stress and anxiety, and ultimately better health.

The more you practice gratitude, the more easily gratitude will come—just like strengthening a muscle. The more you do it, the better you will be at it. So once you recognize how fortunate you are, celebrate it! Toast to good things. Say "thank you"—a lot. Begin and end your day with deliberate thoughts of gratitude. As often as possible, say "yay!" and acknowledge your blessings. It feels so good!

2. Eliminate Complaints and Criticisms

Most of us have a really mean voice in our head. Really, really mean. How many times a day do you say to yourself, "I'm such an idiot." "Yeah, like I need more calories today." "That thing I just said? So stupid." "She's so much prettier than me." "Why do I have to be so fat?!" "Oh never mind, I'll probably just screw it up." Would you ever let someone else speak to you that way? It is so very important that you don't speak to yourself that way either. Your mean voice may or may not use words to beat you up, but it certainly knows how to kick you when you're down. You can't build an amazing life if you fundamentally believe that you don't deserve amazingness. So that mean voice in your head—time for him or her to shut up and go away.

Make time each day to be still and quiet. Observe your thoughts. Each time you hear an unkind thought, push it away by replacing it with a self-affirming thought. To do this, you will need to purposely and thoughtfully compliment yourself. A lot. At first, this will feel silly and cheesy—that's alright, it will get easier with practice. Start by speaking to yourself as you would to a small child. For example, "Look how beautiful you look today!" "I am so proud of you!" "You did a great job! I knew you would." "I love you so much."

Say it like you mean it. No sarcasm allowed. If you can't mean it just yet, at least really want to mean it. You deserve praise and you deserve to feel good. So keep up the compliments! The more you practice, the more authentic the words will feel.

3. Set Personal Boundaries

A huge part of loving yourself is setting clear boundaries. Little things matter. When something aggravates you, say so! In order to befriend yourself, it's important to find your voice. For example, that guy in your office who constantly clicks his pen — trade him for a non-clicking pen. That bra that always itches — get rid of it. Tired of being the go-to person for every project and favor? Try using the most empowering word in the English language … NO.

4. Ask For Help

There is no shame in asking for help when you need it, and there is no glory in going it alone. If you could ease your journey in any way by working with a doctor, a nutritionist, a therapist, a mechanic — any expert you may need, hire one. Love yourself enough to get whatever support you need. You deserve it.

5. Have Fun!

Life is all about the journey, so don't postpone your joy. Do something each day that has no other purpose than making you happy.

I know that my experience of being depleted in mind, body and spirit is not unique. Most of us have an inner mean voice that holds us back and beats us down. Learning to befriend yourself and turn love inward can radically change your life and make your life joyful and abundant, rather than a life to be endured. I hope you will join me and begin your "YOU Renaissance."

•

Dedicated with all my heart to the cast of characters at Wit's End.

I am so grateful to the many people who have been my teachers, mentors, and my own personal cheering section. In particular, I would like to thank Melissa Kopplin, Dr. Patricia Crane and Rick Nichols, Marian Andersen, Erin Olinger, and the bedrock of my life, Joel Davies

~ Meg Davies

Tonia Browne

TONIA BROWNE is an author, a presenter, a teacher and a coach. As a qualified teacher, Tonia has worked in the United Kingdom and internationally for over twenty years and was an Assistant Head for six. She is a strong advocate of inviting fun into our lives and encouraging people to see that there is MORE out there. Tonia is a Heal Your Life® Workshop Leader, Coach and Business Trainer.

She can be contacted at toniabrowne@hotmail.com, Time4T @ facebook.com/ Time4Tonia, toniabrowneblog.wordpress.com, and soon at toniabrowne.com

4 Steps to the Party

 *Participating in the Party of Life*

I had not really appreciated the need to have dialogues with the universe before. Then again, there was a lot I had not appreciated.

How did some people find life so easy? They seemed to find it easy to learn to read, write and remember things. My childhood was full of learning dramas. Adult life was not that easy either. How did people seem to be able to drive, find places, date people, socialise and put together flat-pack furniture?

It was obvious I needed more skills. Many people enter this world with a blue-print of what it is to be human. I appeared to be missing mine. So, towards midlife I accepted the quest to find it. The space I allowed myself in which to question had me in a party frock in 4 Steps!

I am no expert. This is simply my story. It is about how I decided to change my thoughts about myself and about my life, as well as how I organised and made sense of the wonderful information I found available. It is a thank you, an acknowledgement to those who have played a part in making my life so special and a play-it-forward if it can help you or a friend with this magnificent journey we call life.

Are you Participating in the Party of Life?

Do you ever feel:
- like everyone is at a party and you can't find your invite?
- you have been invited but you don't want to go?
- when you arrive at the party you don't belong?

Are you Participating in the Party of Life?

Do you want:
- a life that feels better?
- a chance to change direction and an easy system to support this?
- to feel more of the energy and excitement of life?
- to join the party of life?

Support is out there!
Once you get started it is child's play — hope to C U @ the party!

Throughout this chapter I write about the space for the child and the party of life. These are metaphors for playing with the energy of possibilities so life can help you feel better about yourself and give you more of what you want and need in a more conscious way. The concepts are not my ideas; much of the literature I have read and many of my course leaders have mentioned these in one form or another. I hope this simple, almost childlike approach will encourage you to have a go, to take that first step, if you have not done so already.

On the Landing

I had a lovely early childhood. My parents told me many stories about my energy, positivity and excitement for life. I laughed and loved to play. Yet all this changed in my primary school years.

I was educated in a school system that was very much about right and wrong answers and a fixed way of learning. I was often called a space cadet or given less intriguing labels by my teachers. They were worried for my future and about my ability to achieve. I felt different and a failure. I carried this view into my teenage and adult life. It affected how I responded to life and what I accepted of life. I was a lone ranger. I thought I enjoyed it and in some ways I did.

Yet, this viewpoint was also a driving force in my life. Having been told I was unlikely to get any type of qualification when I was younger meant I spent a lot of energy on attaining as many qualifications as I could later in life. It did not matter how many courses I took and how many passes I achieved, it was not enough. It did not quench my thirst for knowledge nor ease the feeling that I was still undeserving and underachieving. This was my choice and my decision. I played the role well.

I became a bit of a perfectionist and a control freak, setting high standards that I found hard to meet. I worked long hours, constantly trying to prove to myself and others that I could do it. If I could do it, I set the bar higher. If I could not, then it was further proof of my failings.

On the Path

Then one day I wondered if I were on the landing of life with steps before me that I was choosing not to take. Was it me that kept my life on the same plateau? Was *I* the problem and not an external force? This questioning opened up a space for change.

Why did I want to search for another way of thinking and another way of operating? Was it a learning difficulty that continued into adulthood? Was it old programming? Did I really come from another planet? Did I just know that life could be different?

I realised that these questions could be left unanswered. The reality is I was born and wanted the best human experience I could. The important question I needed to answer was what to do next. How could I stop myself sabotaging my own opportunities for happiness? Yes, the answer involved more research and study on my side but this time it felt different. It was not just a qualification to show others, it was a shift in how I felt about being me!

Seeing the Steps

With the high numbers of people experiencing low self-esteem and depression, partly due to a pressure to conform to stereotypes, we need the message that it is okay to be an individual to reach further than it already is. It is from this place of acceptance of self that shifts can happen. There are some great messages from people already, yet the increase in depression and suicide rates suggests however loud the messages are they are not reaching everyone's ears.

My journey has shown me that there is no right or wrong way to be you, only the one that works for you. It is not always easy to make changes. We do not always have the opportunity to make time to consider if our life is working for us. Yet, sometimes, all you need is an encouraging nudge or a little step!

Little Steps

I began to realise that my positive energy and love of play had got lost somewhere between my failure to meet the expectations of school and the need to achieve and survive in a world of my perceived deadlines and seriousness. Who was I trying to prove things to and who or what was I trying to avoid?

These realisations occurred as circumstances had my world of adulthood collide once more with the energy of young children and their play in action. I became a primary school teacher and started to teach early years. The children and I learnt together. We exchanged valuable lessons in order for each of us to grow. I gave them, amongst other things, the gift of reading and writing. They gave me the gift of awe and wonder and the value of play, which in turn awoke my inner child. They showed me that I had become too serious and that life could be more of a game than a course to be achieved. They took my hand and asked me to join them in their party; an invisible world of wonder, as real to them as the shoes on my feet. This coincided with me completing many helpful courses on self-development.

Reflecting on my journey, it is interesting to note, that both my career path and my personal quest to make sense of my life became intrinsically interlinked; another example of the synchronicity of life. Yet let's not get side tracked by my life. Let's get to the 4 Steps. Ready for a new high?

4 Steps

If things seem too complicated or serious with a wrong or right answer, I know people can often opt out in the fear that they might fail. So you can climb anyway you want, maybe with a jump, a hop or a skip up 4 Steps. If things go too fast or do not lead where you want to go, hop down, pause and when you are ready, start again.

With so much time with young children, I like things to be easy, fun and memorable. So here is an overview of the 4 Steps we will cover.

4 Steps to the Party: Participating in the Party of Life
Step 1: The Invitation: Don't miss it — Wish it!
Step 2: The Acceptance: Don't turn — Learn!
Step 3: The Party: Now here — Cheer!
Step 4: A Lifetime Membership: Don't just play — Stay!

✑ Step 1: The Invitation: Don't Miss It — Wish It!

Step 1 is the conscious decision to have change occur in your life and to ask for support for this to happen, knowing that it can.

How often have you heard the expression; 'If you don't ask, you don't get?' or, as I was to learn later, in the style of Abraham; 'Ask and it is Given.'

How much of our life is about conscious decisions? How conscious are we of our thought processes and patterns? This first step involves actively thinking about your thinking in order to realise what invitations you are presently sending out and what you are receiving or rejecting. Step 1 is being clear about your requests, whether they are specific, such as having a bigger car, or open ended such as having more happiness in your life.

We are constantly asking and confirming verbally and non-verbally. Yet, we are often not aware of what we are thinking, saying or asking. We are also not always aware whether our thoughts and language are upbeat and liberating or negative and limiting.

This step is about reflecting on your life experiences to see whether you are okay with where you are. If you want something different you can take action and ask, then take action again from the signs you receive. You do not need to understand how this works, but just be willing to trust that there is a force out there that needs a heads up from you to step in.

Depending who you study, the explanations vary. Gregg Braden, for example, writes about 'The Divine Matrix', whilst Jo Vitale and Dr. Len write about 'Zero Limits.' There seemed to be so many people out there discussing this concept that I decided it was worth a more conscious play. It seemed to me that we use this energy of intention every day anyway, it is just that we may not be conscious that we are doing so or know how it works. We may also not be aware of the advantage of being explicit with our requests. I had not been!

So, this is what I did. As I started to succeed more in my career I wondered why I still felt I operated differently from many of my peers and lacked their confidence. I had been fascinated for a long time about how we communicated in general, as well as what went on in people's minds. Many people I conversed with continued to confirm that there was a mismatch between how my thinking and communication channels worked and theirs. People seemed to talk so clearly in logical, sequential ways. My thoughts seemed to explode with interlinked essentials that meant I would sound in a hurry and all over the place when I tried to get a message across. I was also more interested in the world shown on people's faces than the world they shared through words. I knew these traits could be irritating and frustrating to my linear thinking colleagues. Hence, I wanted to learn more about how communications can be so different and I wanted to be with people who I understood and who understood me.

I had given out a request to the universe for change and understanding and was awaiting a sign. The reality was I had been given signs that could have started my journey of self-discovery much earlier had I been more aware and had I listened more carefully.

Indeed, looking back I remember a conversation with a hairdresser who talked about conjuring up a life you want to lead. Although her life seemed to be going from good to marvelous, I dismissed her sharing as something quite mad! A friend gave me an angel card and talked about how they could help the direction of your day. I remember trying hard not to snigger! I was loaned a book called 'You Can Heal Your Life' by Louise Hay and, at that time, I did not really understand a word of it, although I was fascinated by her life and what she had achieved.

Each sign that I had not consciously acknowledged and those that I had were building up a curiosity within me to learn, ask and question more. This willingness allowed the space within to release a need to control my life. I began to understand that I had only been seeing what I already saw and feeling and responding as I had done before. I decided to believe, like others before, that you *can* change your life. I was willing to think about my thought patterns and to acknowledge the signs. My life started to change.

I met people and read books that talked openly about different ways of thinking and different ways of operating. I learnt about therapies and research that were new to me and I was recommended books about an inner and outer world I had not known of before.

The idea of being conscious of the thoughts and messages in your head, and to live life in the question were common themes in those early days. I began to acknowledge that I had been communicating with the universe all along, but in a complaining and constricting way rather than in an expansive and positive one. Many people saw me as a Pollyanna yet alone in my thoughts I did not have her positivity. I had not appreciated how often I ran the 'I cannot' or the 'I do not fit in' programme. I became crystal clear on this first step and I tried hard to overwrite this thinking with more positive and encouraging thoughts.

It took some time for the momentum to get started yet when it did, it became easier to make positive thinking a more regular practice and to reflect more often on my requests to life. It was no longer necessary to miss opportunities; I could wish for them!

Steps to Entice the Invitation
Be willing to believe that your life can change and that you can support this change—anticipate it, imagine it, feel it
Think about your thinking—give yourself positive thoughts
Reflect on your life and become conscious of your asking—be clear

☙ Step 2: The Acceptance: Don't Turn — Learn!

Happy children at play can demonstrate creativity and human relationships at their best. They have sparkle, energy, excitement and laughter. As you watch them you are soon aware that the merging of reality and fantasy is so smooth and jointly collaborated that the vibe of empathy between the players is often pure perfection. Even the most skilled actors, improvising a scene, are hard fetched to match children at play. Give them party clothes and props and the whole school playtime becomes one incredible party. Most people are included, all they need to do is play too. A child can have such levels of euphoria alone. The same happy child can be seen communicating with empty spaces, commanding the creation of a responding invisible world, all so real to its creator.

There is a positive energy and a contagious excitement during such interactions. This is often missing from the life of an adult. It comes from a place when all is alright in the world; it's a dance, a flow—a magnificence. It is a circle of imagining, seeing, responding and evaluating. We call it play and many undervalue its worth by keeping it in the realm of children. Does it have to be?

How often do we block our own progress due to fear, not being aware or being too focused elsewhere? Step 2 is about saying *yes* to life and taking the opportunities that present themselves if they continue to support your vision of what you want. This step is about being in a state of acceptance and knowing, trusting that all is not a time-space linear outcome reality.

The universe only needs a small request from us for change and change it will. We can help it along by seeing and accepting the signs, and by taking action so the momentum continues. It can be amazing what can happen when we say *yes* to our lives and step out of our limitations. Until we believe it, we can play with the ideas and be willing to believe it!

There can be many gentle changes presented to you through signs that you can respond to. Many authors have written about these potential vehicles for the signs, whether through people, animals, objects or angels, or through colour or smells, to name a few. I remember reading *'The Lightworker's Way'* by Doreen Virtue and enjoying experimenting with the different range of potential signs in order to open myself up more for receiving. The signs are for you. You can accept, dismiss or miss them. If you allow yourself space during the day to check in with the world inside you, as well as the demand from without, you can help this process work for you. It is in this space between choice and decision that possibilities dance.

I cannot really remember the first request for change or my desire to learn about the life force in the world I found myself living in. I do, however, remember the excitement of books and courses cascading into my life. With the internet came ever increasing access to so much. There were many nights that I had little, if any, sleep. I was high on the information buzz that one initial search can provide. I remember clearly, an amazing night, when an initial search on James Twyman had me learning about Indigo and Crystal Children, about invisible grids and a changing world paradigm. Wow! That was a night when my whole brain seemed alive in a way it had never been at school.

Finding amazing authors and lapping up their books and courses and weaving through their web-pages made me feel I was on a mission. I was finding information and experiences that I could relate to. They expressed feelings I felt but had not articulated, explained experiences similar to mine but that I had not understood and they put our planet Earth onto a universal galactic stage. They thought outside the box I had been made to learn in and I loved it.

A friend in those early days explained to me about the Universe's Library and how a book comes to you when the time is right. She passed me a book by Brian Weiss, 'Many Lives, Many Masters'. Not having really read many books since my college days I devoured the book in one weekend. How could there have been so much going on that I had not heard people talk about before? This book was one of so many that the Universe's Library brought my way. A child that teachers were worried may never be an adult reader now had at least two or three non-fiction books on the go and was loving the reading experience. The content held her interest!

Some of the books that impacted my life greatly	
Rosemary Altea: You Own the Power	Gregg Brayden: The Divine Matrix
Paulo Coelho: Brida	Patricia Crane: Ordering from the Cosmic Kitchen
Wayne Dyer: The Power of Intention	Foundation for Inner Peace: A Course in Miracles
Louise Hay: You Can Heal your Life	Annie Kagan: The Afterlife of Billy Fingers
Kyron Writings: Kryon Book VII: Letters from Home	Denise Linn: The Secret Language of Signs
Bruce Lipton: The Biology of Belief	James Redfield: The Celestine Prophecy
Elif Shafak: The Forty Rules of Love	Michael Tellinger: Slave Species of God
James Twyman: Emissary of Light	Doreen Virtue: The Lightworker's Way
Brian Weiss: Many Lives, Many Masters	Marianne Williamson: A Return to Love

The more I read and the more I listened, the more I realised I was saying *yes* to this way of life. It was a *yes* to wanting to build up self-esteem, to mastering the art of manifestation and to learning more. It was a *yes* to being happy and accepting the invitations of life.

My adventures took me into past lives, energy healing, teaching and coaching and so much more. I met new people. I had learnt that life can be a party. What life presents you will be your adventure and your journey, if you wish to accept.

Steps to Support the Acceptance
Be mindful of the conversations you hear around you and articles you see — there may be a message that you had previously dismissed or missed about how to respond and what to respond to next
Research information — there is so much to discover
Trust the signs you are given — say *yes* if it feels right, for they can lead you to wonderful places and can result in miracles

ഇ Step 3: The Party: Now Here — Cheer!

When you look around, it is not always what people have externally that is the cause of their contentment and their happiness. It is not necessarily the money in the bank, their health or their life circumstances. It is how they have navigated their approach to life, how they feel about what they have and how open they are to change.

Step 3 is about congratulating yourself and giving thanks for all that you have, as well as about helping others.

I knew I felt better when my thoughts felt better. Friends appeared and opportunities were presented. I had also given myself signs to help me know if I was still in the flow of life. Are the traffic lights green? Do I still smile throughout the day? Do I continue to have invitations? Do I have time to check in? Was that a positive thought? With each thought we have a choice to accept it or change it. It is a constant dance, sometimes right or left, up or down; never wrong or right. It is just the one you consciously or unconsciously decide on at a given moment using the knowledge you have at that time.

It was one wonderful day when an opportunity to attend the 'Heal Your Life, Achieve your Dreams' workshop training course was presented to me. When I was able to go, I knew something special was happening. By this time I was fascinated by the Hay House Community, initially through reading books by the founder Louise Hay. I had read her book again and this time it connected clearly with me. I read more and they inspired me. This transformational workshop changed me forever. The people and trainers I met, the information that was shared and the strategies and techniques given now play a large part in my everyday life. This was my key to the doorway of an 'Alice in Wonderland' kind of life — my invitation to the party.

Your key or invitation may be the same or different. There are so many ways of learning and so many people out there willing to share. I wanted to learn more and to strengthen my commitment to believe in what was to me a new paradigm of thinking. I had found my passion. Others may find theirs elsewhere, such as in medicine, family, art or business. There is a big world of possibilities out there and each step you take can help you know what serves your happiness and what does not. In finding yourself you help others in many ways. You hold a light to what is possible. When you are happy you change your vibration and this too affects others.

What you want and how you feel can change moment by moment or year by year, so even at the third step I continue to return to the first step to add new choices on a regular basis. I check in to my thoughts to see if they are still positive ones that can improve or maintain my life. I especially focus in if there is change pending or when I want a shift in my life, whether specific or general. The authors in the book 'The Secret' discuss the technique of how to attract something specific into your life and Patricia Crane's 'Ordering from the Cosmic Kitchen' also explains the process beautifully.

Marianne Williamson discusses the difference between magic and miracles. She asks more open-ended questions such as; 'What will you have me be?' This can open up a limitless number of possibilities. It was during our 'Heal Your Life, Achieve your Dreams' workshop training course that we were asked to think about an ideal outcome to a situation and then state; 'This or something better?' I have stopped thinking that I may have the best answers. When you give space for possibilities then the solution and options can be far better than the ones you thought of. It involves a trust in something more than your conscious thought. It is without limitations.

My sense of party continued as I became more involved in the Heal Your Life and Hay House Community. It was a wonderful experience being able to attend the first 'I Can' conference in London. Can you imagine the joy of seeing so many of your favourite authors in one place? I was able to listen to talks and shake hands with some of the authors I had read and studied with. It was an event that I will always remember. I trained further and became a coach. It was wonderful to support other people's transformation when I helped out in some workshops myself. Giving was as, if not more, rewarding as receiving. Yet it also seemed the more I gave, the more I got back.

Steps to Participate in the Party
Give thanks for all you have—gratitude is a signpost that says *more*
Pass it on—there is an abundance in giving
Explore and be open—we all fit in and we do not need to have the answers first. We can find our place and our tribe

✍ Step 4: A Lifetime Membership: Don't Just Play — Stay!

I am still known as a space cadet by some people, but nowadays the term is used with more kindness and respect. It is I who can be heard laughing and talking with enthusiasm to others. I feel I belong, that I have a voice and I want to contribute if it can help. I have found my tribe. I have found love. Life is more a party than a classroom.

Yet life gets busy and it throws up the unexpected. When I feel that I am limiting my choices and putting the brakes on my life again with the negative talk in my head, I slowly and consciously consider the 4 Steps. Indeed, I still have challenges and dilemmas. The difference is that I have more tools that can help during these times. Rather than feed the drama as I did in the past, I try to allow the space for a more interesting and useful solution to materialise, not so much with a specific outcome in mind but more with curiosity.

Checking in on the source of inspiration such as being in nature, meditation, swimming, walking or biking, can help maintain or restore a positive vibration. This allows a space in which to recharge so your inner guidance can communicate with you. It supports your memory of events, helping you to make connections and to give thanks. When you go to a party you bring a gift. Having the gift of gratitude is all encompassing.

There are now many activities that I enjoy that help me stay positive and grateful. My Facebook page contains uplifting positive captions to see throughout my day as well as articles on subjects that fascinate me that I have shared. They help remind me not to engage so much in the drama of life as well as being a reminder of all I have to be grateful for. I also meet with a wonderful group of positive individuals. We engage in a set text, unpicking the meaning to support our understanding. I also listen to some wonderful tele-summits and other amazing recordings available on the internet. They are usually free if you can listen to the interviews in a set time. Alternatively you can purchase them. Some I have time to listen to, others I miss, yet their energy fills my email inbox and serves as a reminder to me to breathe and smile. There are also free resources on many websites, so you do not have to spend, spend, spend. By doing such things I am reminded that beyond the demands and the tribulations of the day is a place that can uplift and liberate. This place of well-being is a good place to stay.

Some of my Favourite On-Line Tele-Summits, Web-Sites/Organisations	
Sonia Choquette	http://www.soniachoquette.com
Patricia Crane	http://www.heartinspired.com
Sheila Gale	http://thesheilashow.com
Lisa Garr	http://theawareshow.com
HayHouse	http://www.hayhouse.com
Dain Heer	http://www.accessconsciousness.com
Deborah King	https://deborahking.com
Jennifer McLean	http://healingwiththemasters.com
The Shift Network	http://theshiftnetwork.com/courses
Maryanne Williamson	http://www.marianne.com

There are many reasons to start a search for a new way of being: a curiosity, an invitation from a friend, a drama or a major crisis or just because you can. There are many support groups and organisations that can help. We do not all need to be the same nor feel bad for not being so.

I have been to school and college, as well as having attended many work training sessions and there has been little, if any, focus on how you think and the choices you have if you become more conscious of your thoughts. In case this is the same for you, it was these 4 Steps that helped me find my way. I did not feel lost but knew I was not at the party. I hope they can help you.

There are many ways of thinking. We are all different. We may also want different things. I found my party—this chapter is an encouragement for you to find yours.

Steps to Stay Past Midnight
Keep participating
Keep believing
Share your experiences
Go through the steps again
Join a group
Start a group
Play it forward

Play in the Party of Life — The Ball

I still run up and down the steps; sometimes frantically and at other times with a hop and a skip!

Depending how my life is feeling, depends how much focus I give to each step. I endeavour to remember the importance of giving myself space for further possibilities and not always to assume I have the answers. I also remind myself of the importance of accepting opportunities and not always playing safe by rejecting them. I appreciate social interactions more now and enjoy the company of others, feeling that I belong.

There is fun in my life. When you are in the vibe some people still dismiss you yet that does not matter so much as having people, including yourself, who enjoy your company and your contributions. You attract your people, your tribe and that tribe just grows. Instead of you seeking them, there comes a time you are the one they seek. It is then you know you are in the dance with the universe and that you have captured that magnificence of play. This is when the world of fantasy and reality combine to give your life meaning, love and satisfaction; through giving as well as receiving.

It took a long time to accept my quirkiness. I have healed some old programming and life is far more peaceful in my head. I hope these steps can act as a spring board for your self-discovery, healing and empowerment.

I would encourage anyone who feels they are not in control of their thinking, as well as those that are entertaining the idea that it may be *they* who are putting the breaks on their lives, to explore more. My gateway to feeling better about myself, and the life around me, was through the 'Heal your Life, Achieve your Dreams' workshop that I also became qualified to deliver. It is amazing when you experience your own life shift and it is phenomenal when you see such shifts in others.

When I was invited to co-author a book on sharing strategies for a better life, it sounded exciting. I had been receiving for so long and it felt right to share. It was not my conscious dream to write, but a wonderful possibility that presented itself when I had sent out the request to give back.

Please remember, there is no need to *play small* in life and sit on the sidelines at the party, nor lose that slipper at midnight. There are, however, many reasons for playing and staying and making this party the ball of your life.

Dedicated to all of us who skip, leap, shuffle or take a step at a time in this journey called life. To those who believed in me and for those that did not. To you who read this book today and for those that will read it tomorrow — thank you.

Thank you to my mum and dad for being there for my first steps, for my friends and family who held my hand as we danced through life and to my darling little sister who skips with me throughout it all. A thank you to the fabulous VIP team who have been amazing to work with, to Louise Hay and the phenomenal speakers and authors I have encountered on my learning quest, and to my husband and best friend, who gave me confidence and space to believe.

~ Tonia Browne

Diane S. Christie

DIANE S. CHRISTIE, SPHR, is an author and a licensed **Heal Your Life**® coach and workshop leader. And, she enjoys her relationship marketing business. Her personal mission is to "Inspire and conspire with others to claim our prosperity in ALL forms." Diane partners with people worldwide to create abundant life results, in her business, and in one conversation at a time.

Diane lives in Olympia, Washington. She is a past recipient of the Governor's Award for Leadership in Management. She and husband, Bill, experience joy through worldwide travel, spiritual adventure, and heart connections with all whom they meet.

Contact Diane at dschristie8@gmail.com

'No'ing to Knowing
 # Whining to Winning

 "An enlightened soul is not one to whom truth
has been revealed, but one who has summoned
it; and not just when they've been driven by pain,
but when life's seas were as calm as glass."

~ TUT, A NOTE FROM THE UNIVERSE

While reflecting about 'empowerment' as a topic, this thought came to mind: "Whenever there's been some comment or an event that challenged me or my way of being, it's *always* turned into a minor or major 'wake-up' call about my life." I've asked … "Now what happens? What do I do with the available information; with my emotions and my feelings?" Then asked myself, how can this intense energy be used to transform? Generally, and especially at uncertain times, questions are my favorite way to propel a conversation to gain understanding, with others and with self.

Looking back, those questions were the tip of the proverbial iceberg at the time of my divorce. I thought I understood how situations had transpired, the beliefs I had that evolved into choices made, how those choices led to such an outcome. Yet, maybe, not so much.

This particular 'wake-up' call went fathoms deep. What to do with life now? None of my plans or expectations for a happy, joy-filled marriage were met. In that present moment, what feelings existed were only disappointment, despair, and discouragement of divorce. I talked, apparently quite a lot, about loss and feeling like a failure. And worried way too much. Until, one day, a dear friend suggested that I take a closer look at myself, my thoughts, attitudes, beliefs, and thus my actions. Wow, that feedback was shocking. However, I listened, swallowed, and followed her suggestion and urging.

There is no agony like bearing an
untold story inside you."

~ ZORA NEALE HURSTON

With a healthy dose of curiosity mixed with courage, I decided to look within, to peer into mental crevasses and to have an experience of guided, mindful exploration. I chose to attend The Excellence Series, three personal assessment programs, developed and presented by Context International. These learning opportunities offer ideas for living, to personally discover and explore how I show up in the world … and then to authentically practice new skills.

The second program in The Excellence Series was aptly named 'The Wall.' Why? Well, even marathon runners hit a performance wall. When they break through that invisible wall, they go on to finish the race. When a person feels fear, has a secret, doesn't want to tell the truth of a circumstance or feeling, there is a wall. What are my fears and walls? Yours? Trust me, we ALL have them. Then, what's behind, or just over that wall?

The purpose of The Wall is to enhance your relationship with yourself. Wow … I was so ready to enhance that relationship! I learned so much during the first program. A switch clicked on and I saw hopeful possibilities. I was very excited and became determined to move quickly in this new direction. I'm like a dog with a bone when I smell results, kind of like Sherlock Holmes. I could hardly wait to enhance the relationship with myself … until I got there. Eeeks! … Are you serious? Given the then current state of my life it was 'Yes. Gulp. Let's go.' Time to take a closer look, figure more stuff out, discover a silver lining.

 "All cats are grey in the dark. So remember that
how much you can see of a situation depends
on how much light you can shine on it."

~ ALEXANDER MCCALL SMITH

Looking back, again. I remember how afraid I was to honestly examine my life. I've heard, and agree, that fear is the emotion I feel when I'm not being me. Within me, the volume of that once still, small voice had grown to whispers. Now it shouted 'Onward!' I felt compelled, at a cell level, to take this risk, and move forward. Time to let light in; assign new meaning to life.

And then came that day at The Wall when the program leader discussed driving needs. Like walls, we ALL have them. And now, we were going to explore and unearth our driving needs. This was new territory and I definitely needed help to understand the concept. Right then, I felt clueless.

At The Wall, there were many exquisitely orchestrated and facilitated exercises; some in silence, some in pairs, some in the larger group. We were asked to remember important times at various stages in our lives and the surrounding circumstances. What happened to or with me and how I responded; how that similar response had showed up throughout my life. And, I remember, a corker of a question ... consider if my responses were truly how I felt or was there something else wanting to be expressed ... which was the authentic me.

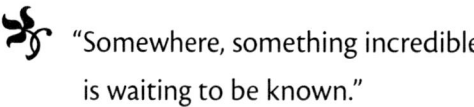 "Somewhere, something incredible
is waiting to be known."

~ CARL SAGAN

Curious, can you remember a time in your life, when you looked different from most everyone around and were teased mercilessly because of that difference? For me, it was my tight, naturally curly hair. When mom combed my wet hair, it hurt, it was so tangled in curls. I cried in frustration, and often pain. I wanted just to be like the other kids; I wanted straight hair so badly. To this day, I remember the boy who sat behind me in History class. He threaded a pencil in my short hair. Tight curls held the pencil in place. He laughed, pointed me, my hair and the pencil out to others. Many others laughed at me. My emotions, however, were anything but laughter. Oh my ... interesting how many times a version of that experience had played out in my life. I felt old pains, over and over.

Another formative episode, from my mom's life ... Growing up, she was on the chubby side. At school, swimming, or at family gatherings she was consistently reminded about being 'pleasantly plump.' A year before my mom died, she again shared the story about the boy in the local grammar school who called her 'fat.' So many decades later, in the telling of that story, tears still came to her eyes. Imagine. Even I could feel her still-present pain. (Interesting footnote about my mom ... no diet or eating plan ever worked for her.)

Upon review of my life, and especially the experiences related to the divorce, I could see and feel a connection between long ago events and how I responded to circumstances in my marriage. I was raised in a family where being independent and expressing independence were expected. We rarely-to-never asked for help of any kind. I learned to believe that asking for help was considered a sign of weakness. These traits, along with the need to be right, were modeled and valued. No judgment here, just the truth. Frankly, each of those values worked quite well under some circumstances. In other situations, not so much. I realized I needed to learn personal discernment and humility.

 "It ain't so much the things we don't know that get us into trouble. It's the things we know that just ain't so."

~ MARK TWAIN

Turns out, I couldn't articulate my true values and driving needs. I had casually adapted my life to others' wants, living out scenarios that others wanted for me because I was unsure what I wanted for myself.

Back to The Wall and driving needs. It was now seriously important to figure out what was happening in my thoughts and actions. Then determine what need was being met. Results didn't take too long in coming. Insights came, like a flood of images floating on what felt like the stormy sea of my brain. To that point in life, I had created some wonderful, life-affirming experiences. I had committed some outrageous, life-damning actions. My work produced tears of joy and shame.

Was there a common theme between the insights? That dig was happening in the mine of my mind. Concepts came to me. Then came words that fit the concepts. We were asked to evaluate our lives and create a short list, three to five, of our essential driving needs. That assignment felt like a tall order. Then, I realized that *IT* was just the assignment I'd been, subconsciously, seeking for years. Themes emerged. Viewing the panorama of my life, I could see most of my decisions and experiences falling into three to five needs. I loved this structure of recall and evaluation! At times, I giggled out loud at the discoveries. Other times, I wept with relief to finally understand what happened. I remembered situations when I knew I MUST speak out and be known. Remember the 1979 movie, *Norma Rae*? She spoke loudly, in action and words, when she felt there was a wrong to be righted. When my inner Norma Rae showed up, it really was a driving need being expressed.

There were also tears of recognition as I thought and occasionally vocalized, *"I'm not the kind of person who would do THAT."* Yes indeed, I had "done THAT." Like times I'd not told the full story because I was afraid of another's reaction which I was unprepared to handle. Oh, there were many waves of truth-telling that occurred. I discovered the power and sheer relief of letting go of excuses and shame. I made commitments... No more self-deception. No more being a saboteur. Time to create anew.

What an intense, joyous journey to explore my life's facets; finding meaningful words to describe my needs and then matching words to concepts. Thoughts and words are power. It felt *so* important to have the right words, right then. Thoughts, words, and deeds ARE the substance of life. This truth is so simply stated by the very first sentence in the book *You Can Heal Your Life:*

 "What we think about ourselves becomes the truth
for us. When we create peace and harmony and
balance in our minds, we will find it in our lives."

~ LOUISE HAY

Next effort: Create my own, very personal Definition of Success (DoS). Aha! Another key to unlock answers to my questions. A DoS was to be easily remembered, verbalized, and used as a life beacon. In other words, when making choices and taking actions, what needs were being met? And, *how* were my needs being met? Those two questions led right to a Random House dictionary definition of power ... *"the ability to do or act, the capability of doing or accomplishing something; giving voice and authority."* Now, it was my *conscious* voice aching to speak up in the authority of my being.

Initially, the detective part of my brain was in overdrive, yet my hands wouldn't move. I struggled to write. I felt stuck, like my spirit needed to be excavated and freed from somewhere deep within. Then, the idea came to use symbols and words that evoked a meaningful, emotional response in my life. I LOVE beautiful stones and creative pieces of jewelry. I love knowing the history of a unique combination of jewels. I feel a special connection to some jewels and honor the legacy of an heirloom. Thus, the jewelry allusion was incorporated into my DoS. Jewels absorb, refract, and reflect light. So do I. Now, I smiled broadly! Then words came easily as inspired expressions of me ... heartfelt, honest, and worthy of living. I had struck gold.

It was pure joy and freedom to be with and in the presence of many others as we wrote and shared our Definitions. None of us was alone. We learned from each other. Each of us asked for support, including me. Each of us gave support, including me. My voice, as others, was tentative at first. We refined and practiced our efforts. The more I spoke my DoS out loud, my voice and authority became clearer, more sure. My belief grew. I surrendered to the surprise of the experience and trusted the process. My commitment solidified to living and loving in accordance with my unique driving needs. To share, in this manner, electrified the cells in my body. I could see life with a clear, diamond-like quality, with a newfound tenderness of spirit. I had lost the sense of uncertainty and found a sense of opportunity. In that setting, I internalized the idea that to seek and experience clarity is a choice. Empowerment, at its core, is self-respect, truth in actions, and living life by making well-informed, wise choices. Moment by moment. OK...I was ready for more *next steps*.

Curious about my DoS and what it is today? I am honored to share the love of those labors. Here it is ...

SUCCESS TO ME IS:

POWER...
Embracing and radiating my divine feminine essence

CONNECTION...
Knowing and growing joyful soul and mind camaraderie

INFLUENCE...
Being seen and heard in a sparkling and illuminating manner

ACHIEVEMENT...
Making a brilliant difference around my world, and

ADVENTURE...
Saying 'yes' to the vibrant rhythm of life

And so it is!

Invitation to Action: Walk with purpose, look into your mirror, have a self chat. Ask 'What am I doing *right now* to enhance the relationship with myself?'

 "You are only one decision away
from a totally different life."

~ ZIG ZIGLAR

A toast to mutual support! It is strength in action. Thank you to those who have participated in this law of giving and receiving. Let's do more.

In gratitude 5GN ... Mary Ellen, Diane, Terry, and Linda.

Love you Bill ... your grin is wide and lights a room; your heart is big and envelops all.

Thank you.

~ Diane S. Christie

Linda Hargesheimer

LINDA HARGESHEIMER has had the opportunity to live in Indiana, Pennsylvania, Alabama, Ohio and Maine. After having her public relations job politically undermined, she searched for healing. Louise Hay's body-mind beliefs made a deep connection with her. In 2011, she designed a three-hour course based on Dr. Candace Pert's proof of the body-mind connection that she teaches for adult education departments in Maine. She has been called "a natural-born teacher." Linda is a Licensed and Certified Heal Your Life® Teacher, numerologist and dream interpreter.

l_hargesheimer@yahoo.com
www.mindbodyemotions.com

Change Your Thoughts ~ Heal Your Body

*C*hange Your Thoughts ~ Heal Your Body is a class I teach based on the body-mind connection which was proven by Dr. Candace Pert at the National Institute of Science in the 1970's. She proved how the limbic system of the brain facilitates your emotions to trigger the chemical reactions in your body to create either health or illness.

At the beginning of the class, we agree that nothing goes out of the room with anyone's name, so the students feel free to speak. I include myself in the class people, because I give many examples.

1. Experiential Meditations

 ∽ Before I discuss the function of the brain or the history of medicine, I begin the class by having the students take a piece of paper and draw a line vertically down the middle of it. Then I ask them to put two more lines on it horizontally at one-third and two-thirds down the page. At this point, I ask the students to put down their pens or pencils and close their eyes. Then I begin the following meditation slowly. I pause after each instruction for them to identify or experience the request.

 ∽ *Now I'm going to have you close your eyes and take three deep breaths (slowly have them breathe), I want you to think about the **worst** thing that ever happened to you in your life. ... Now I want you to identify, **where the worst** thing that ever happened to you in your life is in your body, ... the **worst** thing that ever happened to you in your life. ... Now I want you to identify, **where** in the body you **feel** the **worst** thing that ever happened to you in your life, ... the **worst** thing that ever happened to you in your life. ... Next, we are going to take three more deep breaths (slowly have them breathe). Now I want you to identify the **emotions** you feel from the **worst** thing that ever happened to you in your life, ... the emotions you feel from the **worst** thing that ever happened to you* *in your life. ... I'm going to count backwards from five to one. When you open your eyes, I want you to put on one side of the paper at the top Worst. In the first section, put **where** in your body you felt the worst thing that ever happened to you in your life. In the lower section, I want you to put the **emotions** related to the worst thing that ever happened to you in your life. Five, four, three, two, one. You may open your eyes.*

- I ask for the locations of the worst thing that ever happened to you in your life and list on the board. Next I ask for the emotions affiliated with worst thing that ever happened to you in your life. (At no time, do I ask what it was that was the worst thing that ever happened to them in their lives. That is private to them.) After this listing, I tell them to put their pens or pencils down because we are going to do another exercise.

- Close your eyes and we will again take three deep breaths (slowly have them breathe), ... I want you to think about the **best** thing that even happened to you in your life, ... the **best** thing that ever happened to you in your life. Now I want you to identify, where in the body you feel the **best** thing that ever happened to you in your life, ... the **best** thing that even happened to you in your life. Next, we are going to take three more deep breaths (slowly have them breathe). Now I want you to identify the emotions you feel from **best** thing that ever happened to you in your life, ... the emotions you feel from the **best** thing that ever happened to you in your life. I'm going to count backwards from five to one. When you open your eyes, I want you to put on other side of the paper at the top Best. In the first section, put where in your body you felt the best thing that ever happened to you in your life. In the lower section, I want you to put the emotions related the best thing that ever happened to you in your life. Five, four, three, two, one. You may open your eyes.

- I then put on the board the locations of the best thing that ever happened to them in their life. Then I ask for the emotions affiliated with the best thing that ever happened to you in your life. (That is also private to them.) After this listing, I ask "Which would you rather feel?" Inevitably, they say the best emotions.

- These meditations demonstrate that a major happening in your life, whether positive or negative, can remain as an issue in your body for many years. They also prove the body-mind connection.

- I very briefly cover the history of medicine from Hippocrates, the father of Western medicine in 370 BC who taught that good health depends on a balance of mind, body and environment, to the takeover by pharmaceuticals in the 1950. Then to the 70's when biofeedback and alternative stress reduction options were recognized as valid.

2. How You Become Ill

☙ Next, I draw a full right-above-the-very-top glass on the board. Then I ask them if they have ever seen a glass that was filled just slightly above the open part, but kept from spilling by surface tension. What happens when you add one more drop? The response is: it spills.

☙ I explain that this is what happens when you fill your glass with negative thoughts. It can take anywhere from six months to two years to fill that glass. When it spills over, you get sick.

☙ For example, let's say you are a soldier in the war. You are riding in a truck when the truck in front of you explodes from an IED. Immediately, you have a massive attack of fear. Therefore, every time from then on, when you go out in a truck, you recall that memory and begin to fill your glass with negativity. You might even think about it when you are safe in the barracks. Eventually, your cup will fill and overflow. This is how you might acquire PTSD.

☙ I then ask them to guess how many physical and chemical responses happen in your body when you are in massive fear. From my understanding, research has shown that massive fear triggers more than 1400 known physical and chemical responses and activates more than 30 hormones and neurotransmitters.

3. Exploring Your Health Issues

☙ About mid-class, I give another exercise to the students to explore their life's health issues. I ask them to list their major illnesses and surgeries and put a timeline next to each showing when it first appeared in their lives.

☙ Since an illness takes between six months and two years to manifest, I ask if they find any correlation to the timeline.

☙ Then I hand out Louise Hay's *Heal Your Body* books for them to check to see if they were having those issues prior to them becoming ill. Quite often, I will see many students nodding in the class as they read about their issues.

4. Positives Versus Negatives

☙ The next exercise is to write on their paper a list of negatives in life—fear, anger, guilt resentment, criticism, and self-criticism. Next to each word on the list, I ask them to put the percentage that they feel each negative in their lives. I tell them that column does not have to add up to 100%. It can be more or less. I ask them to total it.

- ↵ Then I ask them to write a list of positives in life—joy, happiness gratitude, hope, pride, love, and serenity. Again, I ask them to put the percentage that they feel each positive in their lives. Again, I tell them that column does not have to add up to 100%. It can be more or less. I ask them to total it. Then I ask them to subtract the lower number from the higher number.

- ↵ At this point, I hold up a Nerf football. I explain that the lighter side represents the 100% positive and the darker side represents the 100% negative. I then ask, "Which percentage is higher for you?" If there is any negativity, then they need to work at clearing out the negatives to find 100% happiness.

5. Exploring Forgiveness

- ↵ From here, I explain forgiveness and why it is important for you and not the other person. We then do a short meditation about dumping our total forgiveness into a boat and letting it float in the river and down into the ocean and over the horizon.

- ↵ Next, I tell them about a powerful technique called clearing letters to assist in clearing out their lack of forgiveness from their body, that they have been holding about an individual or even themselves. I ask them to write these letters on paper, **not** the computer.

- ↵ Begin writing, *Dear _____, I am angry at you because ...,* Then just keep writing to express all your feelings. You will find that you will go from writing on one line to using three lines for words, then six or seven for words, then you will use half a page, then a page per word, and then two pages for a single word.

- ↵ By the time you are done, you have reversed the situation and are down to a single line. Then you can write, "I forgive you" or "I ask God to help me forgive." When you are finished writing, you do NOT mail the letter. You burn it and send it into the ethers. Or, you can tear it up and dispose of it.

6. The Importance Of Words

- ↵ Following this, I discuss the importance of words. The old adage: *"Sticks and stones may break my bones, but words will never hurt me"* is untrue. As proof, I discuss and use pictures from Masaru Emote's work using freezing water with positive and negative words around them.

- Next, we discuss affirmations and affirmation writing. I ask for volunteers to share affirmations. If necessary, we tweak them to eliminate any negatives they may have written.
- I also refer back to the glass of water. I tell them that putting fresh water in drop by drop, or affirmation by affirmation, replaces the negative thoughts so they can heal.

7. Methods To Use To Keep Yourself Healthy

Near the end of the class, we then discuss a list of 14 ways to keep yourself healthy:

- **Consciously control your thoughts.**
  - *Be aware of what you are thinking.*
  - *Say "Stop" out loud to halt thoughts, if in private.*
  - *Snap a rubber band on your wrist, if in public.*
- **Turn negatives into methods of coping.**
  - *Create positive thinking affirmations.*
  - *If it is overwhelming, get some help.*
- **Positively learn to express your emotions. Learn assertiveness.**
  - *Suppressing emotions creates illness.*
- **Take responsibility — Take control.**
  - *Change what you can, i.e. nutrition, environment, thoughts, exercise.*
- **Write down your dreams upon awakening.**
  - *They can tell you what you are worried about, consciously or subconsciously.*
- **Forgive for your sake, not their sake.**
- **Learn to Love.**
  - *Get in touch with your heart.*
- **Touch and hug.**
  - *Good touching is important.*
  - *Give and receive touching and hugging with others or your pets.*
- **Play and laugh.**
- **Exercise.**
  - *Stretch and relax.*
- **Transform your diet to good nutrition.**
- **Find a spiritual center.**
  - *Pray, meditate or enjoy nature.*
- **Relax.**
  - *Find quiet time for yourself.*
- **Practice Gratitude.**

Lastly, I ask the students to write a plan of their own from the above list to become a healthier and happier person.

I hope you enjoyed this explanation of my class. Some of my students have commented that from taking the class, they found *new ways of affirming*, appreciated *a nice blend of science and metaphysics*, learned *coping skills* and *the importance of staying positive."*

If you want to connect with me to discuss more about the class, please email me at l_hargesheimer@yahoo.com. Peace, joy and love, Linda

Dedicated to all the students I have taught over the years. Indirectly, they have also taught me how to improve my class. Also, I dedicate this information to an acquaintance, Lorna Griffin, who recognized that I was "chosen by God to spread peace" and Dr. Caroline Leaf for her book, Who Switched Off My Brain. My goal for the class is to assist others in finding their inner peace, which can move them toward unconditionally loving themselves and others.

With all my heart, I appreciate all the experiences in my life in assisting me to grow into the person I have become. I also thank my husband, Philip, for his unconditional love that encouraged me to pursue the paths I needed to heal and to assist in healing others.

~ Linda Hargesheimer

Robyn Podboy

ROBYN PODBOY is the Owner of RP Life Consulting. She is a Personal Growth Facilitator, Life Coach, International Speaker, Published Author, Certified N.L.P. Practitioner, Infinite Possibilities Law of Attraction Instructor, and a Louise Hay Heal Your Life® Licensed Facilitator.

With enthusiasm and humor Robyn inspires people just like you to change your perspective, thoughts and practices to recreate the life of your dreams. Robyn creates and facilitates empowering workshops and gatherings where you will discover your own personal power, encouraging you to live in true joy, while opening up new vistas of possibilities.

rplifeconsulting.com
happinesscoalition.com

 The Gift of a Gathering

Whether you have been to a workshop, retreat or gathering, there is something magical in getting away to discover something more about yourself. I love the word *Gathering* for this magical time. The definition of Gathering is "to come together" and "to gain or recover." The very first Gathering I attended was facilitated by my mother and her three sisters. Their vision was to create a place for the women of our extended family to come and learn more about each other and connect as women. At the time I received my invitation, I was working full time, taking care of two teenage boys with my husband, who was leaving his current job to start a new career. We were also in the process of moving out of the state. My life was pretty darn busy. I never stopped to think about what I needed. When I reread the invite, I thought, *"I want to go to a tropical island to relax on the beach, not spend time with cousins and family I haven't seen since I was a child. I don't even really know them."*

I shared concerns with my mother that I was feeling emotionally overwhelmed with everything that was happening in my life. I had nothing to offer. "It just wasn't the right time." I remember her response with excitement in her voice saying, *"Honey this is exactly why you should come! You don't have to offer anything just come and Be!"* Huh? "Come and Be?"... now that DID sound interesting! Perhaps this *was* just what I needed.

I arrived at the "Cabin in the Woods." I was a bit apprehensive, but that was released as soon as I saw the excited smiling, happy faces from all the others who arrived before me. They showed me where we would all be sleeping (bunk beds and shared showers). It was summer camp all over again. For a moment I thought to myself, *"What have I done?!"*

As our weekend began, I could feel the magic all around me. We spent our time together sharing what we were experiencing at the different stages of our life. Our ages ranged from 16 to 75 years. Through creative ceremonies, we were able to get to know each other... from fun, crazy free time, to deep conversations of connection.

Yes, we were there to learn about one another, but more importantly, we were there to learn about ourselves. The flow of each fun activity was designed to help us trust in the process and to know that we are not alone in our life's journey. We talked of our life challenges, joys, dreams, goals, kids, husbands, divorce, aging parents … you name it, and we talked about it! We cried together, we laughed together, we danced under the moon and stars together, giggling as we fell asleep. We were emotionally safe, there was no judgment, and in this process we became closer to our own true selves. We created a sisterhood by just Be...ing!

As the weekend came to an end, just like at summer camp, there were tears and laughter with the hugs as we were all saying goodbye. I knew that through laughter, song, dance, and an overwhelming true connection on such an amazing level, I was indeed forever changed. I could not have imagined that one weekend could change my entire life! I still feel an overwhelming sense of gratitude to my mother and her sisters for giving me this amazing gift. A gift of a gathering!

In my business as a life coach, I enjoy guiding people to "live their life on purpose" and to their fullest potential. In pursuit of this passion, one of my greatest joys is creating and facilitating Women Empowering Gatherings for the past ten years. Using my experience and all that I have learned from the many great teachers who I have been nurtured and mentored by, I want to share with everyone the "Gift of a Gathering!"

Here is an outline for how to create a magical Gathering. Feel free to tap into your own flare, trust your intuition, and create your own vision. I am just sharing the basics of what I enjoy most!

When creating a Gathering I feel that it is important to create your intention first, then move into visualization. Think and feel all that you would like to experience. At what location do you feel would be the best setting? How many people you want to attract? What is your end result? How do you want your guests to feel when the Gathering is over? See and feel each moment from when your guests arrive until you are saying goodbye. Your true intention will bring the magic to your gathering. Love the creative process, have fun seeing your vision, and then tap into trust. When you trust, the outcome will be guaranteed.

- ℰℐ I like to find an intimate place where everyone will be in the same location, such as private beach cottages, a private home on a lake or near the ocean, a ski lodge, a ranch etc. Many others have their gatherings at hotels or conference centers, but I love having them at a private place, as this creates real intimacy and the ultimate connection.

૭ After you find your location, think of your theme(s). What is it that you'd like to share or deepen? You can incorporate a few concepts that will flow together nicely. *Example: Forgiveness and Gratitude, or Change your Limited Beliefs to Manifestation, etc.* Don't worry if anyone will be attracted to it. The perfect people whom you are seeking will be the ones you will attract. Trust in yourself and your intention … always! Even if you are an expert on the theme, do more research. During your process to deepen into your theme will come your amazing creativity.

૭ The brainstorming process is the most fun for me to share with a partner. Relax in your intention and before you know it, it's as if you are playing ping-pong. Ideas are flowing back and forth, becoming so amazing, much more than you could ever imagine! You will find yourself being totally amazed at what is coming out of your creative mouths! Make sure you keep good notes, because the ideas will be coming so fast. If you are creating it alone, you will find that it becomes another entity. Either way you are spiritually guided, I have no doubt in this process.

૭ Creating the flow of your vision is important. You want to stay in sequence with your theme(s). The ease of flow from one vision to another is essential and something that your guests will appreciate. When you are in the creative process, don't forget the small details of your gathering. From all the feedback I received from past Gatherings, guests always appreciate and remember (besides their amazing transformation, of course), the simple details and thoughtfulness. It may be something you welcomed them with on their bedside table, a poem or a journal. It could be the food you are serving; is it prepared with love and coming from Mother Earth? Some guests don't mind preparing pre-planned dinners or cleaning up, as it gives everyone the sense that they are contributing and can have great bonding conversations. So don't be afraid to incorporate those things too.

૭ Before you actually begin your Gathering, and once guests have arrived, bring everyone in a circle to go over the logistics. This is when you can skim through the itinerary and set the intentions for the weekend. Let your guests know what is expected of them. *Example: Turn cell phone off, what time is breakfast/yoga etc.* Give each guest a chance to introduce themselves and share a little with the rest of the group. This instantly builds a connection to everyone. Have a basic outline of the timeline, but let them know it may be flexible because sometimes it may change due to unforeseen shifts. Each guest will be bringing their own energy and intention and that is a unique contribution! Again, Trust … It's all good!

ᘓ I always start The Gathering with a sacred ceremony that will complement my theme(s) and set the tone. This is the beginning of the magic. Bring everyone from their daily lives into the space where they can immediately relax, be in the present moment, and begin the connection. Some ideas I have used are: Each guest lighting a candle, smudging, holding a fire ceremony, doing a meditation, using a water ceremony to symbolize oneness, etc. I have found many books on sacred ceremonies that are very powerful. You can check them out at your local book store or at the library in the New Age section. Guests love it!

ᘓ As you begin to allow the gathering to unfold, always have a time when you connect with conversation. Of course your Gathering will be full of valuable information they can use in their life, but you don't want this weekend to be all about the information that you would like to share or your personal story. Your guests want an experience so get *them* involved!

ᘓ Throughout your time together always have some "downtime' scheduled for your guests. During this time they may be able to journal, walk, reflect or even nap. Sometimes the joy of these gatherings is just Be...ing — remember?

ᘓ I love to have a creative activity that they can do. Some people haven't learned how to just Be and this will give them an opportunity to create while just Be.. ing. *For example if The Gathering was a weekend highlighting gratitude, I might have a space where they could create gratitude jars, a gratitude journal, or maybe a vision board of all the gratitude they can affirm in their lives.* Later have a "show and tell" — it's a blast and great fun!

ᘓ It's important to have quiet moments as a group, either through meditation together or a silent meal. (A silent meal can also erupt into laughter with all the munching going on). This is a very powerful exercise for them to appreciate themselves in the silence.

ᘓ Also, another wonderful experience is *breathwork* — any type of breathing is so powerful either through *pranayama yoga* or practicing long, deep breathing as you chant. These are gifts we all have and may have forgotten to utilize to our fullest potential! Find what resonates with your Gathering. These are always a great experience to deepen in!

ↇ Don't forget the importance of music. Quiet soothing music for the mornings or dance music for when you let loose, but make a playlist and always have music!

ↇ At some point over your time together (maybe your last night) leave room for play. Create an activity that is fun and playful. Being playful is the most important element of the Gathering. As we take time out from our lives and the sacred space of the gathering, there needs to be a time for hilarity! It amazes me how many people don't play and laugh in their daily lives. I think it's essential for a happy, healthy life!

  • *Here is an example: The theme of The Gathering was "Stand in Your Truth." We spent a lot of time deepening into the truth, what it means to us and the importance of it in our lives. So after days of standing in our truth, the fun activity that we played was a great game called "Balderdash," where we were encouraged to lie or fib. It brought out so much laughter, bonding and snorting that the gatherers are laughing about it still. Some shared that they hadn't laughed that hard in years!*

ↇ As the time comes to a close, I come full circle in the intention of the Gathering by always ending with another sacred ceremony. This solidifies the experience. Some ideas might be singing together (they know each other by now, so there is no awkwardness) or an acknowledgement of the light that they share in this world with a reading or poem. Sometimes I have ended with the gifts brought to the Gathering by them—their smile, laugh, honesty, compassion…you can get my drift here.

ↇ The finale…as we close, I end with crazy dancing and singing (remember your song list) so everyone can dance in Joy! This leaves everyone with high energy and laughter; it's a perfect way to say goodbye to this amazing Gathering of extraordinary people.

To give the gift of a gathering takes time, organization, and total trust. Make it your own, bring in partners who will enhance it and who share your vision. Whatever you have created and planned for during this amazing time, trust that whoever comes will receive what they came for. What was created in love will be received in love.

"How might your life have been different if there
had been a place for you to go ... a place of women,
to help you learn the ways of women ... a place
where you were nurtured from an ancient flow
sustaining you and steadying you as you sought
to become yourself? A place of women to help
you find and trust the ancient flow already there
within yourself ... waiting to be released ... A place
of women ... How might your life be different?"

~ JUDITH DUERK

Whether you are creating a gathering or attending one, what I know for sure, is your life can be forever changed with The Gift of a Gathering.

In memory of my amazing Mom.

With Love and Gratitude to my amazing husband Tony and my sons Alex and Nate for your love, encouragement and unwavering support. To my beautiful friends Melissa Rocci and Terri Crogan for a friendship full of laughter, support and sisterhood. I am especially grateful to my Mom, Frances Blaesing for loving me as the trees love water and sunshine… helping me grow, prosper and to reach amazing heights!

~Robyn Podboy

Halina Kurowska

HALINA KUROWSKA is an author, writer, speaker, personal mentor, licensed Heal Your Life® teacher and Life Coach. She has an Honours BA in Philosophy from the University of Toronto. Halina spent the last twenty-five years on the path of spiritual development, transcending her own life and then assisting others in their transformations. Halina's unique insight, based on extensive studies of spiritual wisdom and its application in her own life, allows her to help others get in touch with their own inner wisdom. She lovingly empowers people and leads them to joy through her workshops and coaching sessions at *Living With Awe: Awareness, Wisdom, Empowerment.*

Halina is a happy and proud mother of two amazing sons, Wit and Mateusz, grateful to them for sharing this lifetime and their teachings with her. Halina loves nature, hiking, practising meditation, reading, writing and travelling.

www.livingwithawe.com
halina@livingwithawe.com
Facebook: Living With Awe: Awareness, Wisdom, Empowerment

Mirror, Mirror on the Wall

Mirror talk: Steps to achieve tangible results in your own life

 "It is safe to look within."

~ LOUISE HAY

My deep desire to know how life works led me to explore the wisdom of philosophy, psychology and various ancient healing practices. Throughout the years, I poured over many spiritual wisdom texts and incorporated their practical knowledge into my own life, quite often experiencing astounding results. I've used affirmations and meditation, the wisdom of ancient and contemporary philosophers, and a long list of other techniques such as Reiki, Ho'oponopono, and the Sedona Method.

One of the most useful techniques, however, is one that I acquired quite early on in my spiritual journey. Stumbling upon a book by Louise Hay titled *You Can Heal Your Life*, I began implementing mirror work into my daily life. I experienced tremendous results. Mirror work may seem simple, perhaps even silly or vain, yet it is so powerful that it can change your life. It did mine.

So what happens when we gaze deeply into our eyes in the mirror? One of the important things is that negativity is lifted and, with continuous practice, it eventually disappears. This does not mean we suppress or deny our emotions—but rather acknowledge those that surface, fully experience them, be present with every uncomfortable feeling we might have, love ourselves through them, forgive ourselves if we are blaming ourselves in any way, and feel the feelings dissolve.

I have suggested this technique many times in my work as a life coach, to my readers, to my workshop attendees and even to my loved ones. But, unless it is fully explained and properly utilized, mirror work will not get implemented into a person's daily life. This may be because the person is unprepared for the huge wave of emotions coming out of themselves from that first true contact with their Own Self in the mirror. It can be, and usually is, overpowering. Since mirror work is deceptively simple, people often think they will just look into the mirror and happily profess their love for themselves. Yet, we carry around a lot of emotional baggage and before we achieve a real sense of self-love, there is a lot of *unpacking* to be done.

Working with the mirror is a process that can often be quite painful, but it is worthwhile and very rewarding. Here I will be sharing with you a detailed explanation of this technique and providing you with examples to take it even further—from awareness, to acceptance, forgiveness, love and then the creation of a beautiful life for yourself and those around you. Believe me, there is magic in the mirror. I know!

Each of the three methods I am sharing with you builds upon the other, so I strongly recommend mastering one stage before proceeding to the next. Please note that while it is very possible to be your own therapist, there are certain prerequisites that are necessary to success: you must be open and honest with yourself and you must become the witness to yourself in a very loving way. This means that you see your own flaws and shortcomings, but do not condemn or criticize yourself for them. Notice them and resolve to do better or different next time. As Maya Angelou stated it so well: *"Do the best you can until you know better. Then, when you know better, do better."*

Stage One: Love Notes

1. Louise Hay stresses the importance of Mirror Work in order to bring ourselves to the positive state of love and acceptance, thus bringing about wonderful transformations inside ourselves and in the world around us. When we first start looking deeply into our own eyes and seeing our true self, it feels uncomfortable. The moment we gaze at ourselves, we see our flaws—not only outside flaws, like breakouts, wrinkles and grey hair, but also, our inner "defects." Feelings of guilt, shame and self-criticism arise, and in order to continue our healing work we have to forgive ourselves. So, we say: *"I forgive and I love you."* We repeat this process for as many days as we need to until we feel lightness and can say to ourselves with joy, *"I love you!!! I really, really love you!!!"*

2. To help you with this practice, I'm suggesting that you write a Love Note to yourself. Repeat this note to yourself daily as you look yourself in the eye.

    Example A: *"I love you [state your name]. You are my constant companion and I enjoy living my life with you. We went through so much together, so many things happened, and yet my love for you is constant. We are together in this life, we had so many experiences some sad and painful, and there were so many good moments,* *as well. This life is getting better and better, there are so many wonderful moments awaiting us in the future, and a life full of love and joy. All the love begins with us. I love you! I really, really love you!!!"*

Example B:*"[Say your name], I love you. I absolutely love you. You are amazing and awesome, absolutely awesome. I love you unconditionally and I forgive you. I fully accept you and I'm here to support you. I listen to your concerns and I'm here to help you."*

3. When you are talking to yourself in the mirror use "I" but also use the pronoun "you" as if you are talking to your dearest friend. This is, indeed, our Five Dimensional Self talking to our Human Self. You may say, *"I love you and these are the rules to follow now—you are safe and secure with me, from now on I'm taking care of you; we are in this life together and it's good, all good, and it's going to be awesome; we are creating the best life ever."* This process facilitates healing our inner child. In other words, we are parenting ourselves in a good and loving way.

4. Try it! Use it daily. You will be astounded by the wonderful results that this practice will generate. The main purpose of this process is to bring us to the point of experiencing ourselves in a spiritual way, as a *Presence* that is beyond our physical self.

Stage Two: Bring On The Good!

1. Now that we have forgiven ourselves our perceived defects and brought ourselves to a state of love and acceptance, we can take this process even further. We can now start to *invite* good and positivity into our lives.

2. In his manual, *Affirmations to Manifest an Awakened, Empowered and Abundant Life*, Jafree Ozwald suggests stating affirmations into the mirror, but with a slight variation on this technique. Again, looking deeply into our eyes, we affirm that we do deserve to have good things and that they can happen to us. We say, *"I love you and you deserve a good life."* Saying our affirmations often, out loud and with enthusiasm speeds up the process.

3. Here is Ozwald's method, which produces wonderful, powerful results: state each affirmation four times, putting your whole heart into it, but each time say it in a different way. *(Please note, the affirmation I'm providing is for the sake of example only, since it's short and kind of catchy.)*

- The first time, say it loudly as if you are announcing it to the whole Universe: *"I AM A MILLIONAIRE!!!"*
- The second time, repeat it in a very deep, confident voice: ***"I AM A MILLIONAIRE."***
- The third time, say it as a matter of fact, as if you are sharing something normal, ordinary to your friend: *"I am a millionaire."*
- The fourth and final time, still gazing into your eyes, whisper your affirmation softly and gently, as if it was a great secret that you are sharing with yourself now: *"I am a millionaire."* And, it never hurts to add, *"I am a millionaire and I LOVE IT!"*

Stage Three: Connecting Our Selves

1. My final method of mirror work in daily life is based on *Huna Principles*. Huna is an ancient Hawaiian healing practice and philosophy. Within Huna we can find the roots of modern psychology, such as Freud's recognition that the human mind is divided into three parts: id, ego and super ego; and Carl Jung's recognition of our subconscious, conscious and super conscious self. In other words, Huna teaches us to recognize our three selves: the Lower Self (subconscious) which is our body; the Middle Self (consciousness) which is our mind; and the Higher Self—Spirit. Each of these has its own characteristics, and through Huna, we gain understanding of how they interact.

2. This is the basics of Huna. Once you delve into the philosophy, you learn that there are seven principles that govern every moment of our daily life. These principles correspond to the concept of Chakras, the energy centres in our body, and they are the seven principles to freedom. It will take about five to eight minutes to go through them in the mirror, yet the benefits of this daily practice are truly priceless and will lead to profound change. I know, I've experienced it!

3. So, standing in front of the mirror and gazing deeply into your eyes state the following principles. Of course this is just to guide you, use your own words, make it yours, but use it daily. (Again, the reminder about using both "I" and "you" while talking to yourself.)
   - **The World Is What You Think It IS: Be Aware *(corresponds to the Crown Chakra)*** — Say, to yourself, *"Today be aware of your thoughts, they DO create your reality. Today, think only good, positive thoughts, thoughts that bring health, and abundance, goodness and joy into your life. Make sure to do this,*

as this is the blueprint for your life. Today, I'm choosing to think new thoughts that will create the life I want."

- **There Are No Limits: Be Free (Root Chakra)** — Say, *"You are free to create the life you desire. The only limits are your limiting thoughts and feelings."* A Course In Miracles says, "There is no order of difficulty in miracles. One is not *harder* or *bigger* than another. They are all the same. All expressions of love are maximal." Talk to yourself as you would talk to a dear friend, the one you truly care about. Say to yourself, *"whatever limiting beliefs I have, I let go of them now. I let go, I let go. I have the desire, right and determination to heal myself and my relationships and my financial situation."* Fill in whatever you feel you need to work on now.

- **Energy Flows Where Attention Goes: Be Focused (Sacral Chakra)** — Say to yourself, *"My thoughts have power and carry enormous energy within them, they create the circumstances in my life."* Focus on the good that you want to see in your life. Focus on LOVE and on what you would love to attract into your life.

- **Now Is The Moment of Power: Be Present (Solar Plexus Chakra)** — The point of power is in the present moment, so let go of whatever disappointments you encountered yesterday and do not worry about the future. Instead, focus on this moment. Breathe into it with full awareness that this moment is all you have and that this moment is your life. And, it is good, so good.

- **To Love Is To Be Happy With: Be Happy (Heart Chakra)** — So, be happy! Love who you are and what you have and all about you and everything around you. Love yourself deeply and fully because this love is what creates the good in your life and the good life. Love yourself and be gentle with yourself, offer compassion and forgiveness toward yourself and, once your cup is full, it overflows and spills that love and compassion toward others. Then, filled with love, you have something truly valuable to offer to others. So, focus on LOVE.

- **All Power Comes From Within: Be Confident (Throat Chakra)** — You are directly connected to the greatest power and wisdom, so don't dismiss that with feelings and thoughts of unworthiness. Remember your magnificence and your brilliance. As Marianne Williamson said, "Our deepest fear is that we are powerful beyond measure." So, look deeply into your eyes and affirm to yourself, *"Yes, I do have the power within me to create the best life for myself. I am a channel of that Power. I trust my Higher Self and I know that I am loved and supported at all times."*

- **The Effectiveness Is The Measure of Truth: Be Expectant** *(Third Eye Chakra)*— Be positive. Always expect the best, expect good things to come to you. Know and expect that all the work you put into your daily practice will bring wonderful results to you.

This is your program for success. Develop a deep, loving relationship with your own self and watch your life unfold in new and wondrous ways. Tune into your inner guidance, your Inner Wise Self and stay open to the infinite possibilities life has to offer to you. Trust the wisdom the resides deep within you.

I lovingly dedicate this chapter to the brave souls who choose to embrace the journey of healing. Blessed be all of you.

I am grateful to life: for an amazing journey filled with wonder, lessons, growth, love, joy and so many blessings—my heart is full.

I thank my lovely editor Izabela Jaroszynski for her assistance with this chapter. Many thanks to Karen Karall of Energy Matters and Miracles for bringing Hawaiian Huna close to home. Big gratitude to Lisa Hardwick for her inspiring and encouraging guidance. My life is blessed by our deep soulful connection. Thank you Lisa!

~ Halina Kurowska

Paula Obeid

PAULA OBEID loves her role in the world as Chief Inspiration Officer (CIO). Paula supports individuals as they recognize their perfection and that they are love. As a certified Hypnotherapist and life and business coach, she is able to help facilitate healing and achieving an individual's goals through a mind, body, and soul approach. Her passion is providing services, education and products that allow individuals to lovingly move through life with joy and ease.

Please contact her at obeidp@gmail.com

Manifesting Your Dreams

I have been called a *Master Manifester*. I prefer to be known as the *Gangsta of Love* since the high vibration of love and joy is where I want to attract and allow things into my life. We are all a *Master Manifester* and the Universe is standing by waiting to deliver our every thought. You heard me correctly and I said *every thought,* which would also include our negative thoughts. The Universe responds to energy using the Law of Attraction.

You have probably already heard of Law of Attraction tools that exist to help you manifest the life you desire. They are basically tools to help you focus your energy and your thoughts. I like to think of them as tools you use wherever you are on your *magical manifesting journey.* All tools are helpful. As you grow spiritually, you'll find other tools that serve you better at that moment. Think of it as a student on their math journey who first uses little blocks to figure out counting. As the student grows, they may use other tools, such as a number line. Eventually the student will use a calculator and maybe even work up to use a scientific calculator with graphing features. All the tools are helpful at each point in the student's journey to master math and maybe even become an engineer like myself. Manifesting tools that you may hear about in this book or other places are similar in that they appear in your life at the appropriate time so that you can master manifesting.

The basic tool and building block for Law of Attraction is our THOUGHTS. We are taught to choose our words and affirmations carefully. You may have heard and had experiences with vision boards and other tools that help you build a collage of pictures that you can focus upon and set your intentions on manifesting your desires. There are other tools being shared to assist individuals on their manifesting journey and I am going to share my favorite manifesting tool—which is a simple formula or method for manifesting the life of your dreams.

Although there are no wrong ways to manifest your goals, this chapter will include a worksheet to help guide you on the method I use. Just use the tools that feel right to you in the moment. Remember wherever you are on your *magical manifesting journey* that the accelerator to achieving your dreams is keeping your vibration high. A high vibration sets your attraction point for allowing your goals to enter your life. I find that the easiest way to keep a high vibration is to ask yourself, "Do I feel Joy?" If the answer is *no* then shift your thoughts or actions toward joy.

Before we jump into the manifesting tool, I want to talk about feelings and emotions, since they are a part of the manifesting equation. Do you allow yourself to feel all your emotions? I'm sure many, like me, allow ourselves to feel negative or harsh feelings. Our thoughts which are manifesting building blocks then tend to match our feelings which are critical and judgmental on ourselves. The universe will then match those feelings and not the ones that we want to allow and attract into our life. If you don't focus on what you want to create and manifest in your life, your thoughts will put in an order to the universe for you. The manifesting method that I am going to share will help us focus on the positive emotions and feelings that we want to manifest in our lives. We will identify the feelings and emotions that we want to allow in our lives. You can manifest anything you want into your life, but the key to manifesting your heart's desire is to KNOW and FEEL in your soul that you already have it.

Let's start working through the manifesting tool which is the Manifesting Your Dreams Worksheet at the end of the chapter. You can go to my website and down load a .pdf copy of the worksheet as well.

The worksheet has a simple manifesting formula and a method that helps you to pull in the feelings and emotions you want to allow for a specific goal that you want to manifest in your life. The formula I have at the top of the worksheet is:

 THOUGHTS + EMOTIONS + ACTION = MANIFESTING GOALS

Thoughts, Emotions and Action are all required to manifest your goals. As mentioned before, our thoughts are the manifesting building blocks that help us attract what we desire in our lives. This worksheet will help us work through putting intentional focus on our thoughts and emotions, so that we can allow our goals to come to reality. Action could refer to having an action plan to work toward your goals, but more importantly, it is about raising your vibration so that the universe can have an energetic vibrational match for the goals you are manifesting.

Since joy and love are the highest vibration, I recommend coming up with an action plan on how to have more joy in your life. Self-care and surrounding yourself with supportive non-toxic people are also great ways to help bring more joy into your life. When your energy field is resonating with feelings of love, happiness and joy, I would venture to say that you are not having many negative thoughts to which the Universe can respond. Therefore your manifesting goals will come quicker to reality. I suggest developing an action plan that will create joy in your life.

☙ **Let's start off with a quick survey of 5 emotions you want to FEEL currently in your life:**
- Please take three deep breaths and then write on a piece of paper the 5 goals or emotions that you want to attract or have more of in your life.
- From the list you made, pick one that you feel will the make the biggest impact right now in your life. Maybe you chose love or a new career, but whatever ONE you chose, it is what we are going to use to work through the Manifesting Your Dreams Worksheet.

☙ **From the worksheet, circle the area or experience from the ONE you selected:**
- Maybe sit and think why you chose that category for the ONE you selected, since it may mean something different to you than for others.
- Next meditate on and share the reason you desire this manifestation goal. There are no wrong or right answers when using this worksheet, since everything is just an awareness to shed light on what we are asking the universe to deliver in our lives:

The Area or Experience I desire to
manifest using the Law of Attraction is:
Spiritual / Health / Relationship /
Career / Financial / Self-Love / Joy / Social / Other

The Reason(s) I desire this manifestation goal is

....

....

☙ **I open a workshop on manifesting your best life with the question—"If you could manifest one thing in your life right now, what would it be?"**
- Typically people will respond with the standard—a new job, new love or a new car. This is the time I dig a little deeper to see WHY they are choosing that to manifest. When we dig deeper, we find it is typically about something else and connected to some emotions. For example, a person who wants a

new job doesn't want ANY new job. They want to have a job where they are appreciated, have less stress and more money.

- After a few more series of questions, I find what they really want is a job with flexibility and more monetary resources that allows them to travel and enjoy life. I find that when we try to boil down the manifestation goal to one word, we usually find more details to what we want.
- The Golden question is *"When the Universe delivers us that new job, will it be the one we want?"*
- Please take time to meditate and question why this is your manifest goal and fill out the worksheet with your ONE word:

ONE WORD(S) that equates to what the manifestation goal means to me is

....

∾ **I want to continue using the new job manifesting example to work throughout this chapter while explaining how to use the worksheet. Please continue to use the ONE you selected.**

- Many of us have belief systems that are running in our subconscious mind that are impacting us manifesting our desires. I find that taking some time to look at what may be impacting us in achieving our goal can be very beneficial in our manifestation process.
- Let's look at the new job manifesting example to see where there are restrictive thoughts preventing us from getting our accurate order into the universe. Some potential restrictive beliefs around the new goal is a belief that I have to work long hours and that it is hard to make money. Another limiting belief is that my bosses never appreciate my efforts. Now meditate on your restrictive thoughts and document them in the worksheet:

I believe that I might have restrictive thoughts that are preventing me from attracting my desires. My current beliefs and emotions around this manifesting goal are (Be honest & nonjudgmental)

....

....

∾ **If I look at my beliefs that are impacting my manifestation process, I usually can find that they started with a past experience or an individual.**

- So now is the perfect time to reflect and meditate on an experience or individual that I need to do some forgiveness work around and release.

I may find that I have some self-forgiveness work. Please document your awareness in the worksheet:

An experience or individual that I need to release or
forgive including myself related to this goal

- When you have the ability to focus with gratitude on what you desire and can find some examples currently in your life, I feel that is the key to allowing yourself to attract more of what you desire into your life.
  - For the job manifesting example—I desire to be appreciated more by my supervisor. I notice and feel the gratitude from my co-workers and customers. I also find that the Bank Teller after work remarks on how she appreciates my positive interaction when I come into the bank. I start to look around and feel gratitude for all the appreciation that already exist in my life.
  - The gratitude is a signal sent to the universe to send more. I may find at the office next Monday, the supervisor stops by my desk to share how much he appreciates me.
  - Meditate now on your ONE goal and capture in the worksheet where it currently exists in your life and FEEL and the gratitude:

    List aspects of the manifestation goal CURRENTLY in your life
    and why you are grateful. If you can't see and have gratitude for
    what you already have, it is hard to manifest your goal!

- Since you are the creator of your life and can manifest what you desire into being, why not create a detailed list of what you want.
  - I suggest not trying to include "HOW" it should come into your life—since the universe could deliver what you are manifesting in a miraculous way that you cannot not even conceive.
  - For the job manifestation example, I would list attributes of having appreciation by my supervisors. I would see bonus checks for a job well done. I would see a customer telling my supervisor how happy they are with my service. I would hear my supervisor's pride when telling them I am his best employee. I would feel the appreciation. I would feel that I have lots of extra money

for travel and other things that bring me joy. I would see me on my yearly winter trip to Hawaii. I would feel the warm water and sand on my feet.

- Now, it's your turn to dream BIG. Meditate and capture on your worksheet a detailed list of all the attributes of how your ONE shall show up in your life:

Make a detailed list of what attributes you are manifesting.
INCLUDE: What does it feel like? Hear like? Look like? Taste like?
Smell like? How do you feel emotionally when it manifests?

∾ So for each attribute on your detailed list above we want to capture the emotion and feeling of each attribute when it manifests in your life.

- By allowing the feeling we want to be in our energy field, we allow more of that same feeling to come into our lives. The best way to do that is to remember a time in our life that we felt a similar way and capture that memory and emotion. The memory doesn't have to be associated with our goal, but has be a time we felt the same emotion that we want to attract now into our life.
- For the attribute of my supervisor's appreciation in the job manifestation example, I would remember the time my favorite math teacher gave me an appreciation award for tutoring other students. The other students and their parents were also grateful for my help.
- For the attribute of being able to travel and attend other joyful events in my life, I would capture that feeling of the first paycheck from my job in high school. I would remember how excited I was to have extra money for that concert ticket. I could also remember that senior trip to Florida that I paid out of my own savings. I could also capture that first time I went to Hawaii as a young adult and the associated excitement.
- Meditate and capture on the worksheet, the associated emotions for each of the your ONE attributes:

Write down examples from your life experiences when you felt emotions
and thoughts similar to each attribute you captured on your detailed list?
Remember and describe in detail how you felt?

You have completed your manifesting attributes and the way you want to feel when you manifest each into your life. This detailed list completes the formula for manifesting your dreams. Thoughts, Emotions and Action are all required to manifest your goals and the method followed in this worksheet helped you merge that energy into your manifestation list.

 THOUGHTS + EMOTIONS + ACTION = MANIFESTING GOALS

I suggest making a copy of this list and placing it at work and at home. Now spend a few moments going through each attribute on your detailed list for your manifesting goal. Pause for each attribute and visualize that it is already in your life. At the same time, remember to bring in the similar emotion/feeling life experience you captured for each attribute.

I also suggest that you might want to repeat this daily for 21 days, or as guided, to help keep the vibration in your energy field.

Please note that the time and energy in creating this list is done — the next time you run through the list, manifesting will take less time to visualize and bring in the energy of each attribute's emotion and feelings.

Blessings to you as you manifest the life of your dreams!

MANIFESTING YOUR DREAMS WORKSHEET
Paula Obeid 480-239-0660
THOUGHTS + EMOTIONS + ACTION = MANIFESTING GOALS

- ☙ The Area or Experience I desire to manifest using the Law of Attraction is:
  Spiritual / Health / Relationship / Career /
  Financial / Self-Love / Joy / Social / Other

- ☙ The Reason(s) I desire this manifestation goal is:
  ....
  ....
  ....

- ☙ One Word(s) that equates to what the manifestation goal means to me is:
  ....
  ....
  ....

- ☙ I believe that I might have restrictive thoughts that are preventing me from attracting my desires. My current beliefs and emotions around this manifesting goal are (be honest and nonjudgmental):
  ....
  ....
  ....

- ☙ An experience or individual that I need to release or forgive, including myself, related to this goal:
  ....
  ....
  ....

- ☙ List aspects of the manifestation goal CURRENTLY in your life and why you are grateful. If you can't see and have gratitude for what you already have, it is hard to manifest your goal!
  ....
  ....
  ....

- Make a detailed list of what attributes you are manifesting.
  INCLUDE: What does it feel like? Hear like? Look like? Taste like? Smell like? How do you feel emotionally when it manifests?

- Write down examples from your life experiences when you felt emotions and thoughts similar to each attribute you captured on your detailed list? Remember and describe in detail how you felt?

- Now spend a few moments going through each attribute on your detailed list for your manifesting goal. Pause for each attribute and visualize that it is already in your life. At the same time, remember to bring in the emotion/feelings for the similar life experience you captured for each attribute. Repeat daily for 21 days, or as guided, to help keep the vibration in your energy field.

Develop an action plan that will create joy in your life. This will raise your vibration and help your manifestation goal becoming a reality!

My dedication is to the children of the world including my beloved children, Sarah and Adam. My wish for all is that they understand the Universal Law of Attraction that allows them to be the creator of their reality. May they use their power to attract what they desire and deserve!

"All that we are is the result of what we have thought. The mind is everything. What we think, we become." ~ Buddha

I am forever grateful to all the enlightened teachers that have existed throughout time and currently who have shared timeless wisdom to assist us on our soul journey.

~Paula Obeid

Wendy Kitts

WENDY KITTS, at 42, went from a nine-to-five cubicle-gray existence to living in Technicolor as a writer — without ever writing anything before. Fifteen years later, Wendy's written two books and over 200 articles for publications such as *Reader's Digest*.

Wendy's a certified Infinite Possibilities trainer based on Mike Dooley's *Infinite Possibilities: The Art of Living your Dreams.* She's following her dream of writing at the beach year-round, splitting her time between New Brunswick (Canada) and California. Wendy's passionate about helping others follow their writing dreams. Get a free copy of *Write for Profit & Bliss: Sell Your Writing Now!* on her website.

www.wendykitts.ca

Write. Share. Transform.

Do you dream of being a writer but don't know where to start? Do you long for a job where you can skip the morning commute, put in the hours you want, or work in your pajamas all day?

Or maybe you love to travel and need a way to pay for your nomadic habits? Or perhaps you're a speaker with a desire to reach a wider audience? Or maybe you already write "on the side," but are looking for a way to ditch your nine-to-five job and write full-time?

Or maybe, just maybe, you want to spend your time doing something that matters; something that inspires you to get out of bed in the morning? Something that will finally quiet that little voice within that beckons you to put thoughts into words, words onto paper.

Being a freelance writer can give you all of this. It can provide the freedom you're longing for, an income limited only by how much time you want to put into it, and work that seems more like play. And for speakers, coaches and workshop facilitators, writing not only offers another stream of income through magazine articles and "back-of-the-room" book sales, it also adds credibility. You'll be perceived as an expert in your field, which could lead to greater opportunities. And even more importantly, it will help you build the holy grail of the publishing world—a platform.

But the best part—you can do it from anywhere in the world. Whether from home with your children playing nearby, or from an Italian café while drinking Limoncello—all you need is a laptop and an Internet connection. That's it.

Well … that and a belief that it's never too late to be what you wanted to be when you grew up.

When Life Gives You Lemons, Drink Limoncello

Somewhere along the way in my quest to be an adult, I got stuck. I was afraid to follow my childhood dream of an artistic life and settled instead for a life as drab as the walls that surrounded me day after day, year after year, in my accounting job. Then, the worst happened.

Or seemingly.

The fallout of a car accident tore through my life like a tornado, uprooting every aspect that wasn't authentic, and surprisingly ... lovingly ... provided the key to my happiness.

Injured and forced to find work I could do from the comfort of my couch, I scrambled to find a way to support myself. And when all my safe, go-to choices were out of reach, I took the only choice left.

The choice that had been dancing around in the cobwebs of my mind for decades. The choice that refused to die, despite my DNR missive. The only choice I'd been afraid to follow: To leave my nine-to-five comatose-inducing existence for a creative life. A soul-full life.

A life on my terms.

So after a few years of a pity party with a guest list of one, I answered an ad. And at the age of 42, my life went from cubicle-gray ... to Technicolor.

I had no training in writing; I had never even written anything before when I responded to a call for stories about favorite Halloween costumes for my provincial newspaper. Yet my story was chosen as the best, and published. Flash-forward 15 years and I'm a full-time writer who snowbirds in sunny San Diego, writing in my pjs with the Pacific at my door. And, yes, sometimes even a mug of Limoncello nearby.

And it was so easy. Because what I didn't know then that I know now, is that's what it feels like when you follow your passions. Easy.

I grew up believing the opposite. That it was hard; that you couldn't make a living as a writer or an artist. That I'd have to make a choice between expressing my soul, my bliss, and well ... eating. But I eventually chose to replace those beliefs with a few new ones:

You Already Have Everything You Need To Be A Writer

You already have everything you need — right now — to be a writer. You wouldn't have those creative longings within if you also didn't have the means to make your writing dreams a reality. The "how" is inherent in the dream. So the best way to learn how to write is to simply do it. And read, too. Much like an architect learns how to build a house by studying the blueprints of other houses, writers similarly can learn how to write by reading other writers.

And don't let bad grammar or poor spelling stop you. That's what editors are for. Writing is a creative and collaborative act between writer and editor; and it's an editor's job to make your writing shine. Definitely enrol in professional development classes if you need to, work on your craft, but don't let that be the reason to not write.

Besides, the more you write, the better you'll get. And if you're letting a thought like *not being good enough* stop you, you might want to ask yourself why. You have a distinctive view that no one else has, and a voice that the world is waiting to hear.

Writing Is A Growing, Viable Industry

Refuse to believe people who say you can't make a living being a writer. Or that it's too hard to get published, or that it takes too long. Those are their beliefs, their realities — not yours. Today, there are more places to share and publish your writing than in the history of our planet. And without content, none of the publications or websites would exist. Many sites need fresh content daily, or even several times a day.

And even though printed magazines and newspapers are shrinking in size and market share, most have an online presence. Remember, the audience isn't shrinking. Neither is the need for content — there's just a change in how readers consume their information — which translates into more markets, including book markets. Today, there are book publishing options that didn't exist previously, or weren't recognized as valid. Writing is definitely a growth industry.

You Can Be A Writer Right Now — Today

Even if you've never shared your writing publicly before, you can change that right now. This minute. You can stop reading and set up a blog in less than an hour. You could write an article to submit to your favorite magazine or website tonight. Got a weekend free? Write an e-book on your topic of expertise and post it on your website.

Not sure if you have enough information to fill a book? If you are a coach or a workshop leader and have enough material to facilitate a weekend workshop, you have enough content for a book. You also have the advantage of having clients whose stories you can use as case studies.

So just do it. Make today the day you do something towards your writing dream.

Five Tips To Help You Sell Your Writing Now

1. **Build Publication Credits**
   The key to building a professional writing career is getting publication credits. Credits say three things about you as a writer: that you know how to work with an editor; that you can write; and that you can meet a deadline — which is non-negotiable in the publishing world.

It doesn't matter where you got those credits, or even if you got paid for your writing (from an editor's point of view); editors just want to know that you have experience. And sometimes, to get that experience, those publication credits, you may need to write for free—which is the only time you should ever consider it. Writing for free devalues all writers.

Writing is a profession. And professional writers, by definition, get paid. Think about it. A plumber wouldn't work on your pipes for free. Your talent and time are valuable. So if you do it for free, ensure you receive something in return like credits, increased exposure, or promotion.

And there's a difference between simply posting writing online somewhere, versus posting on a juried or reviewed site. It's best if there's some sort of gate-keeper, an editor or review process that you must go through in order to be published. It has to do with credibility and the quality of writing, and most editors will make this distinction.

Once you get your first credit, use it to get the next bigger one. I started out writing for a provincial magazine. I used those credits to get a weekly column and eventually a position as a regular contributor to a national newspaper. And those credentials, along with an anthology credit, helped me successfully pitch my first children's book.

You can go directly to your dream publication. Make big moves when they feel right; if your idea and query is solid, an editor may take a chance on you. But this method allows you to improve your craft and build confidence while learning about the industry.

2. **Target the Right Publication or Website**
Researching target markets and ensuring they are a match to your writing style and the story you want to tell is the single most important thing you can do to get a "yes" from an editor.

And don't limit yourself to consumer magazines. Trade publications are a very lucrative market. They're hungry for content and it's a great way to repurpose stories.

3. **Deliver a Quality Product**
If your desire is to be published in magazines, print or online, a query is usually your first contact with an editor. Query writing is an art and is as important as the story itself, because if you can't sell the idea, you won't sell the story. So it's crucial that you make a good impression, a professional impression.

Keep your query to one page if possible. Ensure you have the most current contact info, as well as the correct spelling of the editor's name. This may seem like a no-brainer, but mistakes on basics like these happen a lot; and lack of attention to details will speak volumes about your writing to an editor.

Open with an engaging fact or question about your subject to hook the editor, followed by a brief paragraph about the story you intend to tell. Include details as to proposed word count, story angle and whom you will interview. Let the editor know why their readers will be interested in this story. End with a brief and relevant bio. Be sure to include anything that demonstrates why you're the best person to tell this story.

Then, deliver what you promised — polished, to word count, and on time. Nothing kills a writing career faster than someone who turns in sloppy work, or misses deadlines.

Queries are also used for agents and editors of traditional publishing. And if you publish independently, hire an editor. You only have one chance to make a first impression on your audience. You want your book to be as polished and professional as any book that may be published through a traditional route.

4. **Visualize Yourself as a Successful Writer**

Studies show that for professional athletes, visualization is more crucial than even skill or talent. Visualization is important for writers, too. Before author Wayne Dyer wrote a book, he had his publisher design a mock-up of the cover which he kept in view as he wrote.

See yourself as a successful writer. See yourself sitting in your chair writing at your computer. Feel the excitement at the thought of seeing your books and your name in print.

5. **Go Within**

Remember, this is *your* message. The message *you* came here to share. The message someone else is waiting to read that will make a difference in his or her life. So be open to sharing yourself on the page. Be vulnerable and aligned with who you really are, not a facsimile of how you think a coach or a speaker would present themselves to the world. Readers and editors respond to real, so don't give them anything less than your Self on the page.

Approach writing by feeling your way there — not only feeling the words, but feeling the spaces between the words. Go within and allow your Self to guide you. If you write from this heart-centred space, it will never steer you wrong.

Write. Share. Transform

This is it. This is your time. Sparkle and shine like only you can. *Write* what is begging to be written, that only *you* can write. Then *share* your unique voice. It will *transform* not only your Self and your life, but, by extension, the world.

And try to enjoy a glass of Limoncello every now and then.

Dedicated to those who follow the writing whispers within — write, share, transform!

Thanks to Lisa Hardwick for this beautiful opportunity to be part of such a heart-centered project. Sending hugs and blisses to Lisa and her entire VIP team for their encouragement and support.

~ Wendy Kitts

Damien Munro

DAMIEN MUNRO is a transformational Life Coach and Motivational Speaker from Melbourne, Australia.

He has travelled throughout Europe, Asia and Australia teaching the principles of Self Love and Acceptance, assisting hundreds of people, just like you, to discover and align to their life purpose and live the life of their dreams.

It is Damien's belief that that we all deserve to live a life filled with love, joy and happiness.

As a complimentary gift to you for purchasing this book, Damien is giving you his eBook free, to download your copy simply go to www.DamienMunro.com/12-Keys

contact@DamienMunro.com
www.DamienMunro.com

Aligning to Your 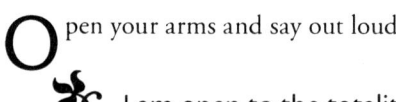 Life's Purpose

Open your arms and say out loud with me:

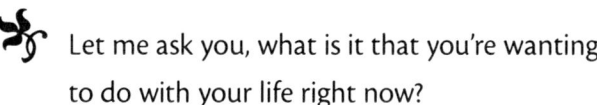 **I am open to the totality of possibilities for my life!**

How does that feel?

Strange? Unusual? Weird? Wrong?

You see, I believe we all deserve to live a life with wondrous possibility, filled with passion and purpose. We all have an amazing gift or talent to share with the world. However, many of us believe that we aren't good enough and nobody will ever be interested in what we have to share.

Let me ask you, what is it that you're wanting to do with your life right now?

Write it down:

....

....

....

....

....

Let yourself express what it is that you really want, it's ok to not know how you will get it, and even for it to be scary. Our thoughts don't always have to be logical and our fears don't need to make sense. For the moment, we are setting sail on new lands of discovery and exploring a whole new way of thinking about ourselves and our lives.

During our time together in this chapter, we are going to spend some time working on drawing your purpose out from your mind and manifesting it into the world.

One thing that I am often asked is, *"Damien, how do you find your life purpose?"* So let's start with that!

1. What Is Life Purpose:

I believe that we are all born with a sense of what it is that we are here to do, it's just that as we've grown from children, we've learned to listen to the beliefs and fears of many "well meaning" adults around us who are wanting to keep us safe.

This is not to blame or ridicule our parents or any other caregivers, they were simply doing the best that they could with the knowledge and information that they had. They possibly even grew up with parents who were scared and didn't know how to make their lives work either.

So the question of purpose is not really *"How do I find it?"* It's more of a question *"How do I reconnect with it?"*

2. We All Have One Purpose:

I really believe that we have all come here with one single purpose, and that is to be of service, and to give and receive love. I really believe that it is that simple. When we are being of service and giving and receiving love in a balanced, non-judgmental way, our lives work, we begin to get what I call the "goodies."

Think of it like the way light travels through a prism. This is our connection to something greater. You may call it Universal Energy, Source, God, Mother Divine, Allah or one of the many names across the many religions.

Our connection is to that of pure love. It enters into us like the light entering a prism, and is then radiated out into the world as colour. This colour is our many skills, talents and abilities. Each of us have at least one and some seem to have many (normally when we have only one, it becomes so much easier — the more confused you feel about what your talents are, the more likely you have many of them). These colours then translate into the work that we do in the world.

This is where I believe the saying *'let your colours shine'* comes from.

The foundation for finding your life purpose is to be comfortable with who you are and where you are in life, right now! I know, this can seem rather backward and I forgive you for thinking I've gone mad. Let me explain … it's true, you may not be feeling happy or fulfilled with where your life is right now. However, simply changing the place where you are is not the answer.

3. The Real Change Comes From Within!

First you must learn to love and approve of yourself—I mean really love and approve of yourself—exactly as you are. When I speak of loving and approving of yourself, I am not talking about vanity or arrogance. That is not love, that is fear.

If you simply change the place where you work without changing the thoughts and feelings you have for yourself, you will simply carry those same old attitudes with you into the next thing that you do. Pretty soon, you'll begin to feel just as unfulfilled in this new place as you did in the old one. Also, you can't try to have a wonderful, successful career or life in order to prove that you are OK, or good enough. You must begin to love yourself and know that you are doing your best where you are right now.

People often think, *"If I were happy with where I am right now, I simply wouldn't bother to make any changes!"*—and this is just not true. When you're happy with who you are and really love yourself, you're full of energy and drive. Changes are easy.

If you blame anyone or anything for not being happy where you are right now, you are going to take that attitude with you. The responsibility of being happy or not is yours and yours alone, no matter where you are in life.

✍ What did you learn about Work and Yourself when you were growing up? (Write down some of the things your parents and other adults told you.)

_____

_____

_____

_____

_____

✍ Did they tell you things like:
- You have to go to school and get good grades so that you could go to university, to get a good job, just so you can earn enough money to get you by.
- Earning money is tough and you have to work hard to get anywhere.
- There's no rest for the wicked.
- Working for yourself is too risky, you could lose everything!
- There is no guarantee that you will always have a job, you could lose it at anytime!
- The job market is … (really tough, too quiet, dried up)
- You can't make enough money doing what you love (art, music, writing, acting, etc.), you may as well not bother.

If you have any of these limiting ideas, it will be extremely difficult for you to align to your life purpose and attract creative work that is fulfilling to you.

Think about and write down how these ideas have affected your life up until now?

....

....

....

....

....

....

႟ One of the beliefs that I used to have was, *"It's so hard to earn money. There simply isn't enough!"* Well, you can imagine the outcome of that thinking—there was definitely never enough money at the end of the week! There was barely enough to cover my bills, and I remember at one stage, there wasn't enough money to eat.

I began to switch my thinking to, *"I find money wherever I turn, life is a joy!"* and within a short period of time, I started to find money left in my pockets or a spare $20 in my bank account, I even found money on the street. In the early stages, I found a $100 monopoly note on the ground, I thanked the universe whole heartedly for the symbol of increased prosperity.

Even if you find 20 cents when you first start out, be thankful, the universe loves gratitude. If you find money and think, *"Oh, that isn't enough,"* the Universe will hear you and you'll cut off this new and improved flow. So please be grateful for even the smallest amount in the beginning. The Universe is ALWAYS listening to you.

႟ We are now choosing to become the authority in our lives and we can choose to change the thoughts that we think, and therefore, change our lives.

We must become aware of our negative thoughts and ideas. These are the very thoughts that continue to keep our good away and we must learn how to turn these statements into positive, powerful statements that build us up, rather than beat us up.

When we change our thinking, we really do change our lives!

Choose one of the negative statements that you wrote earlier and together let's turn it into a positive statement.

For example, if you had, *"You have to work hard to earn a good living,"* it could become, *"Money comes to me easily and effortlessly."*

Practice this positive statement whenever you catch yourself thinking about the negative, and start looking for signs that what you want to attract is coming into your life. The Universe will reward you and give you more of it.

 I really do believe that we all deserve to live a fulfilling and happy life. Yes — you included.

To my ever-growing audience, thank you for your kindness love and support. May your lives continue to expand and grow in the most wonderful ways. Stay beautiful with a splash of gorgeous!

To the many teachers who have shaped my path and shared their wisdom, especially Susie Mulholland, Peter Bruce, Louise Hay, Dr Patricia Crane and Rick Nichols. Matthew Davis for all of your love and support in the work that I do, I love you and couldn't be doing what I was born to without you. Jo Walsh for your promptings to take my journey to the next level. My parents Rod and Leanne Munro for your love, support and early childhood lessons. Without you both, I wouldn't have discovered the lessons I came to this planet to learn.

– Damien Munro

Maggie Cervantes

MAGGIE CERVANTES is a Heal Your Life® workshop leader and coach. She has a Master's Degree in Spiritual Psychology. Maggie has dedicated her life to helping others find their true happiness and self worth. She has co-led workshops on self care, prosperity, meditation, and affirmation writing. In her coaching practice she has worked with women during major transition periods in their lives. Maggie has over 24 years of service in the nonprofit world, assisting low-income families connect with their prosperity.

Maggie lives in sunny Southern California, where she walks her dog everyday giving her time to focus on her walking mediations.

Magcer1027@yahoo.com

❧ Empowered by Spirit

One of the defining *spiritual experiences* in my life was a transformational empowerment journey I embarked on eight years ago. As part of my Master's project in Spiritual Psychology, I chose to walk as a pilgrim on the Santiago de Compostela Camino in Northern Spain. I wanted to experience the physical empowerment of walking in solitude to see where my thoughts wandered, to dig below the surface into any negative or limiting beliefs. I wanted to explore my emotional landscape, to nurture a loving and confident trust in myself and others. And, I wanted to deeply connect and align with my authentic self and spirit.

I had a dream that walking the Camino would be one of those unforgettable experiences in life that would change who I am. And it did. I wanted to jump out of my comfort zone because, for me, empowerment means having the courage to do something that scares me, that brings up resistance or fear, and the desire to find out why. I have always had a need to ask the universe what is next in my life and I usually get an answer, through a feeling, a knowing or a thought. Then I ask myself, "Do I have the courage to confront this?" Curiosity propels me forward.

Before this journey, I had never traveled to a foreign country on my own, so this was a new adventure that both frightened and excited me. I prepared by using the following process to help keep me focused, grounded and centered in meeting my dream of walking the Camino and living my life more closely aligned with spirit.

So how do you prepare your body, mind, heart and spirit when you want to take on something in your life that you know will transform you? It does not have to be an actual physical journey, but could even be simply another form of doing something different, changing a physical habit or practice. So let's say you want to change a mental pattern and the outcome will include a physical action or change in your day-to-day habits

Here is a series of questions to ask. First, start by taking three deep breaths, center yourself (which means to quiet your mind and be in a loving place within yourself). Ask the universe/your spirit guide for guidance as you create a new reality for yourself. Once you feel centered, begin to answer the following questions. You can keep a journal, record your answers on a tape recorder or say them out loud. As an example, my responses are in italics below:

1. **What experience do you want to have?**
   Joyful confidence.

2. **Create an affirmation about your desired experience?**
   I am joyful and confident in every step I take as I lovingly live my life.

3. **Describe what you want to accomplish/experience — what is the outcome you want to achieve? (Make sure it truly resonates with your heart and soul). Write in detail every aspect of what you want to accomplish. Always use self-affirming words that speak to your heart and that you can visualize experiencing.**
   I want to complete a pilgrimage that encompasses a physical, mental, emotional and spiritual journey.
   - **Physical:** *I am enthusiastically building my physical endurance to walk 10 to 15 miles a day. It is exhilarating to walk and practice for my Camino journey. A walking meditation builds my connection to spirit and in every step I feel spirit's presence.*
   - **Mental:** *I love to visualize my walk and I have mentally prepared by doing my homework and research on travel arrangements and lodging. I read books on the Camino that give me a sense of what it is like and I love reading about the history of Spain. I meditate once a day on the wonderful experience I will have and clear my thoughts before I take my practice walks. I am addressing any limiting beliefs that arise, shaking them off and creating new realities for myself on this journey with positive affirmations of who I truly am.*
   - **Emotional:** *I expand my sense of trust and freedom meeting new people while walking. (This was important to me as I grew up fearful of meeting people and had a fear of not being accepted.) I treat myself in a kind and compassionate manner as I know my spirit guides are here to help me connect to my heart and I am filled with grace.*
   - **Spiritual:** *The Camino connects me with my higher self and I carry that connection through all my journeys in life. Spirit's presence is in every step I take in life.*

Giving voice to these four levels of who you are helps solidify your experience. You can update them as you go along and see the remarkable progress you are making on your journey.

One issue that may arise for you when you start a new journey of empowerment is judgment around doing something out of your comfort zone. This came up for me on my own journey. I questioned why I was taking this "frivolous" trip. I feared that the trip was extravagant, that I should not be spending a lot of money while I had many other expenses. Growing up poor, I was raised with the belief that I needed to save my money for practical things. I was holding on to an irrational belief.

So, my issue was about abundance, or lack of it, as I perceived the trip and the amount of money I was going to spend. I also realized I was labeling my spiritual quest as "frivolous." My ego was working overtime to keep me down. I realized I had to have a heart-to-heart talk with myself about my commitment to this journey. I could "just walk it" or I could address my limiting beliefs and feelings of low self-esteem and commit to change my perceptions and feelings.

I pledged to myself to make the deeper commitment. In an exercise of self-forgiveness, I placed my hand over my heart and stated, *"I forgive myself for falling into the limiting belief of not being worthy of this connection with sprit and believing there is a lack of money to make this trip. The truth is that I am a divine being having a human experience and I am worthy of this journey. I am not afraid because there is always a loving presence to help me grow and succeed."*

After going through this process, I set my intention to hold a level of abundance throughout this trip. My intention was to have an easy and comfortable trip. I would treat myself to a fantastic journey that would reward me, beyond belief, with riches and treasures that I discovered for myself, and that outweighed any monetary costs. For me, it was a sense of trusting my spiritual knowing and having the courage to believe in myself to do something that was unusual for me.

So, after a few months of physical, mental, emotional and spiritual training, I set off to discover the Camino and myself. Physically, I endured rain, heat, cold and wind. I trudged up hills, over gravel and onto highways. I savored the beauty of green hills and lush flowers. Mentally and emotionally, I met my first challenge on the second day, after indulging my ego in negative thoughts. My mind began wandering from the present moment and I drifted into a negative pattern of thought about my work back home. I was judging people and situations, stirring up past anger.

I found myself walking through a narrow pathway between two homes. Pilgrims walked ahead of me and behind me at a distance. All of a sudden, a large German Shepherd began barking furiously at me, straining to get through a fence between us. My heart raced. I was startled and confused, hoping it was securely confined.

Almost instantly I made the connection, seeing beauty in the life lesson that had been revealed to me—the dog was mirroring my internal anger and judgmental energy. I was energetically projecting a snarling, angry animal. From that moment on, I realized how my thoughts and feelings defined my life in terms of what I attract.

A few days later, after I had recovered from my mental and emotional hurdle, I began a leisurely seven-mile walk. Even though an intermittent rain fell throughout the day, my mind was happy and free, and I was in a great place. The rural road gave way to a small, beautiful village and my mind rose up to meet it. "I wonder what it would be like to live here?" I asked the universe.

About 10 minutes later, the answer galloped past me. It was a heroic gesture that tested my question to the universe. A man on a brown horse drew up next to me and peered into my face, the only visible part of my body not covered in plastic rain gear, and boldly said, "Come home with me."

"No, I can't, " I replied.

"Are you married?" he asked.

"No," I responded. He pleaded with me to reconsider, as I wiped rain from my face, but I held steadfast in my answer and I didn't want to fall into the mud. I wasn't afraid—he seemed like a nice man.

Finally yielding to my repeated rebuffs, he rode off as abruptly as he had entered my life. It was like a dream, surreal even. The universe had responded gallantly to me, showing me a glimpse of what it would be like to live in this region of Spain—I would be married to a farmer!!!!

I laughed after he left because the universe answered my question in a very unusual, immediate and direct way. I will remember that encounter for the rest of life. And remember that the universe is always responding. When you center yourself, clear your mind and feel from your heart, Spirit is there to respond to your requests, sometimes swiftly.

I set my intention and it came true, I had a wonderful, meaningful experience filled with magical and sacred moments with spirit. In fact, every moment was filled with spirit's guidance and challenges to believe in me, and love myself unconditionally. I now take one step at a time, knowing I am guided, assisted, and loved by the universe. I know that I am empowered physically, mentally, emotionally and spiritually to create a beautiful life for myself.

This empowerment journey helped me create a wonderful affirmation for myself that I live by: *Living from abundance is part of my life purpose.*

I have learned that abundance is more than just monetary security. It is about the fullness and richness I am creating for myself that is heart- and spirit-driven.

It's about living life in a bountiful state and seeing the treasures and prosperity all around me and within me.

 "I've learned that fear limits you and your vision. It serves as blinders to what may be just a few steps down the road for you. The journey is valuable, but believing in your talents, your abilities, and your self-worth can empower you to walk down an even brighter path. Transforming fear into freedom — how great is that?"

~ SOLEDAD O'BRIEN

This chapter is dedicated to all the beautiful and empowered souls who have walked the Camino. With every step we have taken on the Camino, we have lifted our hearts and souls to create more light and love in the world. Thank you to the Heal Your Life® Community of teachers, colleagues and participants for having the courage to explore, heal and live an authentic life.

I would like to thank my family and friends for their guidance and love through the many journeys in my life, especially my mom and sister for the guidance, love and wacky sense of humor that brings joy into my life. I would like to thank my Heal Your Life® workshop partner Linda Lee for her ever-present light and giving spirit.

~ Maggie Cervantes

Kim Sanders

KIM SANDERS has lived in Illinois all of her life and currently resides in the Springfield area. She spends as much time as she can with her two children, Kortni and Kurtis. She enjoys interacting with people and is genuine, personable, and dedicated. Kim has worked for many years in Information Systems with a focus on support and management of software, as it relates to the business side of healthcare.

Though she still enjoys leading short-term projects or training others, this was not her life calling. In the fall of 2014, she graduated from Eastern Illinois University with a degree in Career and Organizational Development. Then, in early 2015 she founded *Kreative Solutions by Kim*. As an independent life coach, she is able to pursue her passion of helping others on their life journey with a witty affection.

Email: kreativesolutionsbykim@gmail.com
Website: www.kreativesolutionsbykim.com

Claiming Your Best (or Better) Self — Now!

Claiming your life purpose is a dynamic journey of empowerment. Opportunities for growth and improvement are out there, but we must be willing to search for and readily embrace them. What holds you back from being the best version of you? Are you missing opportunities of growth and improvement? Can you differentiate between real and self-conceived criteria? In order to reach your full potential, you must maneuver around these roadblocks. While it may seem overwhelming or slow, the process is absolutely worth it because *you* are worth it!

In my past I struggled to understand and implement this concept into my daily life. At times I became idle and opportunities would pass me by without acknowledgment. Other times, I played the endless *"what if"* game. I would reason I was being cautious as I considered every possible outcome, after which I would decide to wait until the *"right moment"* when some seemingly-tangible goal was fulfilled, such as losing weight or getting a new job. I had to *QUALIFY* for my life before I was able to live it.

The process of claiming my life purpose was not quick and easy. I did not wake up one morning to a bright, cheery demeanor and suddenly love and care for myself. As I look back, there were times when I am not certain I was consciously aware of my journey, though, once I committed myself for months on end, the transformation was unavoidable. My awakening into empowerment is a long, fluid movement. I continue the process every minute of every hour of every day, and I face each day with greater focus and diligence.

I do not believe there is a prescriptive method that works for everyone exactly the same, for everyone operates differently. I am sharing my experiences with you and hope you will receive courage, insight, and skills to assist on your journey of empowerment.

Simply put, these are reflections on my journey to claiming my purpose and realizing my better self. You should use this as a motivational guide, and apply it to your life in ways that make the most sense to you:

1. For many years, I pushed my goals farther and farther into the future, telling myself I would surely be capable of accomplishing them the following week, but I always fell short for one reason or another. I formulated plenty of excuses to set my goals aside, and convinced myself I was better off without change.

    In my situation, I justified not seeking a post-secondary education while my ex-husband was in school because there was not enough time or resources for us to both attend. In reality, we could have found a way to make ends meet, but because the situation was not ideal, I hid behind the excuse as a way to avoid change.

    It is in our nature as humans to do anything in our ability to escape from confrontation when we are scared of something. We suddenly become masterminds in picking out every single detail that could go wrong. Say, for example, if a person fears public speaking, they will often flee from situations when expected to communicate to a mass of people. They might believe the crowd will laugh at them and think their efforts are pointless, or maybe they think they will stumble on words and have difficulty conveying the points.

2. To transition beyond this phase, I have categorized these "excuses" into *realistic* and *self-conceived* criteria. This is a time when you have to be completely honest with yourself. You have to draw a line in the sand and stick to it—for it is up to you, and only you, to decide which criteria are self-conceived and which are realistic. The term self-conceived refers to an excuse that is not essential and hinders your ability to complete your goals, and, conversely, a realistic criterion is a legitimate condition fundamental to progress.

3. To properly explain this method, imagine someone looking to take a dance class. Once they have a desire to take the class, a mental checklist evolves. A class with the sought-after dance style, as well as a suitable time and location, will need to be established, and they may be required to register for the class or even purchase a suitable uniform.

    Entwined with these tangible tasks, the idea of actively participating in the class could possibly surface feelings of insecurity in relation to body image or ability to dance—leading to excuses that could impede their goal. To be more specific, let's say their excuses revolve around not being in the best shape or lacking a sense of rhythm. This is when differentiating between realistic and self-conceived criteria can be useful.

Which is which? Personally, I feel that using your body as an excuse is almost always self-conceived. Nobody passionately cares about appearance, and if they are judgmental, they are the ones worse off. And, what about when it comes to lacking rhythm? This is the exact reason to take the class in the first place, to learn and develop a new skill. You have to ask yourself why you believe the excuses restrain you. More often than not, if an excuse revolves around another person's perspective, the excuse is self-conceived. If you have trouble organizing these criteria as thoughts, physically write them down and sort them in that fashion.

4. Time restraints, the third obstacle to empowerment, also have a tendency toward becoming a self-conceived excuse. Time is a valuable commodity that should be respected and managed with an awareness of how it affects the future. Before I cultivated my way of thinking, lack of time was an excuse used liberally that bolstered my avoidance of progress. How can I possibly take classes when I have to work full-time and take care of my family? I simply do not have time! For the most part, scheduling conflicts can be eliminated when the goal is a priority.

Today, if I start using lack of time as an excuse, I know that I need to examine the priority of the goal. To battle this excuse, keep a 'time spent' log and record your activities and how much time was dedicated to them. This will give you an unbiased picture of where your time actually goes. Budgeting your time is essential to keeping on track and realizing your best self!

5. Another trap people fall into is the abyss of *"what if."* This seemingly interminable cycle can greatly affect the outcome of obtaining a goal. Breaking this thought process is integral to the overall journey to empowerment. Now, I am not suggesting that you haphazardly move through life without considering consequences. It is natural and healthy to look out for our best interests. Nonetheless, at some point the *what ifs* become a hurdle to be surmounted.

For as long as I can remember, I have had an overactive *what if* thought process. In elementary school, I would regularly get stuck in the *what if* cycle. What if I volunteer to answer and I am wrong? What if I mispronounce a word while I read aloud? What if people think I am being a know-it-all? The angst followed me through high school and into college. I went so far as to avoid continuing education due to mandatory speech class. Sure, it is completely normal for a developing individual to have these thoughts, but whenever it starts to interfere with education or social advancement, as it did to me, these questions become unhealthy and need to be quelled.

6. At the time, these self-conceived excuses felt comfortable, but in reality they were merely serving as a barrier. Two strategies that help me when I find myself in this cycle are: actively controlling the time spent in the phase, and rewording the *what ifs* from negative to positive.

    The first way I break this cycle is to limit the time I spend on this type of thinking. Taking fifteen minutes to focus on *what ifs* sets a discernible threshold, yet allows the concerns to be mulled over.

    By the same token, rephrasing the *what ifs* from negative to positive helps break through the self-imposed barrier. So what if I stumble on my words? Instead of thinking of the worst possible outcome, I consider that I am setting an example for the next person. I am letting them know it is okay to be human.

As demonstrated, there are essential criteria to execute any goal. However, self-conceived excuses can get in the way if given the opportunity. As I grow, it is becoming easier to recognize when I am using self-conceived excuses. It is my choice to either let it stand in my way or push through. If I allow it to stand in my way, I accept that the goal is not a priority to me; whereas if I push through, I gain the accomplishment.

Will you continue to let self-conceived excuses stand in the way of discovering your best self? What are you willing to do to move forward on your journey of empowerment? As you incorporate the direction found in this book, you are set to become an expert navigator on your journey of empowerment! No one is promising it is easy, but it is worth it—because YOU are worth it!

Dedicated to family and friends for their kind words, loving encouragement, and practical advice. Specifically, to my daughter, Kortni, and son, Kurtis, I am proud of you both and look forward to your journey as it unfolds. Thank you to my nephew, Tyson Navel, for being my sounding board, voice of reason, and most of all, my friend. I am blessed to have such a magnificent network of support. Love and blessings to each of you!

Thank you to my son, Kurtis, for your help in the editing process.

~ Kim Sanders

Linda Lee

LINDA LEE is a certified Heal Your Life® workshop teacher, coach and author who lives in Long Beach, California. She leads workshops with Heal Your Life® teacher Maggie Cervantes throughout Southern California. Previously, she worked for 25 years as an award-winning investigative journalist, travel writer and editor.

lindalee113@verizon.net

 Surrender to Your Power

 "Keep knocking and the Joy inside will eventually open a window and look out to see who's there."

~ RUMI

Many years ago, I read a short story by Leo Tolstoy called "Happy Ever After," and came across this line, which took my breath away: *"And I really was happy, but it tormented me that this happiness cost me no effort, no sacrifice, while my capacity for sacrifice consumed me."* At the time I read this, I knew it hit the mark, that he was writing about ME. I knew it was a piece of the puzzle, I just didn't know where it fit.

I didn't know then that my childhood and religious upbringing had imprinted my mind with a reverence for sacrifice. If Joy was to be experienced, it must come at great sacrifice first, I believed. I was taught that long-suffering, fortitude and patience were virtues, and I practiced them well. I had done many joyous things in my life, felt guilty for some of them, and worked painfully hard for others. The harder it was to attain my goal, the more I enjoyed it, and the less guilt I felt. When things came too easily, it felt like something was missing. It tormented me.

My college roommate once told me, *"Linda, if there is an easy way to do something and a hard way to do it, you always take the hard way."* I knew she didn't mean it as a compliment, but I took pride that she recognized how hard-working I was—that I wasn't afraid to sacrifice to get ahead. As a result, I planned my Joy, days, weeks and months ahead, instead of seizing it every day. I had an equal capacity for Joy and for sacrifice: the scales had to be balanced. If there was too much Joy and reward, I would need to create a hardship to tip the scale.

Over time, the suffering took its toll. I found myself in a health and spiritual crisis for which I could find no easy remedy. One of my many diagnoses was fibromyalgia, which a holistic doctor described to me as *storing emotions in the body's*

113

tissues. Believing there was a mind-body connection to my problems, I initially sought therapy. When my therapist asked me how I *felt*, I was taken aback, annoyed. I was a rational being with great capacity for analyzing all kinds of problems and finding solutions. What difference did it make how I felt? Couldn't we just identify a problem, come up with a solution and give me some homework to DO?

Feelings were not so important in our home. Since I didn't know how to get in touch with my feelings, I sought other solutions. I tried meditation, hypnosis, read books, attended workshops, and as I kept knocking, the door started to open — and so did the feelings. I started finding teachers who taught that I could learn from Joy as well as Pain. Pain can be an impetus for change, but I didn't need to dwell there; Joy was more important than pain. If I changed my thoughts, and surrendered what no longer served me, I could change my life.

The surrendering created new awareness and a life that tilted the balance in favor of Joy. Moving emotions out of my body allowed it to heal. Stress was no longer my power surge — connecting to Spirit and my inner sanctuary was.

 "He was mastered by the sheer surging of life, the tidal wave of being, the perfect joy of each separate muscle, joint, and sinew in that it was everything that was not death, that it was aglow and rampant, expressing itself in movement, flying exultantly under the stars."

~ JACK LONDON

I have a joyful friend with a very wise heart. She giggles easily and often. Years ago, we shared a martial arts class together. As I stood rigidly disciplined in pose, she always tried to make me laugh. I would stare straight ahead, unmoved. After class, she would run full-speed and jump into a large pit filled with foam pieces, yelping loudly. I envied that she could, and would, let loose with such abandon. It took me about six months — I was always a good planner — and finally I ran and jumped into the pit. I still remember being enveloped in soft foam and our laughter. And the sheer Joy of letting go.

 "Joy does not simply happen to us. We have to choose Joy and keep choosing it every day."

~ HENRI NOUWEN

Following my first workshop as a Heal Your Life® workshop leader, one of the women who attended called to tell me a story, which she would like to share with you. She is a mother and a dedicated kindergarten teacher. She and a colleague planned to honor a group of volunteers with a lunch at their school. The theme was "angels" and they wanted to festoon the room with balloons meant to reflect a heavenly morning. She wanted to use white and silver balloons, but her colleague insisted they have pink. She thought the pink was unnecessary, but agreed. A few days later she caught sight of a gorgeous sunrise and saw, as if for the first time, a rosy pink ribbon across the sky. She was stunned. *"I've been so busy with my own boys, and getting everything ready for my class all these years, that I never even noticed the color of the sunrise,"* she said. She sobbed, realizing how many years she had spent trying to create Joy for others, so much so, that she forgot to experience it herself.

She turned her 45-minute commute to work into a joyful journey. She turned off the radio and spoke affirmations to the sun as it spread into lovely pink and white clouds, or simply turned a clear sky golden. Soon after her awareness blossomed, she received a "pink" layoff notice after 25 years of teaching. It was bittersweet; but instead of indulging the bitter, she decided to surrender to the sweet. She decided to focus on the possibilities for more Joy that had unfolded: traveling, reading and relaxing, learning to paint. The awareness she experienced helped to change her thoughts about her willingness for so many years to put herself last. By changing her thoughts and perception about her role as a mother and teacher, she was able to recognize that the pink slip represented an opportunity for growth and self-awareness. She was given a chance to seize her own Joy, in addition to creating Joy for others.

 "When you honor the present moment, all unhappiness and struggle dissolve and life begins to flow with joy and ease."

~ ECKHART TOLLE

We empower ourselves when we are fully present and listen to our wise inner voice. We empower ourselves when we pay attention to the signals embedded in our emotions and manifested in the health of our bodies; when we listen to its cries for attention. We empower ourselves when we release what holds us back and creates unhappiness in our lives. Awareness, acceptance and surrender are the keys.

Are you moving through life with awareness, presence and in full participation? Do you care as much about your own happiness as someone else's? Often, on a conscious or unconscious level, we focus on what we do not want in our lives, or what is not working. We steel ourselves, in a flight or fight mode, bracing to "fight" a person, situation, expectation, habit, whatever is causing us grief. Or, we can be so consumed in our roles, and caring for others, we forget to take care of ourselves and embrace the Joy that is all around us—that *is* us. Power comes in acknowledging and accepting the thing or person we wish to fight and surrendering our negative emotions or attachment to future outcomes. It is also accepting that Joy is available to us, always; it is not a reward. Surrendering is not "giving up," but moving into the present where our power resides, accessing our inner wisdom and learning to trust.

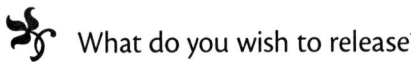 What do you wish to release?

Surrendering means yielding the need to struggle with whomever or whatever diminishes us, hurts us, or angers us. When we focus on the struggle or the fight, we will attract more of that struggle into our lives. Letting go detaches us, creating a distance from the problem itself. It allows us to accept what is in the present moment and to create space to allow light, grace and guidance to move us forward.

Releasing anger and frustration around a problem has physical benefits, creates emotional and mental balance in our lives and makes room for clarity to guide us. Spiritually, it allows us to connect more directly with Source and align with our true selves. It is in this place that we can allow Joy and Love to unfold and lead our lives.

What does Joy look like to you? Is it spontaneity, laughter, being surrounded by family and friends, or is it quiet solitude and reflection? Can you welcome more of these experiences into your life?

Here are two visualization exercises—the first is to help you release problems, situations and emotions; the second is to create a shift in thinking about a particular person.

Exercise 1

 "The more you connect to the power within you,
the more you can be free in all areas of your life."

~ LOUISE HAY

Close your eyes and relax. Let your muscles soften and become aware of your breathing. Tune in and follow its natural rhythm. Be still and ask yourself, *"What is disturbing my peace?" "Am I connected to my inner guidance, or have I tuned that out?"*

Is it a place, a situation, or work that is disturbing? Perhaps it is one situation or event that overshadows all the others; or perhaps it is an accumulation of little irritations that have been building over time. Perhaps it is a habit you want to release, negative thinking, or ideas that no longer serve a purpose for you. Whatever it is, how does it make you feel? It is safe to feel those feelings. Don't judge them. Just observe them. Hover above them, if it helps you. What part of you is needing or allowing this? Ask yourself, *"What would it feel like and look like if I surrendered these feelings, these irritations, this situation?"*

Sit still and FEEL the question in your body. What is your body telling you? Are you ready to surrender what no longer serves you, and replace it with something better?

Imagine that you and a good friend are walking in a beautiful, lush garden overlooking a clear lake. Your friend hands you an exquisitely-carved box made of fine, elegant wood. It has many compartments inside. Now, take particular situations, emotions, patterns or places that are holding you back, and place them all in the box. Small things can be fit in the corners, bigger things can be stacked. Ideas and old thinking can be written down and placed inside. Keep filling your box with everything you want to release.

As you place things you no longer need into the box, thank each one of them for serving its purpose, or teaching you a lesson you needed.

Now imagine you and your friend carrying the box to the edge of the lake. There is a small sailboat near the shore. Place the box into the boat, give the boat a little shove, and watch it disappear across the lake.

Now, feel the lightness in your body. Feel yourself enveloped in a ball of light. Let it flood your new inner spaces. You feel a power surge as you reconnect to Source. The inner space you have created has made room for something new. Clarity. Joy. Love. They are flashing in brilliance and pulsating throughout your body.

Now say to yourself: I am clear. I am Joy. I am Love. I AM. Repeat several times.

Know that you can carry lightness and light, Joy and Love into any situation. No one can diminish your lightness and Joy. Your lightness of being is quiet and strong. Know that if you begin to feel diminished, you can immediately retreat to that still, quiet space inside you, and surrender. And in your surrender, you can allow and accept what is. Allow and trust your inner wisdom to guide your actions.

When you are ready, open your eyes, sit quietly for a few moments, then write what came up for you in your journal.

Exercise 2

 "I do not fix problems. I fix my thinking.
Then problems fix themselves."

~ LOUISE HAY

When I was reading *Compassion in Action* by Ram Dass, he talked about placing photos of people on his altar who needed his forgiveness or compassion. This extended to political figures. I physically cringed reading this, thinking of the array of photos I would have to place on my altar, and wondered if I had the courage to look at them every morning and send them Love and blessings. Negativity, like Love, is expansive (never more so than during election season). It extends from ourselves and our inner circle, to our community and beyond. It affects how we relate to and judge ourselves and the world around us. Acceptance, Love and compassion don't mean we can't recognize the need for change and take action to do so. But being in a place of Love and forgiveness will guide us to take action with a higher level of awareness, without judgment.

True empowerment comes in freeing ourselves of the heavy burden we carry when we hold anger, resentment and critical thoughts of others. It is like a poison invading our thoughts, hearts and bodies. When we use so much space and energy to nurse these hurts, there is little space left for Joy. Relying on outside approval keeps us from seeing our true light and natural goodness. This need, coupled with a desire for "fairness" before we are willing to forgive and release, keeps us locked in fear which burdens our mind, body and spirit. We can learn to replace that fear with Love and Joy.

✌ Close your eyes and relax. Take three long, deep breaths and let your mind clear:

- Imagine a person who needs your forgiveness. Someone who is critical, angry, or in some way has hurt you. Think of the qualities about this person that make you feel uncomfortable, angry or hurt.
- Now, consider if this person is reflecting any similar qualities in yourself. They don't have to be exact, or of the same magnitude. Just be willing to consider that this person is a mirror. If you have strong resistance to this, ask yourself why. Often we will see in someone else, a pattern we may not want to address in ourselves.

- Just look at the resistance that comes up and acknowledge it. Sit quietly with it. Don't fight with, judge it, or engage it; just observe it. Now ask your higher self if there is a lesson for you to learn. Are you willing to learn it? If there is still resistance, that's okay. You have created awareness around this situation and that is the first step.

- Now, relax again and take three long, deep breaths. Imagine that the person who is causing you distress has come to you for guidance. Imagine placing her on your healing table, or on a chair next to you. Let her tell you her story, her wounds, what has led her to this place of anger.

- Now place your hand over your heart and ask what guidance you can give her. She is your student. You are the teacher.

- Notice if there is a shift in how you perceive this person or the situation. Perhaps she has become the teacher and is showing you where to look for your own guidance. When negative thoughts come up about this person, be willing to think of her as your teacher.

- Surround this person in Love, and then release her and all surrounding negativity with a deep breath. Thank her and bless her for being a teacher in disguise, for advancing you on your journey.

- Notice if your body feels lighter. You are creating new space for Love and Joy to replace fear and negativity. Think of an affirmation you can use to reinforce your new thoughts. Perhaps: "I live in harmony and peace with…" Repeat your affirmation several times.

- When you are ready, open your eyes, and write about your experience in your journal.

This chapter is dedicated to my husband, Tim, who has supported my empowerment for more than 20 years. Thank you for empowering everyone around you with your generosity, kindness and collaborative spirit!

I would like to thank Lisa Hardwick, publisher of Visionary Insight Press, for empowering so many voices. A ripple effect is felt throughout the Universe for the wonderful, enlightening work you do! I would also like to thank Chelle Thompson, editor-at-large for Visionary Insight Press, who helps us all empower our words!

~ Linda Lee

Carolee Laffoon

CAROLEE LAFFOON is a certified Heal Your Life˚Coach (www.healyourlifework-shops.com) and Mind-Body Skills Practitioner through The Center for Mind-Body Medicine (www.cmbm.org) and serves on the Faculty of the Mind-Body Center of Louisiana (www.mindbodyla.org).

Carolee resides in south Louisiana where she teaches self-care and personal development skills through workshops and coaching. Her education and professional experience also include an MBA and BS in Chemical Engineering from LSU and 20 years as an environmental consultant. Carolee loves to travel and spend time with her family and friends, and she especially enjoys sharing fun adventures with her husband.

carolee@empoweryourtransition.com
www.empoweryourtransition.com

Ten Super-Effective Actions to Empower Any Transition

Are you struggling with a transition of some sort? Would you like to get from where you are to where you'd like to be with more ease? Whether you desire to improve your health and well-being, change career paths, ease into retirement, find true love, or accomplish any other transition, the following ten simple, yet powerful, actions will help you create the transition you've been dreaming about and yearning to achieve.

Get ready to experience more peacefulness while you supercharge your achievement when you utilize these super-effective actions to fuel your transition.

1. Engage Your Imagination to Create a Detailed Vision.

- All things are created first as a vision in someone's mind. Your house had a blueprint; a trip gets mapped out; a renovation requires a design. Your transition will unfold more easily when you imagine your ideal outcome and focus your attention on your vision often.

- Create a multi-dimensional, multi-sensory vision of what you desire in great detail. Include color, tangible feelings, emotional feelings, people, places, temperature, light, and any other type of detail you can imagine. Write about the transformed you, draw a picture of how you see yourself after your transition, and daydream about your ideal outcome often.

- An inspiring activity that can help you is to create a Vision Album. To make a Vision Album, fill a small photo album (I got one for $1 at Wal-Mart) with pictures and words from magazines, your personal empowering statements, drawings, and any illustrations that capture your ideal transition vision. I love to use an album because you can carry it with you, it is easy to update when your vision becomes clearer or changes, and it has plenty of room to capture new ideas and be creative as your transition comes to fruition!

2. Write Empowering Statements to Inspire Yourself.

I first learned about the power of positive thinking from my mom growing up. She was working hard to create a career for herself after divorcing my dad and she would tape motivational notes to the bathroom mirror to inspire herself.

Create positive statements in the present tense that describe the ideal outcome of your transition and the new ways of thinking you expect to have upon successfully achieving your transition. Here are some examples for a career transition:

- I am fulfilled and financially rewarded beyond my expectations doing work that I love [or insert your new career here].
- My fun, fulfilling work flows effortlessly.
- My career continues to blossom as I learn and grow.

3. Become Super-Aware of Your Words and Thoughts so You Can Align Them More and More with Your Desired Outcome.

Focusing your attention on what you desire to create, rather than what frustrates you, fuels your transition. Don't beat yourself up when you think a thought or speak a word that is not aligned with what you desire to create. Gently remind yourself that what we focus on grows — and switch to more empowering thoughts and words. Seek alignment of what you desire with what you think and say. You may be surprised at how misaligned you are when you raise your awareness and pay closer attention to your words and thoughts — I certainly have been.

4. Love Yourself Just as You Are.

Acceptance of who you are and where you are in your life is key to moving out of the past and can create inner peace to fuel you through your transition. When we love ourselves unconditionally we have more energy available to us and we send a more positive vibe out to the world. Loving yourself makes you more beautiful and healthier. Think about how much energy you spend beating yourself up with *shoulda, coulda, woulda* thoughts, and make a goal to shift that thinking towards supporting achievement of your goals instead.

Telling yourself, *"I love you"* in the mirror is a powerful practice. What comes up for you when you try that? If your initial thought is *"no way!"*... then try *"I am willing to love you."* Create empowering statements to counter other thoughts that come up which are not aligned with love for yourself. Self-criticism is not empowering, so stop doing that to yourself and start loving and supporting yourself unconditionally.

5. Believe You Deserve What You Desire.

We all deserve to be happy and fulfilled no matter where we came from or what has happened to us in the past. If you have a desire in your heart, it was put there for you to explore and enjoy. As Louise Hay advises, if you don't believe something when you say it then try starting the phrase with *"I am willing to"* and work from there.

6. Allow Your Emotions to Flow.

Change has the potential to create a rollercoaster effect with your emotions. Experience the turbulence and know that you will soon be on the next dip or glide. The more you can be in touch with your emotions and allow them to flow, the easier you will continue moving forward. Know that every setback is a learning experience that has the potential to bring you closer to achieving your dream.

7. Focus Your Attention On: 1) Your Ideal Outcome 2) Your Next Step.

Trying to map out every step of your transition can be a fruitless activity because you don't know where the next step may lead you. Inner peace can be created by trusting that all will unfold just as it is supposed to and by focusing your attention on what's next.

8. Connect with Your Inner Wisdom Often.

We have access to an infinite well of information within us, including intuition that can guide us if we provide ourselves the opportunity and are willing to listen. Some of my favorite ways to connect to my inner wisdom are writing and other creative activities, spending time in nature, and participating in personal growth workshops with others. What activities connect you?

9. Relax More and Nurture Yourself to the Max.

Change can be challenging and require a lot of energy, so recharging your mind, body, and spirit is more important than ever when you are in transition. Relaxation is the ultimate stress-buster. Just a few minutes of deep breathing can relax you and create a state of better balance within you. Take extra good care of yourself during times of transition. An excellent resource to help you with this is Cheryl Richardson's book *The Art of Extreme Self Care*.

10. Move Toward Your Dream Everyday.

Even the smallest action can motivate you to keep moving forward and propel you towards your ideal outcome. A body in motion stays in motion, so keep moving even if a baby step is the most you can do on some days. Feeling challenged with what's the next step? Try these simple ones: spend time focusing on your vision, read or write your empowering statements, or reach out to someone to talk with about your ideal outcome. Each action will illuminate your path brighter and show you the next step to your dream.

If any of these actions are difficult for you to execute, seek support from a coach or mentor to help you stay on track. Don't beat yourself up or get demotivated for more than a moment — instead use those thoughts as a cue to choose empowering thoughts and take actions that keep you moving forward on the path to your dream.

You can achieve your transitions with more ease and peacefulness when you visualize your ideal outcome, create empowering statements to inspire you, align your thoughts and actions with achieving your desire, love yourself unconditionally, believe you deserve what you desire, allow your emotions to flow, focus your attention on the outcome and next step, stay connected to your inner wisdom, nurture yourself to the max, and take action every day towards your dream.

Dedicated to my mom, Janice, who taught me about the power of positive thinking when she faced cancer and realized a huge transition was necessary to create a better life for her, me and my brother. Thank you for being courageous and for pursuing your passions. I love you, Mom!

Infinite gratitude to all who inspire me to do what I love. I am especially grateful to Cookie Tuminello, Louise Hay, Dr. Patricia Crane, Dr. Jim Gordon, Toni Bankston, and Denise Palmisano. Your guidance illuminated my path, and I tremendously appreciate the transformative work you do. Thanks to my Heal Your Life® family for shining your light—your inspiration and love are invaluable to me. Thanks to Lisa Hardwick for creating this wonderful opportunity. Thanks to my family and friends for your support and love, especially to my husband and true love treasure, Ace.

~ Caroleee Laffoon

Barbara Simpson

BARBARA SIMPSON is a Healer, Hypnotherapist, Licensed & Certified Heal Your Life® Teacher who also works in the corporate financial world.

She lives in South Australia, where she enjoys spending time with her partner, Michael, daughters Caroline and Camilla, her beautiful friends, animals and garden. She loves travelling and experiencing all different ways of life. She enjoys learning about the universe and everything in it. She is passionate about assisting people to overcome their issues so they can enjoy a wonderful life following their soul's desires. Every client that comes to her for healing leaves her inspired to keep helping others.

Barbara@thehealingcoach.com.au
www.thehealingcoach.com.au

 The Power of Your Soul

 You are a beautiful soul having a human
experience, you are boundless and limitless,
you can and be anything you want.

The Power of Your Soul is a workshop that I conduct in conjunction with my healing work which allows releasement of the ties that bind people to their emotional and physical problems, so that they may feel empowered and become free to choose their path. This material can be used as a mini-workshop, as part of a larger seminar or for personal use.

At the beginning of the workshop it's important to explain that everything that happens in this space is private and confidential, and so that everyone agrees with this, I ask for a show of hands and thank them for respecting everyone's privacy.

Following is a Step-by-step Narrative of the Power of Your Soul Workshop:

Today, you will experience powerful exercises that will help you to release your soul from the issues that are keeping you stuck, overwhelmed or that you wish to let go of. You will also learn about how energy affects you and what you can do to change this. Give yourself permission to begin discarding the baggage of the past and live an amazing life, treading lightly on this earth where you can enjoy each fresh new day with joy in your soul and peace in your heart.

 "Take the first step in faith, you don't have to see
the whole staircase, just take the first step."

~ MARTIN LUTHER KING, JR.

We spend so much time searching for the answers in our lives, but not much time sitting quietly and looking within, learning from within, learning from our soul.

Know that your soul decided before this lifetime what it wanted to learn, experience and when. Being a part of this workshop right now shows that you are ready to move forward and your soul has exciting plans for you.

1. Meditation: (play meditation music)

Sit in a comfortable position and gently close your eyes, place your hands on your lap with the palms facing upwards. Take in a few long, deep breaths from the bottom of your stomach, hold for a couple of seconds and then blow out the breath through your mouth. With each breath allow your body to relax even more.

Imagine in your mind that you have an orange ball resting in the palms of your hands and as you focus on this ball there is a pulsing light that is coming from within the ball. The light is slowly increasing and intensifying and is now flowing in and around you. Now allow the light to completely fill the entire space, clearing and cleansing you and everything in this room. Feel the tingling sensation in your body as the energy lifts, and allow your body to relax into this energy knowing that it is safe and you are in a peaceful location.

With your eyes still closed we will start a mantra using vowels, which will allow your body to feel grounded and centred as you start releasing some blocked energy from your body. We will say each vowel three times, softly and gently out loud (hold the vowel for 5-10 seconds each time). While you are doing this notice where in your body you feel the vibration of your voice. (The vowels are A, E, I, O and U). Now open your eyes and feel the difference both in your energy and the energy in the room (Ask for brief sharing about this experience).

2. Explanation:

In this meditation we cleansed the space around us, grounded and balanced our bodies, so that the energy that we share is calming and relaxing. As the chakras or energy centres in our body are located along the spine where there is fluid, the sound and frequency of our own voices doing the mantra awakens and invigorates our chakras.

Everything around us is made up of energy, sound and frequency, from the chair you are sitting on, to the picture on the wall, the clothes you are wearing, your mobile phone and of course, you.

If you spend intervals with a friend who is generally a negative person you may feel tired or drained after you leave them. This may be because you have absorbed some of their negativity into your own body. You can also bring negativity into your own body by having excessive negative thoughts. That is why it is so important to be mindful of your own thoughts and actions and share time with people who uplift and support you.

After a while, if this negative energy remains in your body, it can make you feel unbalanced emotionally and this can then lead to aches and pains and sickness on a physical level. For example, some people feel a dull ache or pain within the very centre of their bodies just below the ribcage which can then develop into heartburn, reflux or digestive concerns. As this area of our body takes in all of the information from within and around us, this can be a particular spot to focus on for healing and removing any blocked energy.

3. Exercise:

Now we are going to spend about 10 minutes sitting quietly with a writing pad and pen. I would like you to write down some experiences in your life that have challenged you. Particularly events that involve another person, that are stopping you from moving forward or incidents that you are unable to forget. There are no rules just whatever comes into your mind.

4. Visualisation: (play meditation music)

Sit comfortably and quietly in your chair, close your eyes, take some long deep breathes and allow your body to relax. Visualise in your mind walking along a beautiful beach, with fine white sand and crystal clear blue water. There is a gentle breeze flowing through your hair and you can smell the sea air and environment around you. You look out into the distance, and you see a sailing boat slowly gliding closer to the shore. The sailor lowers a small boat into the water and rows this boat to the shore to collect you. You get into the boat and the sailor rows you out to the sailboat. You make your way onto the big boat and from the deck you take in the view of the water and the land ahead of you.

Now walk slowly to the back of the sailboat. As you come to the back of the boat, there you will find a person whom you have had some challenges with in your life. Their soul is right there in front of you. Say to them whatever is on your mind about the experience that you had with them and how it made you feel.

Explain the actual feelings you had—for example sadness, anger, hurt or anxiety—and show them where you felt it in your body. Say to them anything that you wished that you had said to them previously, but were unable to. Take your time with this, there is no rush. Know that they will hear you on a soul level. (allow about 5 minutes)

Once you have done this, allow the other person to express themselves to you.

Now, I would like you to say, either in your mind or out loud, whichever feels more comfortable, "I release the 'feeling' (i.e. sadness, anger, hurt, anxiety) inside of me that was created in the situation and I let it go. I no longer need this in my life." Then repeat for each of the three other feelings, "I release the 'feeling' inside of me that was created in the situation and I let it go, I no longer need this in my life." Now take a few deep breaths in and out.

If you now feel ready to forgive this person, say, "I forgive you, I release you and I let you go." If you are NOT yet ready to forgive say, "I release you and I let you go." (If you wish, you are welcome to hug them and send them love and happiness for their journey.) Your soul says thank you for the lessons and now you choose to move forward.

At this point, you walk up to the front of the sailboat, get into the smaller boat and the sailor rows you back to the shore. You step off the boat and walk along the beach. You find a nice place to sit on the sand, so you can look out at the water and watch as the boat sails off into the distance. Now say to yourself, "I forgive myself for the experience with this person. I love and accept myself just as I am, I am safe, I am well, life is wonderful and I am happy to be here." Know that you have done the best for both you and the other person. Allow your body to be cleansed by the sun shining down upon you; allow the peace of releasement to wash over your whole body. Now slowly bring your awareness back to the room, wiggle your hands and toes and gently open your eyes when ready.

5. Share And Discuss:

Who would like to share any insights from this visualisation? Were you able to forgive and release this person? Were you able to forgive yourself? How does your body feel now?

You can do this with all types of relationships and events. Firstly, it is really important that you acknowledge the situation, to say that it did exist. Then express to the other person what they did that made you feel different, how it made you feel, where in your body you felt it and why it made you feel that way. Be open to how they may have felt also. You may be here to teach them something... for them to experience in this life, in their journey, in their story.

You are an important being on this planet, everything you do affects the world around you. Your choice, then, is how. I loved sharing these moments with each of you, thank you!

Okay, time for a group hug, hug your partner or a teddy! Yay, I love this part!

6. Daily Routine:

If you continue on the path of releasing blocked energy, I recommend starting a daily care routine of cleansing, clearing, healing and protecting your energy, particularly while you are working on yourself. The people around you will notice the difference in you. It is very simple to do and your soul, body and mind will thank you!

- **Start your day with gratitude**—when you wake, be grateful for the day, for the people and things around you and for the wonderful occurrences that are going to fill your day. Use affirmations that have proven to work well for you and set an intention for the day.

- **Cleansing & Healing your body visualisation**—As you shower in the morning, close your eyes and imagine a flow of bright golden light flowing down through the shower head over your entire body, cleansing away all heaviness and darkness, renewing and invigorating your energy and allowing you to feel lighter and clearer. Allow this heaviness and darkness to dissolve away from your body and see it go down the drain below you. Your whole body will feel at peace, energised and ready for the day! (This can also be done at night in the shower, so you will be able to sleep well).

- **Assistance & Support**—know that you are not alone and you are an important person in this world who deserves every happiness. Please contact a friend, your doctor, community service or alternative health professional if you need some assistance, support or healing.

- **Protecting your energy**—If you practice protection each day, it will improve your energy and vitality, it will make you more aware of your energy and how things and people can affect you.

  Whenever you are not feeling like yourself or you are struggling with something in your life, it can open you up to the negative energy around you. In order to protect your own energy, visualise in your mind a stream of light constantly flowing down upon you and it will help you feel better. You can also imagine this light filling up the other people you may be talking with, so that the energy between you is uplifted. Feel free to use a colour of choice—blue is good for protection, green is good for healing, pink is calming and soothing, white and gold are good for everything. You can also use the first meditation from the workshop to clear the spaces in your home or office.

- **Ready to sleep**—As you lay in bed, clear the day's events with a quick visualisation. Begin by placing all your cares and worries of the day's events into a balloon. When you have finished, tie off the balloon and then release the balloon up into the night's sky… watching as it floats up and away releasing you from the day. Place your hands on your heart and say to yourself, *"Thank you for this* *day and the lessons I have learnt,"* and feel the love and warmth coming from your heart and soul. Now it is time to sleep, heal and renew for a fresh day tomorrow.

During this period of change here are some other things that may be helpful: being kind to yourself, drinking lots of water, eating more fresh fruit and vegetables, placing a live plant in your bedroom and spending quiet intervals in nature. Learn about affirmations and how to use them. Be sure to meditate, as this allows you and your soul to have a timeout and brings you into the present moment.

7. References & some of my Favourite books:

- *The Divine Name*—Jonathon Goldman
- *You Can Heal Your Life*—Louise L Hay
- *The Power of Now*—Eckhart Tolle
- *The Celestine Prophecy*—James Redfield
- *Ordering from the Cosmic Kitchen*—Patricia Crane
- *The Lightworker's Way*—Doreen Virtue
- *The Subtle Body*—Cyndi Dale
- *Astrology for the Soul*—Jan Spiller

 Every great master concentrates on
what is right in front of them!

Dedicated to my partner and best friend, Michael, for always encouraging and inspiring me to be the best me I can be!

Thanks to the guardians of the land where I live for allowing me to visit here. For the many teachers and mentors along my path for their wisdom and inspiration to seek further. Particular thanks to Brita Lee for starting my journey to good health and a new life, Lorraine Webb, Asharni, Elisabeth Jensen, Susie Mulholland and authors Louise Hay, Dr Wayne Dyer & Eckhart Tolle, and to Lisa Hardwick and Chelle Thompson for making all this possible.

- Barbara Simpson

Connie Queen

Though born and raised in south Arkansas, CONNIE QUEEN has had the opportunity to live in Alabama, Minnesota, North Carolina, Georgia, Connecticut and Mexico before she and her husband Ross arrived in Arizona on a continuation of her magical life's adventure.

Her primary focus is being a loving wife, mother, grandmother and friend while inspiring others on their own spiritual quest. A writer, mentor, life coach, workshop leader and inspirational speaker, she motivates others to unconditionally love and forgive themselves allowing a newfound freedom and happiness. Believing life is about the journey not arriving at a destination, she continues to be grateful.

connie@conniequeen.com
www.conniequeen.com
facebook.com/ConnieQueen'sFanPage

How to Empower Your
Holidaze with True Joy

As the song *It's The Most Wonderful Time of The Year* implies, the holidays are the hap-happiest season of all with kids jingle belling and everyone telling you to be of good cheer. With the merry parties, marshmallow toasting, and caroling, our hearts should be glowing, because our loved ones are near. Yet, all too often those tales of Christmases long ago are full of painful memories, hurt, sadness and disappointment.

Media hype and the over-stimulation of every single light, jolly sight and joyful sound of the celebratory season always set unreasonable expectations for buying gifts, traveling, and having harmonious interactions with friends and family—to such an extent that on more than one occasion we may become so depressed, anxious and stressed that we are ready to yank our hair out. Therefore, it should be no surprise that the American Psychological Association revealed that over half of women and a third of men report that their stress levels hike during the festive Triduum between Thanksgiving, Christmas and New Year's in comparison to other times of the year.

We go to parties and gatherings, eat unhealthy food, over imbibe and spend uncontrollably, becoming somewhat insanely driven beyond our physical and emotional boundaries. During this period of self-imposed misery and suffering, we choose the path of least resistance staying in old behaviors, even though the consequences of doing so no longer support us in living an empowered life.

"Why, we ask, do we do this to ourselves?" Staying a victim is a choice and it takes massive amounts of courage to make choices that are good for us without guilt or shame. Being free to fully experience, within healthy limits, the joy, sights, smells and sounds of the festivities is also a choice. What's your choice to be? There is hope! Come along with me on an amazing journey of change—and become more fully engaged in your own life during the holidays and beyond. By taking a few suggestions and employing some simple, yet not always easy, actions, we get to enjoy what really, truly matters. So, you are not alone my friend. Welcome to the *Holidaze!*

1. Affirmations For The Holidays

In the hustle and bustle that accompanies this time of the year, stop, breathe deeply, and ingest the spirit of the season. Even though some of our childhood recollections evoke negative emotions, it is important to step through our fear-based feelings. Taking actions in the face of fear makes us feel more at peace while we are transforming our perception of the merrymaking buzz swirling around us. Each new action conquers every doubt, illuminates every shadow, and heals every wound, if we are willing to do the work replacing negative attitudes with positive new thinking. When our hearts feel light, we recall that our life has meaning and purpose.

Using affirmations helps to see the Christmas season with new eyes and new hearts. Each morning and throughout the day repeat the following affirmations. Or, write some of your own — keeping in mind that affirmations are always positive, present tense, and personal statements about the reality you want to create. Affirmations create new beliefs to which your consciousness can respond. Like any new skill, they must be practiced and practiced until they become second nature. As you read the following affirmations, do your best to have them FEEL true for you and see what a difference it makes!

a. *Today the sights and sounds and smells of the season fill me with joy!*

b. *When I make Christmas about sharing, rather than getting, I always feel better.*

c. *Today I feel the joy, peace and love of the season.*

d. *My mind is filled with hope. My heart is filled with joy. It's holiday time and my life is full of limitless possibilities!*

2. Create New Traditions

Sometimes the holidays are associated with feelings of extreme joy. For numerous individuals, however, the signs, smells and sights send them diving into conflict, guilt and confusion. We are torn between what we feel we have to do to make our families happy, and the crucial need to practice extreme self-care. Remembrances of celebrations past can be uncomfortable. Yet, we suit up and show up year after year expecting things to be different, only to get more of the same insanity, feeling disappointed, isolated and alone. One of the easiest ways to get out of our own self-pity is to accept and acknowledge that although this year may not be the joyous occasion we had hoped for, continuing to focus on our less-than-ideal previous celebrations only leaves us feeling like more of a victim. We can always step outside ourselves and find others who are less fortunate and living far away from their homes ... if they even have a home.

Create your own traditions—volunteering at a soup kitchen, for example. Wrapping gifts for Toys-For-Tots or visiting the elderly in a retirement home could have an amazing impact on your holidays. After all the packages are opened and decorations are put away, we are left with one great realization … we have to give love to receive love.

3. Imagine, Create, Believe!

One way to salvage our sanity and peace on Earth is to embrace childlike ways of celebrating the season. For many of us, our skepticism is fueled by many painful flashbacks. However, you CAN alter how you walk through these seemingly impossible days by using gratitude in place of a Scrooge face and a Bah Humbug. Think back to your own childhood, and even if the contemplation is distasteful, take at least ten minutes each day to spend time in self-reflection—searching to find that one special moment when something warmed your heart. Write a letter of thanks and gratitude to the person or people involved, sharing what that event meant to you. Even if they live far away or are deceased, the act of putting the memories into words on paper will be a gift to yourself. Watch one of the many holiday specials on television, complete with hot chocolate and marshmallows. Sing carols, play games and write a letter to Santa. Purchase a kit complete with all the trimmings and build a gingerbread house. Imagine, create and believe!

4. Shop Responsibly

The holiday shopping frenzy may slyly engage your inner shopaholic leaving you with a mound of debt by the New Year. If the shopaholic in you is ready to be unleashed, take steps to control your spending habits. Make a list, check it twice, and do your shopping at emotionally-neutral times. For many who get "caught up" in the festive feelings, the act of shopping and spending is a way to escape feeling alone, particularly when you are tempted to splurge on impulse items or buy unplanned "gifts" for yourself. Don't head to the mall as a form of retail therapy.

Don't fool yourself into thinking, "I really haven't spent that much this season." Make the effort to deal with anger, anxiety, stress, boredom or depression in a healthy way, so that shopping doesn't become an impulsive outlet. If you're stressed or anxious, talk to a close friend or family member, enjoy a relaxing bath or just take a "time out." Shopping responsibly brings an indescribably wonderful feeling of calm while the rest of the world is fighting crowds and going nuts. Making a conscious effort for your holiday shopping to be early, relaxed, and leisurely could turn out to be one new experience you will want to repeat again and again.

5. Make A List, Checking It Twice

The spirit of the season is the essence found in the act of giving. Giving in a spiritual way is based on a generous desire, rather than from a sense of guilt, obligation, pity, or shame. It is giving with no ulterior motive of receiving something in return. In the past, you may have crossed the line into caretaking—running up against an old belief that equates generosity with buying lots of things, with far too much of it bought on credit, leaving you feeling resentful and victimized. Whether it is giving of your time, your talents, your energy, or your money, it must be based on an amount that you can afford. Instead of using giving as an escape from reality in order to feel better about yourself, strive to live in balance proportionate to your income. For starters ask yourself, "What really matters?" and "What are my values?" These are prudent questions to ask especially as Black Friday approaches where exuberance to take advantage of mass savings has a tendency to lead closer to frenzy and hysteria than mindful purchasing.

The best visual I've ever found for prioritizing a holiday budget—or life in general—is a story called "The Jar of Life." For this exercise, you will need a glass jar, large rocks, pebbles and sand. Beginning with the most important things or people, put in the big rocks first—your immediate family and spouse or significant other. Secondly, place the smaller pebbles allowing them to fill the jar around the large rocks—these will be your close friends and cousins, aunts and uncles. Last, fill the remaining space with the sand—the "nice to dos," the greeting cards and gifts for co-workers, and everything and everyone else.

By filling up your holiday budget and shopping list in this order, you'll be sure to stick to your financial plan and maintain your priorities. Get an overall number in mind that you can realistically spend this season and then assign a value to each group of rocks in order of importance. It is tempting to go overboard; but, if you can't afford it don't buy it. Be creative selecting gifts that are in your price range, or make a donation to a charity in your friend or family's name. Make a list, check it twice and adhere to it—taking cash and leaving the plastic at home.

6. Holiday Self-Care

You know drinking too much champagne results in a headache, vomiting, chills, exhaustion, moans, groans and more. It's a bona fide hangover. But what happens when you spend too much time in a situation that poisons your spirit in the way alcohol does your body? You feel tense, isolated, depressed, insecure, angry and completely sad. This is an emotional hangover—and while it may not be as well-known as the physical sort—it is just as painful.

If you find yourself feeling down in the dumps after a family get-together, a company party or even a spontaneous outing with friends, you could be suffering from an emotional hangover or "post-holiday blues." It is imperative to nurse your disposition back to a sound and healthy state. If your emotional hangover is caused by something you did, don't beat yourself up about it by replaying what you could have, should have or wish you would have done differently. Forgive yourself. Be tender with yourself and move forward gently. Nurture your soul.

It is essential that you do something to heal yourself after spending time with people who bring you down. Maybe it's meditation or prayer. Maybe it's exercise. Maybe it's reading, listening to some favorite music or writing in a journal. Or, maybe it's as simple as slowing down in the way you move about your day. The more centered you are, the less likely you are to feel trampled and disoriented in difficult social encounters. Be aware moving forward. The next time you find yourself in a setting that is likely to cause an emotional hangover, be sure to have your own transportation so you can simply go home!

7. Everything Happens For Our Highest Good ... Even The Holidays

Have you ever stopped to consider what the holidays might look like if nothing was wrong? What if everything and everyone, including you, were exactly as it was intended to be at this very moment? At this time of year, people get so busy, wanting to have everything as close to perfection as humanly possible, that they snap. Then any remaining energy is spent beating themselves up for not measuring up to their own expectations.

STOP! Ah-ha moment ... there is nothing wrong ... period! You are playing the game of life as best you know how. We all make mistakes and that allows for growth opportunities. There's no such thing as the way you "should" be. If you do what you enjoy and don't harm other people in the process, you are living a beautiful life.

There are no right or wrong answers. Choose what you think is the best course of action for yourself AND DO IT! As you get new information and grow stronger, you will make different choices. You are powerful! You are beautiful! There is nothing wrong—so, start thinking of good reasons to enjoy this magical time of the year beginning NOW.

One of my favorite affirmations is: *"All is well. Everything is working out for my Highest Good in exactly the right time and space sequence. Out of this situation only good can come. I am safe."*

8. Peace And Good Will

Marvelous acts of giving are realized in our day-to-day lives as we challenge ourselves to express giving in new ways. Each time we forgive our neighbor, whenever we make someone smile, every time we show compassion to the less fortunate, whenever we care for our beloved pets, tend to the beauty in our homes and gardens, and work for peace and good will towards all we are actively giving in the genuine sense of the word.

 Happy Holidays!

Being alive is a gift — living a happy life is a choice!

Dedicated to all those who find themselves feeling dazed during the hustle and bustle of the holiday season. May utilizing these suggested action steps for change help you experience the joy of really, truly living with new eyes and new hearts.

To my children Catherine, Sam and Emily who are the best kids I could have hoped for and who have been my life's greatest teachers. With all my heart, I deeply appreciate your patience, understanding and love. Life wasn't always easy, yet it has been so worth it! I would like to thank my husband and life partner, the love of my life, Ross for standing beside me. He has been my inspiration and motivation for continuing to improve my knowledge and move my career forward. He is my rock, my forever love.

~ Connie Queen

Michelle Prebilic Reese

As a sensitive child, MICHELLE PREBILIC REESE experienced anxiety attacks. Despite her best intentions to heal, her anxiety continued. After years of conventional treatments, she started biofeedback. She reconnected with her body and relearned how to breathe. Today, as an author and Whole Life Coach, she helps others to find balance, relax, and grow from the inside out.

She lives in Walnut Creek, CA, where she enjoys her husband, adult children, and pets. She's gone solar, nurtures a garden, rides a tandem, and shops for whole foods. And she breathes deeply often. She enjoys traveling and embracing other cultures.

info@MichelleReese.com
MichelleReese.com

Give Me Back My Breath!

1. Breathing Techniques

Breathing deeply into our gut is the perfect way for us to unwind, and bring calm and focus to the mind and the body. Something so simple — yet so powerful.

Infants are great at belly breathing. Watch them sleep and you'll see their bellies rise up and down rhythmically; even their lips looked relaxed. We lose this ability at a young age — later, the stresses and demands of life have us breathing in shallow ways and feeling more pressure.

Based on my years of biofeedback training, which is essentially using sensors and breathing to bring balance to the body, I created a playful breathing technique to help my very sensitive and energetic 4-year-old unwind from the stresses of her day. She would arrive at bedtime overly excited without a hint of slowing down. Laying in her bedroom with her cuddled next to me, this became a great way for me to spend intimate time with her and settle her down for a good night's sleep.

As a full-time working mother with two young children and a very busy family life, I needed this break as much as she did. We as parents/caretakers can get so caught up in what has to be done that we forget that the simplest moments can be the most memorable. And the bonus — relaxing can lower cortisol, which can help us feel like we have enough time to get it all done.

2. Balloon Breathing Technique For Four To Ten Year Olds

This meditation focuses on filling balloons. It's a great way to emphasize the exhale, which is the calming and relaxing part of our breath. It's visual, playful, and recommended for children ages 4-10. Check in with your intuition to see if this will work for your child.

Preparations

Minimize Distractions:
- Choose a quiet place
- Play instrumental, calming music to minimize noises (i.e., sirens, neighbors, events, barking dogs, etc.)
- Create white noise by using a relaxation sound machine or a fan
- Dim lights
- Close shades and curtains

Create Comfort:
- Put on comfortable loose clothing
- Select a comfortable place—either on a bed, a comfy chair, a couch, or on pillows on the floor
- Have your child lie on her/his back or sit very comfortably

Invite Love:
- As you breathe along with your child, imagine that your heart is filling up with pure love.
- There is so much love coming into your heart—for you—that it seeps out to your child.
- This love will continue to flow through you to your child as you relax.

Warm Up

Say to the child in a quiet, calm voice:
1. *Take a deep breath in through your nose.*
2. *Notice how the cool air tickles the inside of your nose.*
3. *Feel it move down into your throat, and all the way down into your tummy, as your tummy grows big with the new air.*
4. *Pause.*
5. *Slowly blow the air out of your mouth.*
6. *Hear the warm air leaving your lips with a swishing sound.*
7. *Blow until all the air is gone. Bye-bye air.*

**Repeat steps 1 through 7 two more times,
asking your child to close her/his eyes.**

Filling Balloons

- This time, as you breathe out, imagine that you place a magic yellow balloon to your lips.
- Exhale your warm air into the magic yellow balloon.
- See the yellow balloon start to grow.
- Breathe in slowly until your tummy is big.
- Exhale slowly, hearing the swish of your air going into the balloon.
- See the yellow balloon get bigger each time you exhale. *(Do this a few times)*
- The balloon is full. I am going to knot the balloon, tie a string on it, and put it on the handlebar of your bicycle.
- See the yellow balloon bobbing gently in the wind.
- Now put another balloon up to your lips. This time, as you exhale, blow your warm air into a magic blue balloon.
- See the blue balloon begin to grow.
- Continue to breathe in slowly until your tummy is big.
- Exhale, hearing the swish of your air going into the balloon.
- See the blue balloon get bigger each time you exhale. *(Do this a few times)*
- The balloon is full. I am going to knot the balloon, tie a string on it, and put it on the handlebar of your bicycle.
- See the blue and the yellow balloons bobbing gently in the wind.
- Now put another balloon up to your lips. This time, as you exhale, blow your warm air into a magic green balloon.
- See the green balloon begin to grow.
- Continue to breathe in slowly until your tummy is big.
- Exhale, hearing the swish of your air going into the balloon.
- See the green balloon get bigger each time you exhale. *(Do this a few times)*
- The balloon is full. I am going to knot the balloon, tie a string on it, and put it on the handlebar of your bicycle.
- See the green … the blue … and the yellow balloons blowing gently in the wind.

Cool Down

1. See yourself getting onto your bicycle.
2. Notice the color of your bicycle. Feel the temperature of the handlebars. Hear the wind blowing in the trees near you.
3. Go for a ride. You are totally safe and having fun.

4. Let the balloons blow in the wind. Feel the wind in your hair. *(Stay quiet as you let the child soak in the fun for a few minutes.)*

5. When you are ready, open your eyes, move slowly and bring your thoughts back into the room. *(Or, if the child is asleep, exit quietly.)*

Variations

Interaction. This can be an interactive meditation, where you and your child can pick balloon colors and styles. Listen to your intuition. If interaction is too stimulating, vary it depending on the needs of the day.

Balloon Colors. You can take a moment to have your child pick out the balloons as you settle into the quiet place. Balloons can be any shapes, colors, sizes and patterns that you and your child enjoy.

Bicycle. The bicycles can be anything that your child finds fun (i.e., tricycle, go-cart, motor car). It's most important to maintain that feeling of calm, safety, and comfort.

Groups. This can be used with a group of siblings, children in a daycare, or in a workshop where you are showing parents how to calm their children.

3. Fabulous Friends Breathing Technique For Eleven To Seventeen Year Olds

Adapt this meditation for teenagers as well. If you start teaching teens early—from eleven and up—chances are they'll use these techniques (perhaps without letting you know) into adulthood. Since friendships are the center of a teen's world—and many times their biggest worry—you can have them visualize giving balloons to friends.

Preparations

Minimize Distractions:

- Let the teen choose a quiet place
- Play instrumental, calming music to minimize noises (i.e., sirens, neighbors, events, barking dogs, etc.). It's important that the music does not have words or loud sounds.
- Create white noise by using a relaxation sound machine or a fan
- Dim lights
- Close shades and curtains

Create Comfort:
- Put on comfortable loose clothing
- Have your teen select a comfortable place—either on a bed, a comfy chair, a couch, or on pillows on the floor
- Have your teen lie on her/his back or sit very comfortably

Invite Love:
- As you breathe along with your teen, imagine that your heart is filling up with pure love.
- There is so much love coming into your heart—for you—that it seeps out to your teen.
- This love will continue to flow through you to your teen as you relax.

Warm Up

Say to the teen in a quiet, calm voice:
1. *Take a deep breath in through your nose.*
2. *Notice how the cool air tickles the inside of your nose.*
3. *Feel it move down into your throat, and all the way down into your stomach, as your stomach grows big with the new air.*
4. *Pause.*
5. *Slowly blow the air out of your mouth.*
6. *Hear the warm air leaving your lips with a swishing sound.*
7. *Blow until all the air is gone.*
8. *We will do this two more times. As we do, I want you to pick 4 colors and think of 4 friends. If you are unsure of 4 friends to pick right now, trust that they will show up as we do the meditation. Keep the colors and friends a secret.*

Repeat steps 1 through 7 two more times.

Fabulous Friends

- This time, as you exhale, put a magic balloon to your lips.
- Exhale your warm air into a magic balloon using your first color.
- See the balloon start to grow.
- Breathe in slowly until your stomach is as big as a balloon.
- Exhale slowly, hearing the swish of your air going into the balloon.
- See the balloon get bigger each time you exhale. *(Do this a few times)*

- The balloon is full.
- Knot the balloon and tie a string on it.
- Walk over to your best friend and hand them the balloon *(If the teen is unsure of a best friend, tell your teen to imagine the perfect best friend.)*
- See your friend holding the balloon as it blows in the wind.
- See your friend smile, and feel the happiness beaming from him/her. You know in your heart that she/he is so grateful that you have chosen to give them a balloon. This is a sign of your friendship.
- You both promise to be fabulous friends—thoughtful, loyal, kind, funny, exciting and generous.
- This time, as you exhale, blow your warm air into a magic striped balloon using your next color.
- See the striped balloon start to grow.
- Breathe in slowly until your stomach is as big as a balloon.
- Exhale slowly, hearing the swish of your air going into the balloon.
- See the striped balloon get bigger each time you exhale. *(Do this a few times)*
- The balloon is full.
- Knot the balloon and tie a string on it.
- Walk over to another friend and hand them the balloon *(If the teen is unsure, invite them to imagine the ideal friend.)*
- See your friend standing next to your best friend, and holding the striped balloon as it blows in the wind.
- See your friends smile, and feel the happiness beaming from them. You know in your heart that they feel grateful that you have chosen to give them balloons. This is a sign of your friendships.
- You hug and promise to be fabulous friends—thoughtful, loyal, kind, funny, exciting and generous.
- This time, as you breathe out, blow your warm air into a magic heart-shaped balloon of your favorite color.
- See the heart-shaped balloon start to grow.
- Breathe in slowly until your stomach is as big as a balloon.
- Exhale slowly, hearing the swish of your air going into the balloon.
- See the heart-shaped balloon get bigger each time you exhale. *(Do this a few times)*
- The balloon is full.
- Knot the balloon and tie a string on it.

- Walk over to another friend and hand them the balloon.
- See your friend standing next to your other friends, and holding the heart-shaped balloon as it blows in the wind.
- See your friends smile, hear their joy, and feel the happiness beaming from them. You know in your heart that they feel grateful that you have chosen to give them balloons. This is a sign of your friendships.
- You all promise to be fabulous friends — thoughtful, loyal, kind, funny, exciting and generous.
- This time, as you exhale slowly, blow your warm air into a magic transparent balloon of your favorite color and shape.
- See the transparent balloon start to grow.
- Breathe in slowly until your stomach is as big as a balloon.
- Exhale slowly, hearing the swish of your air going into the balloon.
- See the transparent balloon get bigger each time you blow out. *(Do this a few times)*
- The balloon is full.
- Knot the balloon and tie a string on it.
- Walk over to another friend and hand them the balloon.
- See your friend standing next to your other friends, and holding the transparent balloon as it blows in the wind.
- See your friends smile, hear their joy, and feel the excitement beaming from them. You know in your heart that they love you and want to be your friend no matter what.
- You all promise to stay fabulous friends — thoughtful, loyal, kind, funny, exciting and generous.

Cool Down

1. See yourself hanging out with your friends.
2. See yourself having fun and laughing.
3. Let the balloons blow in the wind. Feel the wind in your hair. Know deep in your heart that your friends deeply love you. They will be with you when you are happy or sad or mad or scared. Because you all know deep inside that a fabulous friend stays by your side. *(Stay quiet as you let your teen soak in the love for a few minutes.)*
4. When you are ready, open your eyes, move slowly and come back into the room.

Variations

Interaction. This can be an interactive meditation, where you and your teen can pick all the details either before you start or during the meditation.

Balloons. Have your teen tell you the balloon colors and styles. Balloons can be any shapes, colors, sizes and patterns that they enjoy.

Friends. Teens can change the friends they choose to give balloons to any time. It's important that they imagine the fabulous friends as happy, kind, healthy, caring and genuine.

Trust You. Listen to your intuition. Modify the words of the meditation depending on your teen's needs. It's most important to maintain that feeling of calm, safety, and comfort.

Dedicated to Daria and Bri, who know how to breathe. Thank you for being on my journey! And to Ellen Place, R.N., B.S.N., Certified Biofeedback Therapist, for teaching me how to listen to my body and to breathe deeply!

I am grateful to all those brave souls striving to bring knowledge, calm and love to the planet through their personal development. I deeply appreciate the organic farmers and food gurus that stay connected to the earth, and tirelessly work to educate us, and to bring us pure, organic, and nutrient-rich sustenance. Thank you to the food and supplement companies with wholesome missions. And for those helping all animals live in healthy, loving, and safe environments. I am grateful for peace, freedom and the great outdoors. Namaste.

~ Michelle Reese

Sandra J. Filer

SANDRA J. FILER, MBA, proprietress of The Happy Goddess, has an amazing zest for Life and infuses everything she does with this energy. "Happie G" is a vibrant artist, author, Goddess retreat creator/host, Empowerment Coach, and co-creator of the Self-emPOWERment PlayShop for Teens. She teaches workshops on radical self-care, creativity as a spiritual practice, and the Divine Feminine. Her Goddess retreats are held several times a year on a magical island.

diosafeliz@hotmail.com
www.thehappygoddess.com

The Roar of the Lioness

It was a typical Saturday morning like any other. I woke up, shuffled down three flights of concrete stairs, and began my day in the fitness room, mindlessly moving my legs up and down on the elliptical machine. Through the window of the fitness room, I could see residents beginning to stake their claim to the lounge chairs, carefully placed around the edges of the resort-style swimming pool. The music began to blare over the loud speakers. And, while the atmosphere was intended to feel uplifting, I felt anything but uplifted. I felt disempowered and lost.

Now, while this manual is not intended to be a memoir, I feel this wee personal story sets the stage for our topic. With that being said, I will continue!

Later that very same day, several of us, the *"newly divorced,"* gathered in our very own area. We consumed adult beverages and made the collective decision to take the party (and discussion) inside. It was during this conversation that I had a complete *come-apart*. It felt like the tears were literally shooting out of my eyes. The others in the room sort of stopped what they were doing to see what all the crying was about. The outpouring of emotion was about me feeling tossed out, cast away, and powerless.

In awkward moments such as these, when the room is brought to silence, many things could have happened. I could have been given a Kleenex along with a sympathetic ear, everyone could have exited stage left, and/or the subject could have been immediately changed to lighten the mood. However, instead, I was handed an empowerment tool. I was given a brochure about an intensive weekend training. An invitation to take action.

After blowing my nose and getting my wits about myself, I walked back home to immediately register for the intensive experience. This, in and of itself, is a step toward personal empowerment – knowing when outside assistance is needed and taking the first step in making it happen.

I'll cut to the chase here. During the weekend, I had an opportunity to face my deepest fear of being *unlovable.* There were 17 women on my team and I waited until almost last to take my turn. I can vividly remember the entire experience as if it were yesterday. It wasn't yesterday though. It was fifteen years ago. So, suffice it to say that when I regained my personal power, it was a memorable and transformative experience.

I shared many of the messages that were haunting me with the staff. After a short huddle, I was given two options. I could either beat something with a bat to release my anger (which they pointed out was the emotion hidden behind all of the sadness) or I could lay on the floor and be covered by a blanket. Once I was covered, staff members would place pillows on top of my body to represent the weight of the messages. WHAT?!

When asked which option had the biggest charge for me, I (bravely) chose the second option, as I am claustrophobic. Slowly, and with my body trembling, I slid under the blanket. The first pillow representing "not pretty enough" was placed upon me. The second pillow representing "not skinny enough" was placed upon me. The third pillow representing "not smart enough" was placed upon me. With each pillow, body weight was applied. It felt constrictive. It felt heavy. I heard the group leader ask me how it felt. I sobbed, *"It hurts. Please stop!"* I then heard another voice say, *"How is this working in your Life, Sandra?"* I cried harder. Another pillow was then placed and yet another and another. I again, through tears, said, *"I don't like this. I want it to stop."* I felt helpless, trapped, and without options. It was then that I heard the voice again ask me, *"Is this how you go about your Life? We are not going to stop. YOU must make us stop."* Ahhhhhhh!!

I honestly don't know what happened next. It was like a wild beast inside of me snapped. I heard a growl rise from deep within and I heard a very loud and long scream. Without even realizing it, that growl and scream came from a place within me that was unrecognizable until that moment. I fought, kicked, and wrestled my way out from under that blanket and all those hurtful messages. When I was out, I realized the scream was my own. I was breathless. I was exhilarated. My heart was pounding. And as odd as it may sound, I felt the corners of my mouth go into a smile. As I looked around, I could see the other 16 women smiling, clapping, and I could hear them applauding me. It was surreal. I felt so POWERFUL. Hell, I had just roared!

After the experience was over, one woman approached me and said, *"Thank you for being so brave. I just watched you face my greatest fear."*

This is where it all started for me. I was given an opportunity to regain my voice. To ask for what I needed. To be supported. To be celebrated. To be witnessed as a woman with incredible personal power. And to be welcomed into a community of other empowered women. As they say in the movie, *The Secrets of the Ya Ya Sisterhood*— *"Ya Ya!"*

Perhaps attending an intensive weekend to reactivate your personal power is not necessarily on your bucket list. I totally get that. So, let me simply offer up some ideas for consideration:

❧ **Mind your mind**. This one idea is extremely important. Our mind is an incredible tool. We must become masterful at tending to our thoughts. Think of your mind as a sacred journal with perfect memory and a projection mechanism. Each thought that you think gets recorded as your truth, and then is projected out into your Life. Any new thought can change the projection of your story.

❧ **Use your voice**. This means to live confidently and speak up! Even if you were told as a child, *"Children are to be seen, not heard."* Know that you are seen and you are here to be heard. Use your voice. Speak your truth. What you have to say matters.

❧ **Know that you are valuable**. Your worth is not defined by anything other than your divinity. You are valuable because you exist. A star is a star. A shell is a shell. A cricket is a cricket. And, you, oh you, are a Divine Expression of Life. Own that!

❧ **Don't take any sh*t**. You deserve to live peacefully. Learn ways in which to create healthy boundaries in your Life. Toxic people and toxic situations do not empower you. They lower your vibration and dull your sparkle. Strengthen your ability to say no!

❧ **Be a woman/man of your word**. Integrity is everything! It's not what you say, it's what you do. When you say what you mean, do what you say, and live by the sword, you will feel more surefooted and confident. It is never wrong to do the right thing. Keep your word impeccable.

❧ **Allow your creativity to be expressed**. We can feel very stifled when we are not expressing ourselves. Being creative allows an energetic flow to happen. It is the spark that can ignite forward movement. It can also create feelings of joy which trigger happy endorphins in our system.

- **Ask for help**!! This is a big one. If I could make the sound of an ambulance's screaming siren right here, I would. Highlight this point! It is an act of self-care to ask for help. You love helping others, right? It feels good. Why would you deprive someone else of that very same feeling? It is an empowered person who asks for help when it is needed. Attempting to do it all by yourself is a fruitless endeavor. Once again, speak up.

- **Find your tribe.** It is imperative to surround yourself with people who share in your beliefs. Who listen from the heart ... support your dreams ... encourage your passions ... hold your hand when you are down ... and, laugh out loud when the mood strikes. Seek out opportunities or communities where like-minded people congregate and jump in with both feet.

- **Stay forward-focused and out of the funk.** Think about a race horse. When it is in competition it has blinders on. This way, it is not distracted. It can only see forward. That is where YOU are headed. Forward. And, while the point of power *is* in the present moment, it is forward that you are headed. Stay out of the funk of negativity. Avoid any gossiping or *"ain't it awful"* conversations. Choose to put the blinders on and forge forward with a renewed skip in your step and lightness of heart!

In closing, I am happy to report that when I wake up on Saturdays, I still head out the door and down the stairs to a fitness room. The difference is that I purposefully move my legs up and down on the elliptical machine. I use my voice when needed, own my value, refuse to take any sh*t, am a woman of my word, express my creativity in a multitude of ways (including putting blue streaks in my platinum hair!), ask for help, have found my tribe, and RUN from negativity.

 While I am unable to forecast or determine what will happen when you fully step into your personal power, here is what I do know. You will not only feel better — you will look better. I promise. Ya Ya!

Dedicated to the tenderhearted. Your sensitivity is a gift!

My heartfelt gratitude to my darling Magico. He blesses me daily by his unwavering love and encouragement. Pamala Oslie for her wisdom that touched me deeply and propelled me forward. Kisty Stephens for being an agent of dream encouragement. And to Lisa Hardwick, my Goddess sister, who relentlessly reminds me to step into my own power and rock it. I love and appreciate each of you!

~ Sandra J. Filer

Maya Giampa

Having been described as a 'catalyst for change,' Maya Giampa gives you tools and guidance to empower and inspire you to live the life you imagine. Maya has experienced a variety of life's lessons and has consciously chosen to be grateful and use them as stepping stones throughout her journey. As well as being blessed with the support of her husband Pat and their 3 children, Maya has chosen to passionately follow her calling and life's purpose to empower others to allow their inner light to shine and be the best version of themselves.

Maya is a highly intuitive Reiki Master Teacher, Licensed and Certified Heal Your Life® Teacher, Meditation Teacher and Holistic Therapist. She successfully runs two of her own businesses, Maya's Healing Space where she offers a range of modalities, classes and workshops, as well as SoulSpace Retreats where she organises day retreats. She is based in Melbourne, Australia, but often travels interstate and internationally to help spread and share her empowerment tools and guidance.

www.mayashealingspace.com.au

The Importance of How You See Yourself

For workshop facilitators and professional presenters

In this chapter I will guide you through a short workshop that I have developed that discusses the importance of how we see ourselves. I have facilitated this workshop in an intimate setting of two people up to a large audience with 45 women, and it has worked well for both groups.

We need to be made aware of how we see ourselves and the ripple effect it may cause. How you see yourself and treat yourself sets a standard for how you allow others to see and treat you.

1. **For the first exercise I ask one of the participants to stand up, and I ask the following questions to bring to her (and the other workshop participants) awareness of how they choose to describe themselves.**
   - What is your name?
   - What do you do? *"I'm just a hairdresser"* What do you really do? *"I cut and colour hair."* Ok, granted, but what are YOU really doing? So what you are trying to say is that "you are able to transform the appearance of your clients, and make them feel great about themselves when they leave you." *"Yes!"* So why didn't you just say that?
   - The responses may vary from *"I'm shy, nervous, doubtful, not sure what people will think, don't want to sound up myself."*
   - Who else feels this?? *We ALL Do!!!* But why?
   - And why are we continuing it? Is this what we would want to encourage our friends and daughters to do?

   You may give some time during this point for each participant to sit and bring their awareness to when it was in their life that they learnt these limiting thought processes and from where. It is very important to stress that this is not to place blame on the individual or institution where it came from. Realising where it has stemmed from provides you with the opportunity to realise that it is not *your* belief system, it is one you have learnt, and therefore, have the power to unlearn, and to choose a new belief system that is beneficial to your life at this moment and in this present-day society.

2.   **During the workshop I usually have a full mirror on display or to the side of where I am facilitating. If you do not have one it is perfectly fine to pretend that you are in front of a mirror. I usually perform the following role play example:**

 ↝   How many of you get up in the morning, get dressed, look at yourself in the mirror and say, *"You are amazing, you are going to rock today, go get em"*? Or how many look in the mirror like this, tuck your bottom in, stomach in, stick breasts out, look at bottom, look at side, look again … those who put your hands up, keep them up.

 ↝   How many of you have daughters?

 ↝   Do your daughters watch you, even distantly, getting dressed?

 ↝   Do they hear what you are saying to the mirror? Or what your actions are implying? Have you seen how they look at themselves in the mirror now?

 ↝   Our own personal experiences, beliefs and thoughts shape our perception, and no two people will see the same thing in the mirror. For instance (grab mirror and place it in front of a workshop participant's face) ask the participant to describe what she sees. Then give it to the woman next to her, and ask her to describe what she sees in that other participant.

 ↝   Can you see now that your thoughts, doubts and insecurities are yours and yours alone? The person next to you does not see what you do, so don't believe that.

 ↝   With every thought you think, stop and ask yourself the question, would I say this to my best friend? If the answer is no, why are you saying it to yourself?

3.   **The next exercise is taken from the Heal Your Life® workshops I facilitate, I hand out a hand mirror to every participant just before I begin this exercise.**

 Let's now take a moment and bring our awareness to how you see yourself. In front of everyone is a mirror, I invite you to pick up the mirror and look directly into your eyes, JUST your eyes. Not your nose, cheeks, or any other part of your face. What are seeing? What are you feeling? What are you thinking??

 ↝   Do these thoughts you are thinking belong to you or have you learnt to believe them from someone else?

- ❧ Can you look yourself in the eyes and say, "I love you, I really love you"? If you struggle, that is ok, just be *willing* to love you, so say, "I am willing to love you."
- ❧ Place the mirror down and place your hand on your heart, do you feel that? This is you, alive, beautiful, worthy, deserving … enough. It is ok to love yourself. It's actually not just ok, it is a necessity. It's ok to let your love shine, to let you shine. You are perfect, as you are. Perfectly you.
- ❧ I then ask all the participants to stand up and walk around to the other participants in the group and to tell them 3 things you love about them.
- ❧ Did you find it easy to give compliments? Did you find it easy to receive compliments?
- ❧ How do you feel now after giving and receiving? Awesome isn't it?
- ❧ Imagine how life would be if we all did this instead of judging others.

Be the change you want to see, its starts with you.

Change your thoughts and change your world.

I'm going to leave you with my favourite quote by Marianne Williamson:

 "Our deepest fear is not that we are inadequate. Our deepest fear is that we are powerful beyond measure. It is our light, not our darkness that most frightens us. We ask ourselves, who am I to be brilliant, gorgeous, talented, fabulous? Actually, who are you not to be? You are a child of God. Your playing small does not serve the world. There is nothing enlightened about shrinking so that other people won't feel insecure around you. We are all meant to shine, as children do. We were born to manifest the glory of God that is within us. It's not just in some of us; it's in everyone. And as we let our own light shine, we unconsciously give other people permission to do the same. As we are liberated from our own fear, our presence automatically liberates others."

Kalpana Parekh

KALPANA PAREKH, MSW, LCSW is a holistic, positive psychology-based psycho-therapist, life and executive coach, speaker, author, workshop facilitator and singer. She is the Founder and Owner of *Wellness Around The World, LLC*, an international practice whose mission is to inspire people and to empower them with the tools they need to live flourishing lives. Kalpana, who earned her MSW from Columbia University in New York City, holds a certificate in applied positive psychology, is a certified yoga teacher, a licensed Heal Your Life® teacher, a Flourishing Skills group facilitator, and has studied Reiki and pranic healing. She sings Indian spiritual, pop and classical music, as well as American pop music, has released several CDs in Indian music and has a certificate in music therapy from India. She is the founder of the Facebook-based project *"Letters From The Heart"* (visit "Letters From The Heart" Facebook Community Page).

Kalpana would love to hear from you! To learn more about her practice, you can visit her website, or send her an e-mail.

www.wellnessaroundworld.com
E-mail: wellness1027@gmail.com

Hold On To The Paperclip

"*Sir, how can you not do anything about this?*" An assistant watched his boss read an abusive letter from a critic, contemplate the words, carefully remove and set aside the paperclip, tear up the letter and gently throw it into the recycling bin. His boss went on with his business, and the assistant was dumbfounded. The boss responded, *"I took what was useful and let go of the rest."* The boss had thoughtfully considered whether there were any helpful suggestions worthy of heeding, and when he determined there were none, he saved his precious energy to do the important work ahead of him, without generating negativity towards his critic. He remained environmentally conscious by holding on to *the paperclip*, and spiritually conscious, by *focusing on what was important and letting go of the rest.* The boss was none other than Mahatma Gandhi, the spiritual giant who led India to independence through non-violent civil disobedience.

Listening to stories like this one, by my grandmother's side, were some of the best moments of my childhood, as she passed on important lessons to me from great leaders and ancient Indian epics. At the age of nine, this simple story made a deep and lasting impression, as I too felt the indignation that Gandhi's assistant did, and wondered how Gandhi could remain so calm, focused and unaffected. My grandmother taught me that human life is precious, gifted to us after thousands of births (according to the theory of reincarnation), and therefore, not to be wasted. She taught me to think carefully about my life — what kind of person I want to be, how I want to live, and what I would like to create. Gandhi's story revealed to me that, in any situation, we always have the creative choice of how to respond — we can choose what to hold on to and what to let go of, and by doing so, conserve and focus our precious life energy.

The Sanskrit word *shakti* means the Divine strength, power and creative energy that each of us has within. According to yoga science and philosophy, our true self (which is unchanging) is joy, gratitude, love, and abundance. Though our responses to various life circumstances may disconnect us from our true self, it is ever-present. I believe that to *empower* means to let someone in on the ancient secret that there is tremendous power lying dormant within, waiting to be unleashed at any time—simply by giving one's self permission to do so, and then using the proper tools to connect with this power. Connecting with our inner power elevates our consciousness to a level higher than the challenges we are facing, allowing us to thrive through adversity and write our own story—to be *creators*, and not victims.

There are countless ways to connect with our inner power. My grandmother knew that in a world with multiple challenges, and one where I was raised in two cultures as an Indian-American, I would need practices that could keep me plugged in to positive energy. She planted the seeds of meditation, yoga, Ayurveda, the power of inspirational reading and discourse, classical music, acupressure and many other healing practices and traditions early in my childhood. As a result of her positive influence, I started a company at age eight, whose mission was to make people happy. These seedlings blossomed over time and have led to my lifelong commitment to well-being and a career as a holistic, positive psychology-based psychotherapist, life & executive coach, speaker, workshop facilitator, writer, singer and Founder/Owner of Wellness Around The World, LLC, an international practice, whose mission is to inspire people and empower them with the tools they need to live happy, flourishing lives.

In the challenging, often overwhelming and fast-paced world in which we live, we need simple and concrete tools to find our power in any situation. I have integrated various tools in my work with individuals and audiences over the years, and hope to share some strategies with you, dear reader, that have helped me personally, and numerous clients.

Holding on to the paperclip, the idea of holding on to what is useful, positive, or relevant and letting go or recycling what is not, can be applied in myriad ways. While it is true that life is not always 'black-or-white,' computers work entirely on the binary system of 0's and 1's, and this kind of efficiency may often be needed to simplify our lives in times of overwhelming choice.

Here are a few tools I created and/or was introduced to, that I hope will help you on your journey:

1. The Power of the Pen

If I had reached Gandhi's spiritual height, I might have been able to ignore the letter too, but what could someone like me do to remain centered, to connect with my inner power and respond appropriately to life? *Write!* The pen has always been a powerful tool and a friend that allows me to focus, forget, let go and recycle. Since the age of 15,

I have faithfully written in my journal. It is my sacred place of privacy, refuge, release, self-expression, exploration, discovery and insight. It is a place where my inner-most being has the permission to dance, sing, cry, get angry, question, or inquire.

Negative and draining thoughts and feelings are often what stand between us and our inner power. What if we could use the pen to take us on a journey from negativity to positivity, from victim to creator—where we are writing the story of our lives, and where we get to choose what to hold on to and what to let go of? Dr. James Pennabaker, a social psychologist, has done extensive research on the emotional and physical health benefits of therapeutic writing. Just as we visit a spa to have our body aches massaged, we need a place that welcomes and pampers our emotions. Given a stage to perform on and express themselves, as opposed to keeping them cooped up backstage, our emotions will tend to be satisfied and move on.

The heart is the center of our spiritual being, and filled with power. I let myself write from my heart, without abandon, about life's events, my initial reactions, and my deepest thoughts and feelings. Knowing my journal is confidential (and password-protected!), uncensored and not being graded or evaluated is validating, cathartic, and empowering.

At times, instead of a journal entry, I may choose to write an unsent letter to someone to whom I would like to express my feelings. Everything that once swarmed around in my head and occupied the energy of all my cells is now out on paper and has less of a hold on my being. When the cobwebs of negative thoughts and feelings are cleared away, the inner power starts to emerge. Now, the events of my life, thoughts and feelings are like clay—ready for me to mold, reshape and create into something new.

After a cathartic cleansing in my journal, my creativity can take charge. I ask myself powerful questions that help me focus on what is useful and positive, such as: *"What did I learn from this experience?"*— *"What am I grateful for today?"*—or *"What was the best part of today?"* In his journal, Benjamin Franklin used to ask himself every morning, *"What good shall I do this day?"* and at the end of each day, *"What good have I done this day?"*

The beauty of being human is the granted ability to think and perceive *as we choose*. When we think differently, we feel differently, and we then experience life differently. This is the heart of resilience. When I left my job in investment banking to follow my dream of becoming a psychotherapist, I faced many critics. I wrote for days about the pain I felt from others' disappointment and about the questions I had in my mind about whether I had done the right thing, but as I dug deeper, I found I could reach the gold. My inner power was my conscience telling me that this is the work I was meant to do. Through my writing, I could release, reflect, and recycle my experience of leaving an unfulfilling career into helping others do the same. There will never be another you in this world, so write about your experiences for your own personal growth, and you may find that it will help someone else in the future too.

2. Your Zone of Control

This is a simple but powerful tool I created in 2000 while working with HIV/AIDS patients who had difficulty accepting their new diagnosis: Whenever you are faced with a challenge, I encourage you to draw a circle and draw a line through the center. In one half of the circle, write 'CONTROL' and in the other half, write 'NO CONTROL.' In the NO CONTROL zone, write down every part of the situation over which you feel you have absolutely no control. For example, a newly diagnosed patient could write: *"My diagnosis, my past actions, regrets, other peoples' reactions and behavior."* In the CONTROL zone, one could write: *"My thoughts, researching my condition, choice of doctor, developing a wellness plan, remaining positive, writing a life plan."*

It is human nature to spend an inordinate amount of energy on the things over which we have no control. However, doing this is like banging our head on a brick wall and hoping it will move; the only thing that happens is we start to bleed. Instead, our precious life energy is better spent releasing that over which we have no control and focusing on our zone of control. Efficient focus of our energy brings vitality. At times, our zone of control will be miniscule, but focusing on that can make all the difference.

Dr. Viktor Frankl stated he had no control over any area of his life while at Auschwitz, except for the attitude he chose to take. A giving and positive attitude allowed him to survive the atrocities, find meaning through service, and help others for many years after he was out of this situation. In the film, *A Beautiful Life,* Roberto Benigni knew that his fate was out of his control in the concentration camps, but he put all his energy into maintaining a playful attitude for the sake of his son, who ultimately survived. Focusing on our zone of control helps us to remain solution-focused and stand in our power.

3. Haa-Guru, Naa-Guru (Yes-Guru, No-Guru)

My spiritual master, Dr. Viren Shah, taught me that we can learn in each moment from *Haa-* (Yes) Gurus and *Naa-* (No) Gurus. Yes-Gurus are those teachers that exemplify something/someone we want to emulate, whereas No-Gurus teach us how *not* to be. Knowing this is empowering as we come to realize that everything in our life serves a purpose. Even the boss who is yelling at us becomes a Guru, a No-Guru teaching us how *not* to be when we become a boss.

We can find both a Yes-Guru and a No-Guru in one person, who has both admirable and undesirable qualities. We can ask ourselves: *"What qualities, stories or beliefs do I want to hold on to and what am I ready to let go of?"* Asking yourself in your daily journal who your Yes-Gurus and No-Gurus are will make for a life-long journey of learning. Our Gurus can be people, books, quotes, a phrase we overheard, anything that teaches us! One Yes-Guru for me is the violet flower, for Mark Twain once wrote, *"Forgiveness is the fragrance the violet sheds on the heel that has crushed it."*

4. Plug in to Positivity

My grandmother believed that mental nourishment is just as important as physical nourishment. She encouraged me to eat an *inspiration 'sandwich'* everyday — by reading something uplifting first thing in the morning and right before going to bed at night. Positive energy empowers me to transcend negative energy I face in various life situations on a daily basis. Positive emotions can broaden our scope of thought, creativity, and our ability to perform. One way to cultivate positive emotions is to collect and savor all the positive experiences of your life (your paperclips). I created a PowerPoint called 'My Positive Experiences,' including words and images that remind me of my best times. When I need a boost, I look at each slide and savor each past positive experience utilizing all five senses and reactivating the thoughts and feelings I had. I immediately feel joy, gratitude, love and an abundance of other positive emotions. The beauty of savoring is that it can be done repeatedly, beyond the experience itself.

Some of the experiences I included were not always positive, but became so after journaling; my perception of them had changed, and they became stepping-stones, not stumbling blocks. Some of my positive experiences were *"visiting the lavender farm in Maui, recording my first CD in a professional studio, enjoying a meal with my best friend by the ocean..."* The powers of memory and imagination help us focus on positive experiences. In the midst of a negative circumstance, focus on one of these situations, or listen in your mind to a song you love, as a soundtrack to the challenging scene you are experiencing at the moment.

5. Be Clear On Your Life Vision

Write freely in your journal about your highest vision for your life. Imagine you are at the end of your journey, and looking back. Ask yourself, *"Who would I like to have been? What would I like to have experienced and accomplished?"* When this vision is clear in your mind, hold on to that vision. Keep the vision in front of you, make a vision board or create a picture on your computer or phone and look at it frequently.

Then, with any decision in life, you can ask yourself, *"Will this choice bring me closer to my vision or further away?"*

6. Your Energetic Footprint

I believe that being conscious of our energetic footprint on the Universe is just as important as our carbon footprint. How do we show up in the world with our family, friends, and co-workers? Do we bring positive energy into the world or are we spreading negative energy? Either one is equally contagious. *Holding on to the Paperclip,* as a philosophy, can help us to be positive, solution-focused, strength-based leaders in the world. We can use our power to "be the change" we wish to see in the world and to spread positive energy.

I founded a project this year called *"Letters From The Heart"* whose mission is to encourage people around the world to write a positive letter or note of encouragement or inspiration to someone who may be in need. I encourage you to write someone a positive note regularly. The more positivity we share and spread, the more positive power we feel within.

So ... hold on to the paperclips of your life!

*Stay tuned for the book I am writing with the same title, to be released in the near future. Please share your 'paperclips' with me at wellness1027@gmail.com!

I dedicate "Hold On To The Paperclip" to my dearest grandparents, the late Ramniklal Daftary ('Kaka') and Jayalaxmi Daftary ('Kaki'). Kaki, my grandmother, will be turning 90 years old this year. She was my first spiritual teacher in life and continues to be, and will always be, the foundation of my spiritual life. Kaka and Kaki, everything you shared with me in childhood and beyond will always be with me. May your teachings spread far and wide to touch the hearts of people everywhere, as they have always touched mine. I love you forever. I also dedicate my chapter to the late Dr. Wayne Dyer, who has been a spiritual rock throughout my life. Dr. Dyer, you gave me the courage to share my music with the world, and you inspired me to become a speaker and writer. You will always be a guiding light.

I want to thank my parents (Jawahar & Vasanti Parekh), grandparents (Respected Ramniklal & Jayalaxmi Daftary), my uncle and aunt (Dr. Suresh & Malini Parekh), my immediate and extended family, and my spiritual Gurus (Respected Dr. Viren Shah, Mr. Jayantilal Shah & Mr. Ghulam Mir) for everything! Your continuous support, encouragement, and belief in me have allowed me to realize so many dreams and continue to keep soaring higher and higher. A special thanks to all the Haa-Gurus and Naa-Gurus of my life who have brought me to this point, and to my nephews, Ketan & Kiran, the apples of my eye, who are my inspiration.

- Kalpana Parekh

Melissa Kim Corter

MELISSA KIM CORTER has never been one to follow the rules, color inside the lines, or be led by the crowd; her work has taken a similar path.

As a spiritual photographer, teacher, and transformational guide, Melissa helps people release fear, removing emotional amour from life experiences and beliefs. Through a variety of modalities, coupled with her heightened intuition, she connects with your spirit for deeper truth and guidance on how to shift limiting beliefs. This leads to transformation; opening the heart, and transitioning through the fears that can hold people back. She enjoys watching the magic unfold in her client's lives when they begin to consciously create what they desire.

Melissa lives in magical Sedona, Arizona, wither her two fur-babies, husband of 12 years and 11-year-old son. She teaches classes online and hosts workshops and retreats. Her clients have deemed her the "Soul artist," capturing the essence of who they are and showcasing it in her portraiture.

www.melissacorter.com

🌿 The Art of Self-Awareness for Manifesting

In my work creativity is the foundation of everything. My professional imagery services, helping women move through fear, and coaching clients to redirect their energy and intention is crucial. We are all creating every moment of every day, yet making it a conscious choice instead of a default reaction is the goal. This is where people get tripped up. On one hand they believe in their ability to manifest desires, create their lives, and open up to a prosperous way of life. Then why are so many of them still struggling and spending enormous amounts of money to find "the secret" to getting what they want?

In my work and personal experience, I have discovered five main reasons why people get stuck and do not produce results. Each of the five reasons will come with a journal exercise to help you break-through to the deeper awarenesses that are waiting to surface. The five main areas individuals have trouble with (conscious) manifestation are:

1. *Knowing is different than applying.*
2. *It involves a great deal of trust in oneself.*
3. *Seeking acceptance gets in the way of fortitude.*
4. *You do not have to know it all, it is not your job.*
5. *Creating involves constant involvement and discipline of the mind.*

Awareness #1: Knowing is Different than Applying

Knowing for the most part, can be a very intellectual experience; although we can also "know" something to our core, most people know things from the level of the mind, not the heart. Understanding the Law of Attraction, energy, and the power of your thoughts through theory is completely different than applying the principles in your everyday life because you know it to be your personal truth. When you experience something as deep truth, there is no question, and very little room for outside influences to deter you from your belief. Most people love the idea of their beliefs, yet there is a superficial level of trust in them that will be tested when faith is required.

> *Awareness #1 Journal Prompt*—How do you practice and/or apply your beliefs on a regular basis? If you believe in abundance for all, do you hesitate when spending money on something that is greatly needed? If you believe in Law of Attraction, are you honing in on the areas of your life that are attracting less than stellar results?

Awareness #2: It Involves a Great Deal of Trust in Oneself

Most people do not have any inkling that they do not trust themselves to make the right choices and decisions. Often they go to someone else for feedback, ask others to decide for them, or follow in the footsteps of someone they trust or admire, instead of trusting in the one person who matters the most. In order to go forward with complete trust in yourself, there is an opportunity for some forgiveness work. Letting the past go, learning from the mistakes, and stopping the cycle of self-sabotage is an important key to manifestation. You cannot hide your feelings from yourself—you may be in denial, but your body, mind, and spirit always know. Become your greatest ally, learn to trust yourself, then when you reach out for feedback you will feel the difference in whether it resonates with you or not.

> *Awareness #2 Journal Exercise*—Do you keep commitments to others as well as yourself? Do you find yourself changing your mind constantly or avoiding making decisions? What does the self-talk within your mind sound like? How can you show up more for YOU?

Awareness #3: Seeking Acceptance Gets in the Way of Fortitude

Human beings seek approval, acceptance, and want to be a part of something greater than themselves. It is an innate quality to want to belong to the "tribe," also know as family. At a young age this process begins, looking for signs of approval, whether it is a glance from a parent, a smile from a teacher, or a nod from one of the "cool" kids in school. Although it is absolutely normal to seek approval, there is a fine line between wanting to belong and not having the confidence to stand alone in your beliefs or decisions. This is where things get muddy.

I remember a time when I told people I wanted to move to Sedona, my current city of residence. I was met head on with all sorts of excuses and reasons why it would not work for me and my family—all coming from friends, colleagues, and family members. Thankfully, there were some supportive people as well, and they were the ones I would consult with when feeling doubt. All in all, it was truly an inside job. I spent countless hours daily, visualizing what I wanted, and more importantly, feeling myself already living there. In the end, my efforts paid off and everything fell into place.

The lesson here is, you must find the stillness within, the knowing deep inside that keeps you going. I know that even those who could not support me, still loved me and wanted the best for me, they were just giving advice through their own filters, fears, and limitations. When I stopped reaching outside of myself, it all came together. Sometimes you have to share the news *after* it has manifested.

> ᴄᴧ *Awareness #3 Journal Exercise*—Think about the type of support system you have; do they tend to speak to you through their own fears? Are they able to hold space for you and see the vision with you? It is ok if they cannot, the important thing is the recognition that you may need to find that support elsewhere, and spend more time going within yourself for support.

Awareness #4: You Do Not Have to Know It All, It's Not Your Job

It becomes very easy to get caught in the trap of always wanting a guarantee before taking a step forward. Wanting to know what will happen and how this will all come together makes logical sense, but it is actually backwards. It is not your job to know how things will manifest, it is your job to decide what you want. The "wanting" starts a process of discernment—if you open your eyes to see the subtle evidence forming. Things will shift, sometimes below the surface of visibility, yet they are shifting.

This is where I like to think of the quote, *"Do not give up five minutes before the miracle"* (author unknown). It is in that time that your focused attention is needed, believing wholeheartedly that you can accomplish your goal, dream, or task. If you start thinking of *how,* you have stepped into the territory of the universe, and are now trying to take control. Fear and getting stuck in the head space will usually prompt this behavior. The only job you have to do is to decide what you want, what it would feel like to have it…and then pour your entire being into it. Use as many senses as you can, release the fears, and this will set you up for success.

One small disclaimer, it is my belief that there is also an aspect of universal involvement here, meaning not everything is going to manifest, if it is *not* in alignment for your highest good. Ask for what you want, and also include, *"always for my highest good."*

✑ *Awareness #4 Journal Exercise*—Close your eyes and imagine yourself receiving and being in the exact manifestation of what you are called to. If it is a new home, see yourself in it. If it is living without anxiety, feel the peace in your body. Whatever it is you desire, see it in your mind's eye and slowly bring in the other senses and feel it. Feel the breeze on your skin, the fresh air, the sound of the front door; feel it all and give it as much color as you can. See yourself performing certain tasks from this place of living the manifestation. After you have witnessed in your mind's eye, journal the entire experience. Practice this exercise every morning or night for 30 days and watch the magic unfold.

Awareness #5: Creating Involves Constant Involvement and Discipline of the Mind

Creative, holistically-minded people and artists will sometimes receive the labels of being too flighty, ungrounded, and often *woo-woo*. Many people have a belief that they are scatter-brained and living like gypsies (not that I am judging, I love gypsies). My personal belief on this is that sometimes the way their message is conveyed, coming from the right hemisphere of the brain and often with the excitement of the creative process, appears to have less focus on the business or strategy side of their endeavors. Creativity comes from everyone, grounding that idea down into a tangible form takes discipline. Many creators stay in that phase and rarely put anything out into the world that will result in sustaining a lifestyle to be supported by their creativity. This is the reason you can meet one of the most talented people, see their gifts and how they could serve others, only to find that they are blocked when it comes to self promotion, or charging appropriately for their work. Hand in hand with this comes value and how we perceive the value of what we are creating.

It takes discipline of the mind and your thoughts to move into the phase of bringing an idea into form. You have to move past the self doubt and mental chatter, get beyond the insecurities and remember why you do what you do … to express and connect with others who resonate with your message. It does not matter if your medium for this message is artwork, writing a book, speaking in public, or simply sharing a kind word with a stranger at the grocery store. It is all important, and it is selfish to stay small and hide your gifts from this world; so get out there and trust that your spirit knows how to help you accomplish this.

✑ *Awareness #5 Exercise*—Divide a page in half by drawing a line straight down the center of the paper. On the left side, top of the page, write the word *Excuses*. Next, under the word *Excuses*, use the rest of the column to write down every reason why you cannot move forward with a project, experience, or situation. It can be anything you are struggling to move forward with, personally or professionally. After you finish go to the right column, top of the page and write the word *Truth*.

Now take a deep breath and ask your higher self for clarity. Is it true that you cannot do these things, or is that you just do not know the next step? Is it true that you will fail, or is it true that you have some fear about moving forward? Take any "excuse" and one by one break it down to the essence of why it feels heavy or overwhelming. Sometimes acknowledging the underlying feeling is all that is really needed to break through.

There is an extra step to this if you are ready and that is to take the things you want to do and create a separate page for *Actions Ready to Be Taken*. One by one you write down the action that you feel is right to move forward and then schedule it in to your calendar so that you begin to tackle it. This is discipline, having awareness of perceived limitations, yet the willingness to persevere through them step by step.

The End Result

All of the steps take time, each one will have a different pace for you depending where you are in the process, in your life, and comfort zone. There is no right or wrong way, and if you are guided you may skip a step or revisit the same one over and over again. Practice makes perfect, and once you surrender to your higher self the evidence of manifestation can actually move through your life experience more rapidly.

The end result may shock you, witnessing the power of your own mind is empowering and the more you practice consciously creating, the more certain lessons begin to leave your experience, for others to surface. You learn to trust your spirit, and become your own best friend.

Give yourself credit for how far you have come, and allow the answers and guidance from your higher self to arise. You will always be supported. Sometimes the greatest way to hear that guidance is to get really quiet and still, reducing the chatter of the mind so the voice of your spirit can reach you. I wish you well always, and in all ways, Namasté.

To every person in my life who believed in me, thank you. For every person who did not believe in me, thank you — I became a better person from the lessons you taught me. I dedicate this work to every student and client who showed up for themselves, I am grateful for the opportunity to see your spirit, thank you for opening up and letting me in.

To my son Jared, thank you for being one of my greatest teachers, I love you to Terraria and back. Kristopher, my husband, I would never have dreamed that I would be the person I am today, I know that is because you have been my partner and best friend, guiding me when I couldn't find my own light — I am forever grateful.

~ Melissa Kim Corter

Sharon Gambrill

SHARON GAMBRILL (also fondly known as 'Shazza') is a Sydney-based come-dian, actor, writer, Laughter Yoga Leader, and licensed Heal Your Life® Workshop Teacher and Personal Coach. During a year of medical and holistic treatment fol-lowing a mastectomy in 2011, Sharon decided it was time to 'go within' to examine the mind/body health connection and come to terms with a worried childhood being her mother's parent—then her mother's subsequent suicide in 2001, absent father abandonment issues, and her lifelong struggle with obesity. What a year! It was a transformational time with healing occurring on a deep, emotional level by studying the philosophies of Louise L. Hay and using her bestselling book, *You Can Heal Your Life,* as a guide. Other healthy practises used were laughter, nutrition, Tapping, Reiki, walking, meditation, music, and visualisation. While at times an excruciating process and at other times smooth flowing, Sharon persevered reading numerous books on health and emotional healing which led her to the Laughter Yoga and Heal Your Life® certification trainings—being the modalities she found to be of the most benefit. Sharon has written a number of children's story books and is currently working with an illustrator to bring them to life. Sharon always writes from the heart and is warm, open, honest, funny, and inspiring. Sharon continues to uplift everyone around her and is now on a personal mission to encourage others to accept themselves unconditionally, release the past, and create a life filled with love, laughter, and excellent health!

For workshops, personal coaching sessions or speaking events, please contact Sharon at:

info@sharongambrill.com
www.sharongambrill.com
Or connect with her on Facebook, Twitter, Instagram or Meetup.

I Am Alive!

Empowerment is a strong vital-sounding word. It can imply status or power, but for the purpose of this chapter I am going to refer to empowerment as — *a feeling of safety and security within ourselves in the present moment, and confidence in the future no matter what is happening in our life right now.* To feel safe and secure is to feel empowered. In the midst of a crisis, feeling empowered disappears and is replaced with fear, panic, and shock. At this time of extreme challenge it is of prime importance to feel calm again and in this chapter I will be sharing techniques that can be included as part of a health and healing workshop, or done by an individual in a quiet place, as a daily practice. After reading about the health benefits of deep breathing, smiling, meditation, and visualisation, I have included these elements. Along with medical care, I would also recommend Tapping, walking, and good nutrition.

This chapter is especially written for any women who have received the worst possible news after a biopsy. Feeling lost, alone, and terrified is something I know about. My world changed in 2011 with the shocking discovery of a tiny, little hard granule inside a soft breast lump. This was followed by a rush of biopsies, scans, and calm-but-concerned-looking doctors who give you the impression they are getting you prepared for something serious. I felt completely disempowered, vulnerable, and panicked. The floor fell away, as did any feelings of security I had.

What a diagnosis like this can do is bring up any unresolved issues in our life and heighten our emotional state. Whilst in hospital recovering from a mastectomy, I found myself grieving for my mother who had suicided 10 years earlier, and wishing I had taken better care of myself emotionally and physically after a childhood of looking after my mother when she was depressed, and being angry at my father for leaving us. Added to that the guilt, I felt that I had somehow contributed to the condition from years of eating junk food, bouts of obesity, and doing little exercise. Imagine what an emotion-charged week it was lying in that hospital bed with drainage tubes coming out of my flat, left chest. Glad that's over!

This is why I have written this chapter based on what I learnt that helped me dig myself out of that misery, and have included techniques that I use when I teach workshops and support groups for women who are recovering from breast surgery, as well as with other groups who have different health challenges and chronic illnesses. I continue to practice these techniques daily. I have forgiven myself and others. Feeling strong, healthy, and empowered is my wish for you, too, so let's get started!

The first part of this workshop is a *Guided Relaxation Meditation* and the second part is what we refer to in a Heal Your Life® coaching session as *Growth Work*. Both are designed to benefit your health and recovery process.

Part 1: Guided Relaxation Meditation

1. **Deep Breathing**—Sit in a comfortable chair, put phones on silent, and minimise all noise. This is your time. Close your eyes. Breathe in slowly through the nose to a count of four; hold for four, exhale through the mouth to a count of four. In between each breath gently say this Louise L. Hay Power Thought Affirmation—*I Am Safe*. This is designed to associate safety with relaxation. Do this three times.

2. **Smile Meditation**—Feel your body relax and allow your mind to calm. Put a smile on your face. Imagine a big beautiful smile, of any colour that appeals to you, floating from the air and down into the top of your head. As it passes into your head and down into your neck and shoulders, feel your whole body relax and your breathing deepen. Continue to smile yourself, as you imagine this big beautiful smile flowing down each arm, past your elbows, into your hands, through your stomach and back, down each leg and into your ankles and feet. Keep smiling and see this big beautiful smile fill up your entire body, as all your internal organs relax and start glowing with health. Well done!

3. **Healthy Cell Visualisation**—You can relax your mouth now, but continue to feel that big beautiful smile within you and keep your eyes closed. While in this comfortable seated position, say the following out aloud and imagine each descriptive word filling your entire body—*Every Cell In My Body Is Alive With Happiness!* Imagine thousands of tiny smiling faces looking up at you representing each cell in your body. *Every Cell In My Body Is Alive With Love*—imagine thousands of love hearts looking up at you and each cell is filled with love. *Every Cell In My Body Is Alive With Vibrant Tremendous Health*—imagine every one of your cells as a bright, glowing sun filled with glowing health.

4. **Going For A Walk Visualisation**—Now let's imagine we are going for a walk. See yourself walking in a lovely park or by a beach, whichever place pops into your mind first. It is a lovely sunny day, the exact temperature you like, and the air smells clean and fresh. You are dressed exactly as you are today. As you walk, imagine you see your favourite flower or scented blossom tree. Lean in and appreciate how fragrant it is and how happy the simple act of smelling a flower makes you feel. Smile. Now keep walking and next you see a friendly little dog, cat, rabbit, horse (any animal you like). Stop and pet this friendly animal and have a little laugh, as it playfully jumps around you and gives you unconditional love and acceptance in that moment. As you walk a little further notice how light and happy you feel. Breathe in the fresh air. Next you unexpectedly see a trusted friend, neighbour, work colleague, or family member. This must be someone who always uplifts you and makes you feel good in their company. Greet each other with a big joyous hug and laugh in amazement that you are both here at the same time. Now I want you to imagine that this person looks at you and says, *"Wow you look fantastic! How wonderful!"* and you reply with, *"Thank you. I feel great!"*

5. **Affirmations**—Open your eyes, smile, and say the following Louise L. Hay Affirmations aloud with enthusiasm!

> *My Immune System Is Strong And Healthy—My Body Is Strong And Healthy—Every Cell In My Body Is Alive—I Am So Glad To Be Alive—I Love Life And Life Loves Me—I Look Forward To Every Day—I Lovingly Live Life To The Fullest—I Am Healthy, Beautiful And Filled With Energy—I Lovingly Forgive And Release All Of The Past—I Choose To Fill My World With Joy—I Love And Approve Of Myself—I Bless My Body With Love—Thank You For My Healing—All Is Well.*

Now take a deep breath in and exhale. You can look up *You Can Heal Your Life*® by Louise L. Hay to see more affirmations for specific health conditions.

Part 2: Growth Work

1. Create a picture or vision board filled with photos and pictures of adults or children with happy smiling faces. This can be people you know or strangers cut out of a magazine or shopping catalogue. Add fit healthy-looking people as well. Sports store catalogues are good for this. Also cut out or write words in pretty colours such as *Health, Love, Energy, Life, Joy, Happiness, Bliss, Thank-You,* and

arrange them on your vision board, a piece of cardboard, or place them around where you live … and even in your car to reinforce in your subconscious mind the idea of health. Enjoy looking at these words and saying them out aloud.

2. Go to a park, sports ground, or beach and watch people socialising, walking, or exercising. Enjoy seeing children playing energetically at a playground and having fun. This can be *you* too!

3. Accept help from others and nurture yourself. Your health comes first now.

4. Listen to upbeat, lively music or music videos. Dance around, if you can, or just sing along.

5. Laugh! Research shows laughter produces a response in the part of our brain that releases endorphins and other healthy hormones into our blood stream which improve our immune system and assist in cellular repair. Deep breathing from laughter brings in more oxygen to our brain and cells which is good for our health and makes us feel more alert, energised, and less anxious. Turn off the news, stop reading your medical reports, and watch a funny movie or TV show. My Laughter Yoga workshops show people that we can laugh doing fun, laughter activities and pretend laughter to receive the same health benefits as if we are laughing for real at something, in particular like a joke. So let's laugh for no reason right now. Ha-ha-ha! Promoting unconditional inner joy and child-like happiness is good for our health!

So despite the circumstances of my transformation in 2011, and the fact that it was virtually forced upon me, I can now say that I have never been healthier or happier.

 Transformation can be empowering. So my wish for you, dear reader, is a calm, happy future — filled with love, laughter, and good health. I am alive and so are you!

I dedicate this chapter to all the women who have sat in a doctor's office and received news they did not want to hear. With this writing I send my loving wishes to each one, plus the intention to inspire and empower them with the knowledge and confidence to know that they have a future and it is bright, healthy and filled with laughter!

I would like to acknowledge and thank the wonderful Louise L. Hay and her ground breaking book, You Can Heal Your Life. This book literally changed my life! I also wish to acknowledge and thank Dr. Patricia Crane for creating the Heal Your Life® teacher training program and taking it worldwide, plus the Australian/New Zealand teacher trainer, Susie Mulholland, for her care and mentoring. Finally, I would like to acknowledge and thank my beautiful and sensitive mother Lesley. My mother was the person who gave me a personally-signed copy of You Can Heal Your Life after she met Louise in Sydney in 1986. She must have known I would need it one day. I largely ignored the book for 25 years until 2011 when it became my lifeline. To these four women go my love and thanks.

Sharon Gambrill

Antoinette Coleman-Kelly

ANTOINETTE COLEMAN-KELLY from Ireland is an International DeNA "Light-Up" Activator, Presenter and Transformative Coach, **Heal Your Life®** Leader, Coach and Business Trainer.

She is a lifelong spiritual traveller with an inspiring, positive, happy and grateful outlook on life.

She is dedicated to motivating people to discover change and achieve their highest and best potential.

www.lifehealing.ie.

 The Power of Thank You

D o you have the "Thank You" gene? We all have free will and it is our choice to bring beautiful positivity into our lives by being grateful.

Being thankful can lead to a wonderful sense of joy, feeling cherished, peaceful and contented—a powerful feeling of gratitude dramatically improves us, our lives and those around us:

- ✌ The dictionary describes gratitude as a feeling of being grateful (from the Latin *gratus* meaning "grateful/thankful") and associated words include thanks, thankfulness, gratefulness and appreciation.

- ✌ As children, we were taught to be polite, generous, to say thank you, and this is regarded as good manners. As an adult we are grateful when someone does something good for us; for example, opening a door for us, presenting a gift, passing us a compliment, cooking dinner and so forth. In addition, what about everything else that the Universe/God supplies?

- ✌ Be thankful for the weather, seasons, mountains, sea, nature, smiles, thoughts and feelings, fun, work, wisdom and knowledge, our health and our thinking and so on. Imagine how awesome it is to say *"Thank You"* to the Universe/God and allow an abundance of this beauty to keep appearing for us.

- ✌ What we focus on can expand, and the energy of gratitude in our everyday lives can magnetically draw the things we desire directly to us. The Universe magnifies it. Being thankful is not just to be noted on an annual basis, but many times every day, as the simple practice of saying thank you can bring extraordinary results to each of us.

- ✌ Gratitude is my rocket fuel. As I wake up every day, the thought *"Something wonderful is happening to-day"* automatically pops into my head. I also believe in keeping a gratitude journal and writing four things that I am grateful for every day. I strongly suggest you do likewise. Now I know there shall be days when you might want to write one hundred and four and I say go for it, perhaps some days four might be too much. When we live with a grateful heart, it is more difficult for fear or guilt to enter.

- ✐ Find a little pebble/stone/rock and keep it in your purse/pocket as a "gratitude stone" as a reminder to be more grateful every day. Thank you, are just two small words, but they are massively effective.
- ✐ It is a known fact that you cannot be thankful and unhappy at the same time. Gratitude allows us clarity and vision and frees us from stress and frustration. Many great philosophers have encouraged people to cultivate the habit of appreciation.
- ✐ While this is my perception on gratitude I invite you to try being grateful for thirty days and notice the amazing results.

I have had so many occasions and things to be grateful for in my life, too many to mention, but one occasion that stands high was a spiritual trip to Northern India a couple of years ago. While travelling deep in the Himalayas we visited many beautiful temples, where many Masters have walked, one temple in particular really spoke to me.

This was the beautiful *Chandrabadani Devi Temple* known affectionately as "Mother Temple." On this occasion, we walked up a very windy, difficult path several kilometres in length to the base of "Mother Temple," and then climbed the sixty plus steps to reach the Temple itself. As I rang the bell to announce my arrival, I was thankful to say I had arrived to honour the Divine. We were so high up on the mountain that I really thought, if I had another step to take, surely, I would have been stepping into Heaven. The views were totally stunning and we could see Mount Everest to the left, Tibet and China in the far distance.

It is important for me to explain that at this time I was suffering greatly with my right hip. I am so utterly grateful to the most amazing teachers and group, as I often struggled walking; but despite this, I succeeded in fully participating in all trips, including reaching "Mother Temple." The blessings I received were inspiring and remain very special to me. I am forever and eternally thankful.

Within a month of my return to Ireland I was in hospital, recovering from a total hip replacement, feeling very vulnerable and affirming that my healing was well in progress, feeling extremely thankful that the surgery was a success and that I woke up!

On the day following the surgery, the physiotherapist appeared, introduced me to two crutches and I thought, *"Oh my goodness, is this really possible?"* As you know, one does not argue with the physiotherapist! I gingerly and slowly walked with the crutches! I could not believe that I could walk. I was feeling huge gratitude. I kept silently repeating *"Thank You God, Thank You God,"* and thus began my challenge on learning to walk again.

Within weeks, I had a return visit with my Consultant and had x-rays ... all was going to plan. I felt I was receiving unbelievable blessings. He told me to use a cane (in my left hand) and that I could drive on week six. *Whoo hoo*, what music to my ears! I was walking with my fabulous cane/stick. (May I add a beautifully coloured cane?)

The physiotherapy continued and the pain was tolerable! Many of the exercises were excruciating, yet with practice, it did get a little easier, eventually! I was thankful that I could actually walk so well.

I believed it was mind over matter, no matter how painful my hip was, I would not give in. I affirmed on a daily basis *"I am enjoying vibrant health and my hip is in perfect working order."*

Ten months following the surgery, I returned to Northern India and the Himalayas in massive gratitude for my wellbeing and my ability to walk, and yes, I went back to visit the beautiful "Mother Temple" to say Thank You.

The amazing feeling of gratitude I felt was rather overwhelming, I was almost dizzy. I thought I would explode with this most awesome feeling, this gift of life. Every breath and every step was a miracle. I felt very humbled and I really truly thanked God for my life.

Gratitude is a paradigm shift allowing us to move from feeling stuck to creativity—and from fear to love. I invite you right now, using your ten fingers, close your eyes, name and count ten blessings you have in your life today.

Being thankful is an emotional response that wells up when one is confronted by the most miraculous design of life. Focusing on being grateful for all the wonderful gifts in our lives, allows more of the magic from the Universe to flow abundantly into our lives.

Thank You.
Namasté

Awesome gratitude to my family and friends for their uncon-
ditional love and support.

~ Antoinette Coleman-Kelly

Tonya Thomas

TONYA THOMAS, M.S. is a Habits & Relationship Coach, family therapist, Reiki Master/Teacher and author. She has a Bachelor's Degree in business and a Master's Degree in Marriage and Family Therapy, and will soon complete her doctorate in Psychology.

She resides in central California and enjoys traveling to her home state spending time with her children, grandchildren, family and friends. She also enjoys sharing Reiki through both giving sessions and training others. Her deepest passion is helping people by challenging their limiting beliefs towards finding the love within and empowering them to live their life to the fullest.

The Power of Meditation and Visualization!

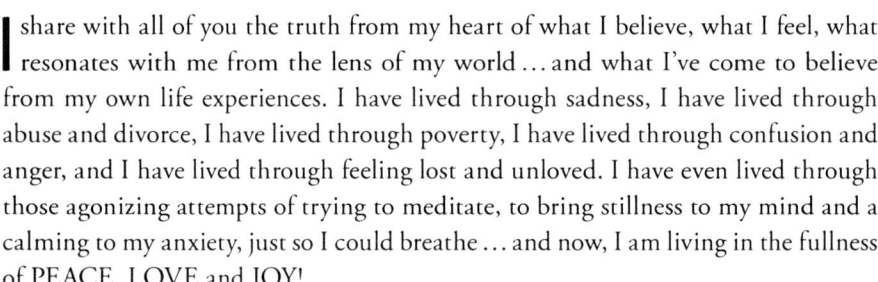

I share with all of you the truth from my heart of what I believe, what I feel, what resonates with me from the lens of my world ... and what I've come to believe from my own life experiences. I have lived through sadness, I have lived through abuse and divorce, I have lived through poverty, I have lived through confusion and anger, and I have lived through feeling lost and unloved. I have even lived through those agonizing attempts of trying to meditate, to bring stillness to my mind and a calming to my anxiety, just so I could breathe ... and now, I am living in the fullness of PEACE, LOVE and JOY!

As a child, I learned how to survive around sadness, anxiety, and fear. We lived in poverty, with my mother barely earning enough to feed us, and her in a world of depression, many times having to lean on our grandparents for our physical and emotional needs. At seven years old, I witnessed my mother in her deepest sadness, wanting to end her life and take us with her. After my mother told us to lay on our bed made of blankets on a hardwood floor, I watched her carefully place towels under the doors, turn on the gas stove, and blow out the flame. Our lives were in her hands and about to be extinguished, along with her depression. But something happened, and instead she choose for us all to stay alive. Soon after this horrific event, my mother met a man who became my step-father, and oh, how she was in love ... and my world forever changed.

And so the next 11 years were filled with childhood sexual abuse, anxiety, and chaos. I learned how to stuff my pain and hide my feelings. How to be silent and invisible. I learned how to separate me from my body, and how not to feel. And then, the next 21 years was spent dodging my feelings and pushing away all my childhood memories, stuffing them deep inside my body, giving me a false sense of peace.

However, that sense of peace was turned upside down in 1996 when I got divorced, throwing me into a whole different type of chaos. By 2001, I was married a second time, divorced for the second time, and then ended up in bankruptcy. This time I hit a wall, and could no longer keep stuffing my pain. I became so angry, I would explode from the slightest trigger, leaving others wondering, *"Who is this person?"* I was no longer silent nor wanting to stay invisible. It was time to release the darkness I had allowed to reside deep within me, to find a way to love life—and most importantly, to love me.

Soon after hitting my emotional brick wall, I met a friend who started me on my spiritual journey. She guided me through a past life journey using active meditation, and had me visualize and describe what I experienced using all my senses. She then took me to a group gathering where she was learning hypnotherapy, and I went on another guided journey. This too was a type of active meditation where I visualized and described my experience with all my senses. As I was guided down some stairs, I came upon a darkness that I was unable to pass through, so I ended the session.

Then a few years later during an existential class for my doctorate studies, I was introduced to "wake dreaming." Another type of active meditation where a guide started me on a visual journey in a meditative state, me again describing my experience while using all of my senses. This time however, I walked up the stairs and into an open and well-lit ballroom. As I climbed the stairs, I could see to my right some doors that were closed with a railing that blocked me from entering. I had a "knowing," a feeling that behind those doors were chapters of my life safely tucked away, and that one day I would be prepared to open those doors when I was ready.

As a child of sexual abuse, I was very good at stuffing and masking my pain from others, but my body was not allowing me to keep it all stuffed away anymore. My mind would not stop creating thoughts that continued to manifest anxiety in my body, and I was attracting poor relationships to feed the cycle I was in.

Then one day in 2006, I happened to open up a community college flyer and came across a class to learn Reiki. I had heard about Reiki, but I had never experienced it. I felt a strong pull to learn, so I signed up and went to the class. I was the lucky one who got to lay on the table while others practiced their hand placements and I felt tingling in my legs while seeing swirls of color, something I had never experienced before. I then started practicing on others and experienced so much more. I'm not one to follow exact instructions, so even though I was told I should keep my eyes open while practicing Reiki, I preferred to close my eyes and allow myself to become at one with the person while meditating. It wasn't long before I began to see colors that tied to different chakras and feel the energy flowing through me to areas of their body that needed it most. I even began to feel as if I were levitating off the ground and that my body and the other person's body had merged into one. Of course, it spooked me at first and I opened my eyes to see that my feet were still touching the ground, but the experience allowed me to open my senses to more than I had ever known.

Now, I am not like many others who are able to sit down each day at a specific time, in a specific position, and hold my arms and fingers a certain way in order to meditate. So Reiki helped me to connect with the practice of meditation and visualization even more. I'm also not saying that you must learn Reiki to be able to meditate or to use visualizing techniques either. This practice needs to resonate and work for you, wherever you are. Maybe you might want a guide who will walk you through an active meditation, allowing you to visualize a journey or coach you to breathe in and then breathe out. Maybe it's taking a nature walk or a run along the beach where you find your peace and calm state. Maybe its journaling, as you ask questions and then receive the answers through writing from your higher self, the angels, or your old soul. Maybe it's through dance or gazing upon a painting. Meditation to me is connecting with my inner self, allowing feelings in my body to surface, and listening to the messages or answers to my questions. It is finding that place within me to release and let go, allowing the God within me to heal those places where I so carefully carried my pain, and to forgive both myself and others.

You may now be wondering to yourself, *"So now what? How do I actually do this?"* Here are some ideas that have worked for me. Again, if it resonates with you, then go for it. If not, make slight changes in what I have shared or continue researching for what works for you.

Allowing and Tapping Into Your Emotions

1. **Give yourself permission to allow without any judgment or control of the experience.**

    Do not give up if you don't quickly resonate with or get the results you believe should happen. Limiting beliefs are major roadblocks in all areas of our lives, and may need to be acknowledged, accepted and then released before one is able to freely open up to the experience.

2. **Tap into your body by listening to what your thoughts (self-talk) are saying.**

    Feel the physical changes (anxiety or excitement) in your body, and what emotion (sadness or joy) you are experiencing with each choice or non-choice you make. Be sure to write in the margins what is happening externally as well. Such as, you got stuck in a traffic jam for two hours, you got in a fight with your boss, or you just got finished with a relaxing bubble bath with no interruptions… *ah, Calgon take me away!* If you are experiencing a depressed mood, consistent anxiety, or even happiness, score the day or each half of your day, from 0-10, with 0 meaning "not at all" to a 10 meaning "extremely high." Again, journal without making any judgment or analyzing the why's or why not's. After some time has passed, such as a week or even a month depending on how much you have written down, go back and highlight the connections of the event to the emotion.

3. **About now you're likely asking, what does this have to do with meditation or visualization?**

Well, the first two steps are breaking old belief patterns that may be blocking you from continuing this practice and teaching you how to tap into your body to HEAR the messages coming to you. It is listening to what your body is telling you by how you FEEL … sadness, anxiety, or joy! It allows you to tap into the messages you are receiving and teaches you how to LISTEN to what your body is expressing. Messages are always being sent and our emotions are the receivers of those messages. If a message is causing your body to feel anxiety or pain in your stomach area, and is ignored over and over again, it may very well end up in permanent body pain or illness, such as an ulcer or serious digestive problems. If time is taken to track these past patterns (and I am not recommending this needs to be done), you will most assuredly find the beginning mark is some event that was ignored and stuffed away that is currently causing health issues. I see all emotions as messengers, such as when anxiety rears its head, there is something that needs to be faced, dealt with or changed. I like to think of anxiety as a "change agent" with a large megaphone calling out, *"It's time …"*

4. **Ok, let's continue. Visualization is a technique many use to see oneself succeeding at such things as giving a speech before an audience, winning a sport, or even dreaming a vision.**

Some people easily see pictures in their mind, and yet others have a "knowing" or a feeling. I was one of those who only saw black when I closed my eyes. But after being attuned to Reiki and practicing for a while, I began to see colors, and then sometimes images. However, for the most part, I'm more of the sensing and feeling type. Again, it's tapping into the emotion that you are feeling and where in your body you feel this emotion.

5. **To help guide you to make some kind of sense of the experience, there are many different resources you can tap into on the meaning of color, smell, sound, and even the chakras.**

Again, find what resonates with you. For those I attune to Reiki, I ask that they look at a chakra color chart or anything else that is similar to that color to attune themselves to "seeing colors." When I practice Reiki, and then discuss the experience with the one receiving, I will share what I see or feel (a "knowing" or message), but I also have the person connect to and find their *own* meaning with their experience.

6. **Now, let's try a little experiential activity. Go outside and look at a leaf**.

    Pick up the leaf and hold it in your hands. Take the time in your mind to describe its shape, its color, its movement, and anything else you see, feel and smell. What memories does it bring up? What emotions are you feeling? Use all your senses to really connect with this leaf. Listen to how your body feels, listen to what thoughts come to you … become one with that leaf. Close your eyes and see that leaf in your mind, again with all your senses. Keep practicing this with anything you choose, it doesn't matter what you pick. It's the practice of attuning yourself to visualize in your mind. Again, you may never actually see it, but instead will have a "knowing" or sense of what a leaf is without having to look at it.

7. **Here is a technique I have used with both my Reiki and therapy clients**.

    I combine visualization with deep breathing and have them see and feel "love, happy, or good" moving into their body as they breathe in, and then have them see and feel "anger, sadness, or pain" leaving their body as they breathe out. If actual visuals are needed to help make this happen, use them. Find red hearts to represent love, or a picture of someone you feel love for, or a happy event or place you have been to that represents what you "breathe in."

    I really don't think you need to actually visualize darkness or pain, as the body already knows this all too well. However, finding something that represents love may be difficult at first if the body and mind have been conditioned to only recognize hurt or pain. This may take some time and you may have to do some deep searching of when there was a time you did "feel" this loving emotion. A gratitude or appreciation journal is a great way to tap into some positive past emotions. But, if it is still too difficult, dream a little into the future and pretend how you might feel to be happy. Really pay attention to your body and how different it feels from what you are used to feeling. If it feels good and right … you've got it!

8. **Dancing is another form of meditation I have used. It has always been therapy to my soul.**

When I was first divorced in '96, I found dancing to be more than just moving my body around on a dance floor. For me it was a release of so many years of stuffing pain deep inside myself. When I felt extreme anxiety and was unable to let go, I would move the furniture out of my way, turn on music that resonated with me at that time, closed my eyes, and danced. I let the music guide my movements, releasing all the pent-up anxiety in my body. It helps to find music that gives you that "high" feeling, so that when you have something you need to "release and let go," you can simply turn it on and move. Again, it really doesn't matter if you dance, or run, or walk. Just get up and move your body with the intent of releasing.

I am not of the norm when it comes to meditation and I believe there are many ways we are able to quiet our minds, tap into our inner self ... to release, allow and receive. I enjoy sitting at the beach, and allowing the sounds of the ocean waves to bring in the love and release the chaos. I may be on a nature walk and decide to sit for a while, close my eyes and allow the sounds of the wind to carry me to that calm place. Meditation has allowed me to connect to the God within, helping me to release old pains, and keeping me safe in a life of chaos. It is a means of visualizing my life to be different than the one I was experiencing ... one of LOVE instead of pain. Visualization has helped me to see a different future, and to manifest my life dreams. I've learned to forgive, to release and let go, and I've learned to allow my heart to feel. I now embrace all that life brings, both the good and not so good, and I've learned to simply BE in ... PEACE, LOVE, and JOY.

 When you feel you have come to the end ...

it's really just the beginning!

Dedicated to my first love, my maternal grandmother Jessie Mae Hopkins — because of you, my heart always remains open to love. Dedicated to my children and grandchildren — because of you, the light in my heart continues to shine.

A special thank you to all teachers and learners of life who continue to cross my path and provide me with incredible opportunities for growth.

~ Tonya Thomas

Dawn Amberley

DAWN AMBERLEY was born and bred an English rose, with an endless passion for helping others overcome their limitations and obstacles. In support of this she strives to understand the mind-body connection with certifications in Reiki and hypnosis and is currently studying Neuro Linguistic Programming (NLP).

Dawn now resides in Phoenix, Arizona where she finds wonder in the sun setting on the desert mountains and inspiration in the starry skies at night. She firmly believes that what you give out to the world you get back – ten-fold, so best make it amazing!

dawnamberley@yahoo.com
facebook.com/DawnAmberley

 Inspirations and a Cupcake

Ever feel like you've had just one too many challenges thrown at you? Or that you don't match up to other people? Are you feeling undervalued and wondering why you are being tested quite this far? I get how you feel. I consider I have attended the school of life and learned by experience from many challenging personal situations. When I came alone to work in the USA, I had to find a way through the loneliness and self-doubt to make a new life for myself.

When negative relationships rocked my core beliefs, I had to establish my true values and boundaries in order to move on. When my long-term boyfriend was diagnosed with pancreatic cancer, I suddenly had a new role as his sole caregiver. I had to dig deep to find strengths I never knew I had. When he died I had to find a new kind of strength to overcome the enormous grief. During some of these times, there were days when I could barely put one foot in front of the other, I had to learn to believe in the power of me and trust there was a brighter world waiting for me. I would like to share with you some of the inspirations that pushed me to keep my feet moving and ultimately change my life.

You need to know that you are an amazing, worthy, valuable and loveable human being. You are worth every possible thing your heart could dream of. You can have and do anything you want, because YOU are worth it ... but there are steps to getting there, of removing the obstacles in your path and to seeing that light peeking through the dark forest, that maybe you feel you are wandering through right now. If you are going through a challenging time, reach inside yourself for that little bit of knowing that things can be different, that life can be better, that you deserve peace and happiness. Know it. It's there. Once you can find even a little tiny corner of that knowing, you can start to believe, and when you believe, magical things start happening. Wouldn't you like to feel some of that magic?

Here are some of the crucial steps that I feel helped me get through my own personal forest of darkness. I've broken it down to three main subjects, accepting yourself, trusting your intuition, and setting boundaries:

1. Accepting Yourself

You are perfect as you are, body and mind. I have put this first as it's so important, but this is a tough one, as we are met with so many media idealizations about body image and how we should look. Couple that with other people's judgments on our personalities and how we should behave and it can become a source of much pain. I could tell you to just ignore every article or every comment, but that won't make any difference until you can change the way you feel inside.

Be proud of who you are! Be authentic! Consider what really lights up your day. Aim to take actions that move you toward that "feeling good" feeling. Make a list of what you love to do. What really makes you happy? When you can really come to grips with who you are and what lights you up inside, it makes life decisions so much easier. You are meant to be living a life of joy. You are not meant to be unhappy! So stop battling with yourself and trying to be someone you are not. Here are some suggestions to help you …

- Think about the security talk on a plane before it takes off. The cabin crew reminds you that in the event of oxygen being required, you must first put on your own oxygen mask before you help anyone else. This is true of life. You must put yourself first or you'll not be able to help others.

- The first thing that can really help is to change your body posture. Have you noticed that if you are having a bad day, or you don't feel well that your body slumps or you find yourself slouching in a chair? Changing your posture can have a dramatic effect on how you feel. Stand up straight! Sit up straight! Head up! No shoulder hunching or slouching. Every time you catch yourself slouching, pick yourself back up. Take a deep breath in, then breathe out slowly and relax your shoulders. Not only is this better for your body, but it gives you an instant boost. Also, making a constant effort to adjust your posture takes your mind off of whatever is worrying you!

- The next thing to remember is that people will treat you how you treat yourself. Find some quiet time and identify your fears and limiting beliefs. If you feel that no one loves you, find ways to give more love to yourself. If you feel people have no respect for you, think of the ways that you are not giving yourself enough respect and change that. Taking the time to put yourself first can have wonderful consequences to your self esteem. Try something small each day. This may mean taking the time to pamper yourself or getting some quiet time for thirty minutes. You may have to ask for someone else's help in order to get some alone time, but just do it. You deserve it. It may also mean talking to yourself more kindly. How do you talk to yourself in your head? If you are constantly berating yourself, you will never get the respect and love you want and deserve. Look at yourself in the mirror and tell yourself how beautiful or handsome you are. Learn to love your body however it is and tell yourself—daily. You are worthy and you are valued, but it all starts with you. Believe. Once you start being kind to yourself and treating YOU the way you deserve, other people will do the same.

ↈ Next is to forgive your past. Whatever you did or didn't do, it's over. Whatever someone else did, that is also over. It's already happened and there is not a thing you can do about it to change it. I know it's hard to just forget the bad things that have happened, but instead of dwelling on them, think about how you can use them to your advantage and change your life going forward. Whatever mistakes were made, think about how you would react today if the same situation presented itself. I'm sure you would react very differently, and when you realize that, you know you have made a huge step forward. Whatever went wrong was a lesson for you and you won't ever make the same mistake again. But—we are all human, and if for some reason you do, then you know that you just need to make some tweaks in order to change the outcome. All negatives can be turned into positives. There are no wrongs. Only lessons to help you on your true path.

2. Trusting Your Intuition

Your intuition is your complete inner guidance system and the path to your happiness. Once you learn to trust your intuition your entire life changes. It's as simple as that.

The first big realization of my intuition was at the age of 23 when my brother-in-law was rushed to hospital with a brain hemorrhage. He'd had one the previous year and had made a full recovery, so I had no real reason to feel bad, but this time something was different. It was as if every cell in my body knew the absolute truth. I could feel it in my whole body from the top of my head to my toes and to the very end of my fingertips. I knew he was going to die. He remained in a coma for 2 days and in that time my conscious mind took over, trying to rationalize and find a positive outcome. I completely overrode my 'feelings' as a way of avoiding the pain of the truth. But the inevitable happened. And with that came the understanding that we are more than our brains—so much more than our thoughts.

You'd think that after such a huge awakening, I would be totally guided by my intuition from that day forward. Wrong! Although I have definitely tuned in to my intuition to help me find better jobs and situations over the years, it's through ignoring my intuition that I have learned my biggest life lessons.

So what is intuition? And how do you use it? Well, it's all about being in the present moment. Inside of us we have all the knowledge and answers we could possibly need. That funny feeling we have in the pit of our stomachs when we don't think someone is telling the truth—Intuition. The way the hairs on the back of our necks stand up if we are in a potentially dangerous situation—that's intuition. The overwhelming feeling of joy and happiness if we are doing something we love—Intuition... and our inner guidance system telling us we are on the right path! If we just take the time to be still—be quiet and listen to our bodies, feel our emotions, we will always know the right path—what is best for us and only us.

- ✍ Find a quiet place where you can relax and go inwards. Intuition will always be a feeling not a thought, so bring your attention below the level of your thoughts.

- ✍ Focus on your breathing and the feelings inside your body and you will start to get intuitive messages. It doesn't matter if your mind chatter gets in the way—as you know it will. Just gently re-focus on your breathing and being in the present moment.

- ✍ It may take a while to grasp, but once you get comfortable with trusting your inner guidance system, you can gain confidence in who you are and learn to say no to the people and the paths that feel wrong. Suddenly, you know what you want and you find you have freedom because of that! Think how happy and contented you would feel. You just need to tune in and listen.

3. Setting Boundaries

It is said that our weakness is our strength. Whatever is perceived to be a weakness, just turn it around. Use your skills to your advantage. There's never anything wrong with you, you're just using your abilities in the wrong way.

Here's an example. Maybe you have been criticized for being bossy and outspoken. Other people don't like this and maybe you have tried to fit the mould and be in a humdrum job that you despise. But, what about if you use that outspokenness to your benefit? You would be a great leader. Or, an advocate for a charity that you are passionate about. There are so many roles where you would be a great fit! Think about who you really are and what lights your fire. Acknowledge your feelings to get those intuitive messages. You can be and do whatever you want and whatever feels right for YOU. Once you tap into those feelings, you will find the perfect job or situation for you. In fact, it's likely to find you.

I have been told my entire life that I am too "nice." Still told that sometimes now, actually. But what does that mean? I like being nice. It's who I am. Being nasty makes me feel very uncomfortable inside. So after a long time of beating myself up for being who I like to be, I decided to think about it more. There is a difference between being nice and being walked over. And that's where we "nice" people need to draw the line. You can be a nice, kind person, but again you need to look inside yourself and check your feelings as to what is right and wrong — to you.

- You must set boundaries to protect your kind heart. You do not have to do anything that feels wrong to you. In fact, you don't have to put up with any situation that you feel is wrong. But remember, a boundary is only a boundary if you uphold it. People will always try to push your boundaries so it's up to you to stick to them.

- Don't let other people define your boundaries, either. While other people may have good intentions, their advice is likely to be clouded by their own experiences and they cannot know what is best for you, so, as always, go inside to feel how YOU feel about a situation. Stop saying yes and learn to say NO. It doesn't make you a bad person! Walk away from anything that does not feel right for you.

Overall, my suggestion to you is to not take life too seriously. We are here to enjoy ourselves and BE JOY! When you can see the fun in life, every day seems a little bit easier and brighter. Get out of your comfort zone, do something a little bit scary. Travel to somewhere you have never been. LOVE YOURSELF! DO WHAT YOU LOVE! Remember, you are worth it.

And if people try to bring you down, I have one last idea to help. Picture that person with a silly outfit on, or turn them into an object or animal with just their face showing. It's amazing how differently you can view that grumpy neighbor or boss when you now see them as a huge cupcake with their face peeking through the vanilla icing and their arms and legs dangling from the sides. Waddling along as they try to walk. Try it! Your imagination can conjure up all kinds of images and the more stupid they are, the better you are likely to feel about that thorn in your side…and you will never see them in the same light again.

Thank you so much for talking the time to read my message. I hope this has given you some ideas to make life a little brighter and helped to show how worthy and valued you really are.

This chapter is dedicated to my Mum and Sister; strong women who have provided me with a lifetime of inspirations and giggles and the strength to get up and go when my get up had gone!

Namasté

Which means — The light in me honors the light in you.

~ Dawn Amberley

Tressa Wood

TRESSA WOOD is an author, poet and Coach. Tressa has lived in both the United States and Canada. After many years working in the Financial Industry, she chose to pursue her dream of becoming a Life and Business Coach and attended the highly-regarded Coach Training Program through Accomplishment Coaching. Tressa is a powerhouse of love and life, a believer in miracles, an angel in high heels and a grateful spirit!

Tressa.Coach@gmail.com
www.tressawood.com

Don't Just Leave Your Legacy — Live It!

While sharing breakfast with a dear friend recently, we were having a very emotional conversation about our legacy and what we would leave this world; what would we want that to look like, feel like, truly mean? Later that day, I was struck by an overpowering thought, *"I don't want to just leave a legacy, I want to LIVE IT!"*

What would I be choosing, really choosing, if I were living my legacy? It wasn't that long ago that I would have described my world as "very small." I had taken a close look at a few of the relationships in my "very small" world:

- *With one, I had thought, "I don't know what else to do — I will try and make this work."*
- *In another, what I believed was, "I am really just not enough, maybe this will fix everything — and, prove that I'm finally worth it."*
- *And, in yet another relationship, I chose to believe that, "I can save them — I can finally prove that I am good enough."*

What could my life look like, my legacy, if I were to create a whole new relationship with myself? Where would I be choosing from, if I were truly wanting to live my legacy? These were bold questions! And, these questions provided a space to open up a very small world in service of creating one that was so much larger — one that was fully experienced — a life lived. As I began to reconnect with my life, it was like rekindling a relationship with an old friend that you hadn't seen for years ... oh, how I had missed myself!

"It takes courage to grow up and be who you really are."

~ E. E. CUMMINGS

So, what is next when you are choosing to create a whole new relationship with yourself? Consider that there is nothing to fix, you aren't a problem to be fixed. You are not broken; you are a whole and capable being. Once I chose to see myself as the whole and capable being that I truly am, my world began to shift. I started to recognize that I am the creator of my world, my relationships, my experience — my everything.

Your world is whatever you say it is. Once you know this, you cannot *"un-know"* it. You cannot go back to pretending that everything that is *"wrong with your life"* is because of someone else ... what they did, what they didn't do, what they should've done, could've done. Or, if only things were different, I could be happy — I could have the job I really wanted, the relationship, the money, the house, the car, the body, all of it — if only things were different.

What could it mean to be fully responsible for yourself? Now, I will be honest with you, being responsible doesn't really sound like a lot of fun ... actually, it sounds kind of heavy, it starts to sound like the "burden" of life and it begins to feel very uncomfortable. While starting this new adventure of creating a whole new relationship with myself, I also began to look at words differently, too. Was I willing to move outside of what I knew, outside of what was comfortable? What if owning *"my world is whatever I say it is"* could be the most empowering choice I could ever make — and, what if this choice, to be responsible for myself and my world, came from a place of self love?

 "It was a time when the unthinkable became the thinkable and the impossible really happened."

~ ARUNDHATI ROY

I became open to being uncomfortable, and actually started to become very aware of being uncomfortable; what was I noticing? What body sensations, feelings and thoughts emerged as I was practicing being responsible for myself? In the beginning, it felt like a revolt ... my body, my feelings and my thoughts threw a fit! This *"being responsible for my world"* wasn't going over very well — part of me wanted to slip back into the old ways, the well-worn ways — I knew those ways. What if I were to offer myself even more self love? And, what if I were to ask myself if I would be willing to practice being responsible for myself just a little bit more each day.

This wasn't a race, this wasn't about *"doing responsible"* it was about developing and creating a whole new relationship with myself and *"being responsible."*

One of the most transformative awarenesses I have received is the distinct difference between "doing" and "being." You see, most of my life, I have based my self-worth and my value on what I do — what I do for work, what I do for others, what I did today, what I'll do tomorrow — it has all been about the "doing." When everything is about the doing, there isn't any room left to experience the "being."

Consider how much of your life, this life you are creating, is about the "doing." What would your life be like, what would your relationship with yourself be like, if it were about the *experience of being*? How present are you in this moment to your *Beingness*? In this quiet moment, when you are not *doing*, you are free to listen to your body, your heart, your spirit and everything it wishes to communicate with you. You are open to hear the gentle reminders that you are a child of God, you were made to love and be loved, you are the heavens and the universe, you are the stuff of stars, an ocean of wonders and depths unknown, you are infinite ... you are forever and you are here now, *being* in this moment.

What will your legacy be? And, if you were choosing from the most empowered place, how would you be living your legacy every day? What if it were a practice of choosing, just a little more each day?

 Knowing there is nothing to fix, what do you see is possible if you were to practice from a place of self love, responsibility and being? What if this were the most courageous and fearless choice you could make in service of living your legacy each and every day ...

Dedicated to those who are willing to be a leader for love, miracles and possibility; to those who are willing to make the bold choice, the choice that may have you on your knees calling all angels for support, all in service of lighting the way for self love.

Thank you to my Mother and Stepfather for always supporting me in all of my writing endeavors, AC Team & Leadership for showing me that Unstoppable Together exists and my dear friend, Diane Christie, I am grateful for who you be.

~ Tressa Wood

Katina F. Gillespie

KATINA F. GILLESPIE is trained, certified, and licensed as a Peace Love Wings, Mind Body Spirit Practitioner and Workshop Facilitator, an author and active volunteer. Katina grew up on a farm in central Illinois and suffered a traumatic brain injury when she was 17 and was faced with challenges and adversity at a young age. She moved to Memphis during her rehabilitation to study neuropsychology with a focus on traumatic head injuries.

Life happened and she became a restaurant manager after completing her Bachelor of Science in Psychology. She has an extensive background in restaurant and hotel management. She worked in several cities and various restaurants and hotels at many levels. Katina returned to her calling of helping others and created *Emotional Harmony and Wellness* so that she may encourage others to find their best self and inner wisdom.

EmotionalHarmonyWellness.com
katina@emotionalharmonywellness.com

Manager of the Year

I was employed by a large worldwide hospitality company as a human resources manager. I loved my job and all of the craziness that went along with the responsibilities. Out of all of my duties training is what I enjoyed the most. In this capacity, I was responsible for providing team members history of the company, informing them about the tools the company provided, and work with the department managers and directors to ensure everyone had the information and tools needed to perform their duties. I also counseled team members on personal, professional, and inner-departmental matters. I loved that so many individuals trusted that I could give them needed advice and point them in the right direction.

On the flip side, the job also included disciplinary action. I never enjoyed this aspect but I continuously had to remind myself that the individuals put themselves in the position of job loss, not me. I was just the messenger. It is difficult to get yourself terminated in a corporate company. One must do the same thing five times. One verbal warning, a written warning, a second written, a final written warning and the FIFTH time they do the EXACT same thing, they will lose their job. It takes away from any possible favoritism, but also makes it difficult to terminate low-performing individuals.

I enjoyed the persons that I worked with, but was not able to get too personal with ANY of them due to my position. I would attempt to socialize outside of work, but undoubtedly topics that I could not discuss would come into conversations, such as salaries, promotions, employment status, etc. I had to limit outings and conversations. I'm sure it came across as anti-social, but it is the nature of the beast when you work in human resources—and maybe there were truths I didn't want anyone to know.

There were many things in the hotel that I had knowledge of that no one else was privy to. Some things were personal and some were professional. I still don't discuss this information even after years of not being at the Resort. "I know nothing" is and will be my response to inquiries.

One thing that was personal to me that others did not know was my home environment. The person I reported to had noticed changes in my behavior. He asked me to come to his office and shut the door behind me. He sat next to me, looked me in the eye and asked, "What is he doing to you?" I was not expecting that question one bit. I was living with my boyfriend at the time and had been since before I started working with this company. I had done EVERYTHING to hide any signs. I played dumb, "I don't know what you're talking about?"

He told me a story of an abusive relationship that he had been in a few years earlier. I had not told ANYONE! How did he know? I couldn't hold it in any longer. I took a deep breath and broke down in tears. Actually, I HAD told someone and that was my best friend from high school. She and I had not spoken in years and were now catching up and beginning to speak on a regular basis. One night, a few days before I was in the office with my director, she asked me the same question. She could hear it in my voice. He had not hurt me physically per se or in any way that one could see with their eyes, so I thought it was nothing. The truth is that he had isolated me, verbally abused me daily, and threatened my life on many occasions. My Director was amazing. He provided me with phone numbers and shelters to contact. I was not ready to admit the abuse and felt that other women needed the services more than I needed them, so I decided not to contact them.

My director had just purchased a house and his townhouse was empty and on the market. He said that I could stay there, but I would need to pack everything away every morning so his realtor could show the house during the day. I slept on an air mattress with my dog and would read or watch TV on my laptop and eat out every night. It was a gated community and safe. My boyfriend did not know the location. I did this for almost a month. Then the townhouse sold.

I didn't know where to go or what to do, so I arranged a meeting with my boyfriend in a public place. We talked and agreed that I would come back to our house, but as 'roommates.' I continued to pay half of all of the bills. We slept in separate rooms though I never fully fell asleep, as I feared what he may do to me. I did my best to make this work, but I couldn't continue any longer, so I went to the General Manager of the hotel and discussed my situation. He allowed me to stay in the hotel with my dog on nights that we were under a certain occupancy. We would put the room out of order for the night, so no one would know I was there. On the nights that I needed to vacate the room, I would bring my dog to the office. My dog was amazing through it all. He slept quietly under my desk and very few people knew he was there. I would sometimes be able to get a room at sister properties and other times, I would sleep in my car.

I had a friend who was remodeling a condo that had belonged to her grand-mother. It was unfinished and a construction zone, but I slept there on my air mattress for a couple of weeks. There was running water and electricity, but no heat or functioning kitchen. Again, it was safe and better than my car. I had very little money, as was still paying half of everything on the house that I shared with my alcoholic, mentally and emotionally abusive boyfriend. One night when I was staying at a hotel, he had taken all of my things and threw them out on the street, in a drunken rage. At this point, I felt NOTHING! I was numb of all emotion. I almost wanted to feel anger, embarrassment, and humiliation, but I didn't. I simply gathered my belongings moved them back into the house. The next day a friend brought his truck over and I moved what I could not fit in my car into another friend's garage.

Somehow I was able to maintain appearances and things at work were going well, but my direct report manager was going through some personal issues and was absent from work frequently. I was basically acting Director of HR in his absence. He came into work intermittently. I was never sure if I should expect him on any given day. The days he was there I spent catching him up on what he had missed. He had given me a safe haven and allowed me to realize the hell that I was living in, so I was eternally grateful. The only two people at work that knew what was going on outside of work were the Director of HR and the General Manager.

Holiday Season was on us and this is a very busy time for the Resort and especially HR. We had the holiday party to plan and purchase/acquire donations for raffle prizes, invitations, menus, decorating, PowerPoint presentation that summarized the year, etc. A big event at the holiday party was the announcement of the Team Member of the year and the Manager of the Year. Each quarter a team member and manager are chosen for their performance and achievements, and then one of those winners are chosen to get the yearly honor. I had been awarded the fourth quarter manager, so I was in the running for Manager of the Year. This year was unique because the HR Director was very quiet about all of it. Generally the HR Coordinator and I assist in the announcement and prizes for the winners.

The night came, I went to the party alone, but did not feel lonely. I would rather be at work than anywhere with HIM. Out of pure desperation, I had returned to staying at the house I shared with my now ex-boyfriend due to the high occupancy during the holiday season of the hotels and the condo that was no longer an option. I was monitoring all of the activities at the party to ensure the team was enjoying the festivities. It came time for the announcement of yearly awards and the HR Coordinator and I were both given the honors respectively! It is unheard of for HR to get any awards. It is normally awarded to the more public positions. I could not believe it! There were harsh feelings from the other managers thinking that I was not worthy. However, they had no idea what I had gone through both inside and outside of work. Actually, I did not believe myself to be worthy either. I was pretty much at the lowest low I had ever felt due to the psychological abuse and fear I was receiving at home and doing the dual job of director and manager while at work.

That night I was speaking with one of my co-workers and it came out that I was having issues at home. He and his partner offered their spare bedroom to me and my dog for as long as I needed it! It was the most wonderful gift! That night I went home and tried to share my accomplishment with my then 'roommate' and he found a way to twist it around into some jealous rage that made me feel inadequate. It should have been one of the best nights of my life and I ended up crying myself to sleep. I went to work the next day and finished up the work week. That Saturday, I packed all of my things and headed to my temporary home. They were wonderful! I felt secure and was able to sleep for the first time in months. I did not have to sleep with one eye open in fear that I may lose my life, and I was in a REAL bed. I am eternally grateful for them welcoming me and providing shelter without asking anything in return.

Things at work continued to get even crazier. Months before I had applied for a training position at a much larger new property in another city. I received a call to see if I was still interested in the job. I had just been awarded manager of the year, but I had no place to live and my director was still intermittently coming in to work. Something had to change! Maybe this was my opportunity? I agreed to travel to the job interview. It went very well and I was offered the position the same day of the multiple interviews. As I drove back to the city I was living in, I was on cloud nine! Were my prayers really being answered? Did the universe grant me a way out of my scary and humiliating situation? Were my dreams coming true?

Unfortunately, those euphoric feelings ended quickly. How was I going to tell my GM and director who had saved me from being homeless and/or abused AND kept my secret away from others? I was offered my dream job and I was filled with **guilt**. Was I being selfish and ungrateful? Should I wait? Should I stay? If I stayed, I would be doing the job of a director, getting half the pay and I would be in fear for my life in the event my ex-boyfriend would locate me or show up where I work. I put all of these questions up in my 'Angel Box' and put it in the hands of the universe.

I agreed to accept the position in the other city and things moved VERY quickly. I went home to my family farm for the holidays and was excited and proud to announce my promotion. I kept most of my battles from my family, as I did not want them to worry about my well-being. I was raised in a small farm community in Central Illinois with a family of Christian values and very little time spent in large cities outside of the Midwest. I knew they were concerned enough with me being

1,500 miles away from them. All they needed to know is that I had broken up with my boyfriend, was awarded with Manager of the Year, and I was starting over in a new city with a promotion. I put on my stage face just like I had done while I was at work. When I returned to work from the holiday, I assisted in finding my replacement for the job I was leaving, started looking for apartments to relocate, and organized my projects so whoever took my position would be able to easily pick up where I left off.

I worked until Friday, January 29th and was to report to work at the new location on Monday, February 1st. I was given a weekend to move. I had another couple of friends offer me a room to stay while I transitioned to the new property and agreed to watch my dog when I returned on weekends. It had been arranged that I could stay in the new property with my dog until I found a new place to live, but I would travel back and forth on weekends to slowly gather and move my belongings that had been stored in various places. The transition with my dog, working full time at a new property in a new city, securing a place to live, purchasing furniture, and getting all utilities turned on was very difficult to do alone. The good thing was that my ex-boyfriend did not know where I was working or living.

Somehow, I did it and did it with grace. How? I decided that I was bigger than any injury (mental or physical) and better than what this job did to me. I pulled up my bootstraps and I put one foot in front of the other and did what needed to be done. I will not provide you with all of the details of the torment and darkness. In this process I discovered a strength and courage that will never be able to be taken away. I was blessed with friends and family along the way who offered assistance and ears to listen. They were amazing in that they never told me what to do. I had to make those choices on my own.

There is no recipe or checklist for how to get yourself out of challenges and difficult times. You must discover that strength within. It sounds cliché and impossible when you are in the darkness. If you look *outside* of yourself, then the fix is only temporary. You are full of light and everything you experience — good, bad or ugly — holds a lesson. Be gentle on yourself and be careful not to be too harsh or judgmental of your responses to what life brings your way. We all make poor choices. We are human. It is important to forgive yourself for these choices when they don't work out as planned and embrace them. We are our own worst enemy and the most difficult person to forgive is ourselves. I tend to take the road less traveled and it is not always the best decision or in my best interest. My personal 'school of life' has been full of lessons. I've chosen to have no regrets, only lessons. I replace the regrets with love and confidence. There are MANY things that I have done that I am not proud of and would do differently if I were given an opportunity, but that does not mean they are regrets.

I now know how I would choose in the event history attempts to repeat:

1. **In order to process these life lessons I have found that journaling is an excellent tool to allow yourself to sort and review thoughts and changes in the tides.**

    ↝ The River of Life is not always calm and flowing. There can be stagnate, tidal, or harsh conditions. Create a habit of taking time EACH day to journal. It does not need to be a long period of time, whatever is achievable with your schedule and lifestyle. Find what works best for YOU. Some days will be longer than others, as there is more or less to process. Consider it preventative maintenance for your mental health and life balance. There are no rules or regulations for what you include or not include in your journal.

    ↝ I choose to call mine "brain puke." I write down whatever comes to mind. This allows you to bring awareness to your emotions and how you are feeling about a situation. Half the battle is emotional awareness. Often times I do not know what I'm thinking until I write it down. I keep a journal next to my bed so that I can write before I go to bed, when I start my day and/or if I wake from a dream that I want to remember. Honestly, I rarely read what I wrote, but the act of writing puts it out into the universe.

    ↝ Your thoughts control your world, so I do my best to write about the positive things that I am grateful for and the things that I desire to happen in my life, instead of venting and continuing the negativity that occurs. Although sometimes venting is needed to determine what I'm feeling and to decide how I will respond. The power of positive thought is real. Write down your positive affirmations, goals, and achievements. You will be amazed in how this changes the energy that surrounds your world.

2. **Another ritual that got me through and continues to keep me balanced is taking a minimum of twenty minutes per day to quiet your "monkey brain" and meditate.**

    ↝ If you don't have time, *take an hour.* Be still. Breathe deeply. Lay flat or sit comfortably, relax, and flex every muscle group. Start with your toes, then your feet, your calves, knees, inner thighs, outer thighs, quads, hips, buttocks, lower abs, mid abs, upper abs, shoulders, biceps, triceps, hands, fingers, neck, facial muscles, etc. All the time concentrate on your breath. As thoughts come into your mind, don't get frustrated. Simply acknowledge them and release them. Go back to relaxing every muscle group and focus on breath. In with the good, out with the bad.

ↄ Tell yourself how much you love YOU! Find your happy place and your mantra that bring you inner peace and stillness. Self-confidence, self-worth, and self-love will ALWAYS pull you through! Invest in YOU! This takes time and dedication to create positive habits and develop a relationship with your higher self. YOU ARE WORTHY! YOU ARE ABUNDANT! YOU ARE LOVE!

Dedicated and grateful for each person and situation that has brought me to where I am right now! Because of you ... I know and love myself more freely.

Thank you Nikki, Joseph, Andreas, Michele, Brian, Jamie, Terry, Dane, and the team at HFLBR who allowed me to find my path and shine my light when I only saw darkness. And to Lisa—thank you for your continued belief in me to share my story. Namaste!

~ Katina Gillespie

Kisty Marie Stephens

KISTY MARIE STEPHENS is an author, life coach, presenter, motivational speaker. Specializing in motivational psychology. Kisty is also an expert in Heart Centered Leadership as well as Positive Psychology techniques. Kisty is also the Founder and Executive Director of Sparrows Voice Inc. a Non Profit Organization focused on educating our youth about Heart Centered Leadership, as well as Heal Your Life Workshops.

www.sparrowsvoice.com
www.begreatcon.com
www.kistys@gmail.com

"Chutzpah"

EMPOWERMENT? What is it all about? What emPOWERS you? Is it something big — is it something you have accomplished, or is it a feeling you have after doing something that scares you.

 "The spirit is larger than the body — the body is pathetic compared to what we have inside of us."

~ DIANA NYAD

Diana Nyad is the woman who bravely swam from Florida to Cuba at the "tender" age of 64! WOW … that's a long swim! I feel very empowered when I read about her tremendous triumph — not to swim from Florida to Cuba, but to do something GREAT. That feeling you get in the pit of your stomach that rises to the top of your chest and seems to just burst out of your heart — that's EMPOWERMENT!

Here is another quote that I love, written by Mark Nepo, *"Every human has an unfathomable gift that only meeting life head on will reveal."* What a beautiful invitation to live an inspired and courageous life — to live out loud and without fear.

I can now say, as I enter my fifth decade, that I live with less fear and much more gusto or as my grandfather called it *"chutzpah."*

Chutzpah must be the Yiddish word for confident empowerment. I remember playing in the backyard of our old house on Madison Street with my little sister. I was standing on top of the swing set slide yelling to my invisible audience, "I HAVE CHUTZPAH!" and then jumping undaunted into the crowd, which was really just a big pile of leaves that would pad my leap of faith. I didn't know what chutzpah meant exactly, but I knew I wanted it, because it sounded important and my grandpa had it! I was on the path of enlightened empowerment at the innocent age of 7. Way to go me!

I have always aspired to live a compelling and meaningful life. I've used many different approaches and attempts, some of course were miserable attempts, but none the less it was movement in the right direction. It has taken me decades to realize what this all really means and what living an empowered life even looks like.

 "Do something every day that scares you."

~ ELEANOR ROOSEVELT

Fear — oh yes — fear is a four-letter word. I have many fears. Let me name just a few: fear of success, fear of speaking to an audience, fear of flying over the ocean, fear of my own light sometimes, fear of being vulnerable, fear of being left out. Facing my anxieties … one by one … as horrible and scary as they were, brought me to this place of living an authentic and humbled life. This is when the magic happens — it does not get any better than this! When you know the thing you feared more than fear itself was nothing more than a test, you have achieved something many will never experience.

When you walk on coals and don't get burned, you have then mastered your apprehension and only then does enlightenment and a sense of empowerment occur. If you are a person that has dared to face your fears, even just one, I say congratulations for living your life and not hiding from your own trepidations and confusion!

That my friend is living emPOWERED. As Janis Joplin so eloquently sang — *"Freedom is just another word for nothing left to lose."* Janis had the magic, she knew the way to fame was walking through the fire, not around it.

Most of us are searching for more enlightenment, more insight, more understanding, more motivation. At any given time there is uplifting energy swirling around and through us that we can tap into whenever we want. It is there for each of us to use — it's Universal and it's eternally available.

What if I told you, that all of the answers you are looking for don't exist outside of yourself. The answers you are reaching for are within you … everything you are seeking can be found by looking in the mirror. Remember the old adage — *as within so without.*

Empowerment is awareness, and for me, awareness means living in spirit — inspired — or as some call it dwelling in my higher and empowered self. Living in your higher self allows you to exist in alignment with your integrity and with your purpose. Everyone has a divine purpose and calling and it is up to each of us to figure that out. What is your calling? What keeps you up at night? What encourages and exhilarates you? Do you want to go big...are you ready to shake your fear and stop hiding?

Elizabeth Gilbert teaches us about answering the call and how to set our fear aside—if only for a day—to answer that call. One of the easiest ways to go higher is to acknowledge the lessons and the challenges in your life as opportunities for growth. When we answer the call we are coming from an enlightened and inspired place of growth. We are ready to face the obstacles that stand in our way. We know that every impediment prepares us for battle and every battle empowers us to face our fear...once we lose our anxieties we then are able to answer the call. I love everything about divine awareness and the ability to live in my higher self. Do you feel *empowered* to answer your calling? Does it make perfect sense that every battle is preparing you for your life purpose? Expect to be challenged and expect to be hurt...but answer the call anyway...let your life work for you the way it was intended!

To live in the power of your own light is to live an empowered life. Awareness is key in my daily routine and in my spiritual practice. The doorway to deeper truth is awareness. It is paying attention to, and holding up, the vision of truth. Without awareness enlightenment does not exist. Our lifetime is a journey out of darkness and into the light. The more you act from your truth and stay in line with your integrity the more evolved you become.

If I can leave you with something that inspires and empowers you, then I have accomplished something worthwhile.

We are as unique as our fingerprint—you are here to do much more and if you are reading this right now—you already know this. The time has come to:

- Stop hiding—it is not serving anyone and certainly not serving your greater good!
- Answer the call—you cannot live empowered or inspired if you don't answer the call.
- Share your magic—start a group or join a mastermind group—join something.
- DO IT!—What are you really waiting for?
- Start before you are ready—very successful people do this.
- It does not have to make perfect sense right now—plant the seed and let it unfold.
- Open the door—face your fears...one day at a time. Rome wasn't built in a day.

I look forward to reading your blog—your book—to being invited to your *"Be GREAT Presentation."* I know it's scary, but start anyway, start now and start where you are. I have flown over the ocean, I have spoken to a large audiences, I have been on death's doorstep, and I no longer have a fear of my own light.

 Let's use our light to illuminate the world, to make
the world a better place for all who come after us.
I hope you are empowered now to go out there
and Be GREAT! I know you can do it! Namaste!

A very special dedication to my little brother, Buddy. Thank you for being the constant love and light in my life. You are my Earth Angel and the wind beneath my wings. You have always been my inspiration. This chapter is dedicated to all of those who suffer silently—thank you for not giving up. You know who you are and you inspire me. Sparrows, I salute you. My life would not be the same if I hadn't known you. Amy Jo, Rachel, Garrett, Alisha—I love you more than you know. To all of you who live with Chutzpah—this one is for you, with love.

~ Kisty Marie Stephens

Catherine Madeira

CATHERINE MADEIRA is a freelance writer and artist. She has been receiving ethereal information for years and is now sharing it in the hope of helping others in their life's journeys.

Catherine is from the Reno / Tahoe area with her 2 children, Jason who has always demanded an intellectual approach to life, and Daughter Kendal who was born a very old soul. Catherine has been documenting her experiences for years. Subsequently, she has been able to receive, evaluate, and compile the information to pass to others.

Umbriel03@gmail.com

Empowerment in Adjustable Foresight

When I was 21 I had an extremely jarring Out of Body experience. It wasn't a near death nor was it astral projection. These are three conditions similar, but very different. Astral projection is the act of projecting the consciousness to different locations, but the soul remains in and attached to the physical form.

My belief is *The Near Death* and *Out of Body* are the same in the sense that the soul or spirit itself actually separates from the physical form. The Near Death, as we know, occurs in a Near Death situation and the soul that is experiencing this will usually be accompanied by others (angels, family members, friends, etc.). This soul is usually shown where he will be going after passing and is often given the decision to stay or go, or is sent back to earth against his will because he hasn't completed his journey.

In the case of the Out of Body, the separated soul will usually be alone and the separation is for an unknown purpose to the *separatee*. The reasons will vary as widely as each existence varies. In my case, *my* soul left my body spontaneously. I lost all sense of my body because I wasn't in my body, (it was over on the other side of the room) as I was flying around completely out of control. Because I didn't understand what was happening until I saw myself laying over on the other side of the room ... it was a very frightening experience. Once I finally saw myself I then realized I had left my body. I started repeating to myself, *"Go back, go back!"* and that drove me back over to my body and I lowered down into myself. The reinsertion was very painful because all my nerve endings reactivated as I dropped down into my body.

The Out of Body altered my life completely and it taught me many things. For instance, we do continue living after we die, and I also realized that I knew more upon my return. I had always been sensitive, but following the separation, my abilities were expanded greatly and I was hit with a tidal wave of knowledge. It is a simple knowledge. The truth is that we all know everything we are meant to know. When given new information we realize we already knew it and we just have to be reminded.

I knew that this existence in this place is a giant teaching mechanism. We live and interact with souls that we have been traveling with for eons, at the same time we are all connected as one. When we pass and return to the point of origin, the occurrences in this life are very trivial. What in the end is the Love and the connections we have maintained and achieved with our fellow travelers. This includes all life here.

I needed to tell you of the previous information so you could better understand my views and reason for arriving at my theories in regards to the actual topic that we will be covering today. We will move further through the Out of Body experiences in a later correspondence, as our topic today walks us more deeply through Foresight, Visions, and Premonitions in an attempt to reassure you to believe in things you are shown, no matter what happens in the long run.

I have spoken in previous writings of different kinds of premonitions. Today we speak of one variation. The premonition that may be altered when seen by the right individual who has the power to change it. Let's call this Adjustable Foresight.

Through the years we have all heard people talking of premonitions of terrible and frightening events that they had encountered in visions. For example, Gordon Michael Scallion, clearly witnessed a catastrophic case in California. He watched a magnitude 9 plus earthquake hit California and it was total destruction. He saw the people trying to evacuate the region and he was even shown the newspaper headlines. He is a noted, proven clairvoyant and healer with a large following, including myself. It was Mr. Scallion who created the new world maps. He is a man I still respect greatly, primarily because I understand why his vision has not yet hit.

These people see these occurrences in perfect detail thus feeling empowered and having an urgency to tell others and share what is coming because of their certainty of the approach of the event. So they do share their premonitions with others in various ways. In some cases the information concerns and does frighten large masses of people. But then the premonition does not come to pass. When it doesn't happen, the person who had the vision is then viewed as a nut and is ridiculed. What I think is actually happening here is, the premonition is so impactful on the Clairvoyant that was shown the information that the Clairvoyant himself alters the oncoming event. Through the sheer WILL of not wanting to see this thing happen I believe *he alone* causes change and the event is avoided.

Let's imagine that I receive a premonition that an asteroid is approaching this planet, I am shown and live this premonition as though it actually happened. I don't want it to happen so much that *my* WILL causes the far distant object to veer just a millimeter, but due to the distance from our planet as the astral body moves along its trajectory is more and more driven in the alternate direction, thus causing it to miss the mark. Subsequently the premonition does not come to pass.

The Clairvoyant has no idea that it was his WILL that thwarted the coming impact. So he is left to question his visions and suffer the ridicule of those people he had informed. I am obligated to write the following in regards to this dilemma, *Adjustable Foresight*. This is a poem that flowed from me like water once the concept of what was happening in these situations became clear to me. This ode was put to paper in hopes of helping the visionaries that have experienced this lonely plight:

 BRIDLED

Striding, yet bridled in each Soul's WILL

Is the whole power of The God Energy

The individual who bears the gift of premonition

Must also shoulder the burden of the empath

Because one walks hand in hand with the other

He who stands witness to future's approach

Also may unsheathe the power of his WILL

For the empathic WILL is all that may change

A destined future's course

The lonely burden looms, in his mind and soul

For he has, through his vision, and his WILL

Altered the future, he has foreseen

Thereby, only he, could see and prevent

the approach of Cataclysm

Rather than the minds of the masses

believing in the possibility

Of the strength inside the WILL of the ONE

The masses choose to remain blind and powerless

And Banter at HIM, that he is CRAZED

~ CATHERINE MADEIRA

I wrote this poem, as a brief way to describe the dilemma of Adjustable Foresight.

As we go forward, please keep in mind that I am very reclusive, subsequently I haven't reached out to many people with my visions or abilities. I wouldn't dream of placing myself in the company of the Great Clairvoyants, however, I do have information that must be shared; so, like many other Visionaries, I have had enough premonitions that did later happen that I trust what I am being shown. I had a premonition that was so real it enveloped me with dread. I and my loved ones did not survive this experience along with countless others. Being compelled as other Visionaries are, I told people about what was coming. I then dwelled on it and wished it away with all of the power within me.

What follows was the premonition and what I am now referring to as Adjustable Foresight:

- I was sitting passenger-side in a cream-colored, long bed fleet-side Ford truck with my son, Jason. I was wearing light colored jeans, a white shirt and a blue flannel over the top. The month is March, but I don't know the year.

- As I entered this premonition, I already knew the circumstances; there was a small asteroid approaching this planet. The media had been reporting on the potential impact for only three days. They had reported that they weren't sure as to the point of entry or impact. They further reported that it may not even hit, and if it did, it wouldn't be too harmful. They instructed people to prepare the same as you would for a hurricane or earthquake, with five days of water, food, batteries, flashlights, candles, blankets, etc. They suggested to retreat to your basement or a secure spot in the home would be sufficient. We followed the instructions, as we were not too concerned about our safety.

- As I said, it's March, sometime between 10:00 a.m. and 11:00 a.m. and the morning felt crisp, as it had been raining most of the night. The remaining clouds were billowy and sparsely placed. The sky was crystal blue following the nights cleansing … it was brisk and clean to inhale.

- We were in Reno, Nevada, and riding home from the store after picking up the remaining supplies needed to be prepared. My daughter Kendal was waiting for us in the house. We were listening to the updates on the radio as we drove, as the fly-by was getting nearer.

- We pulled up to the house and into the driveway on the south side, got out of the truck and grabbed two paper bags each. I had walked around the front of the truck and onto the damp grass with Jason ahead of me on the walkway, and I was then 15 feet from the front door.

꙯ At that moment, the sound was distant at first, but then instantly began growing louder, like a horrible rumble, a tearing and ripping sound and it began shredding the calm clean pristine silence. *(The following took only seconds to run its course. But time slows down in these moments.)*

꙯ I'm thinking, "OH NO! I AM NOT HEARING THIS!" The indescribable planet-smashing roar was growing louder and it was deafening. I tightened and experienced an instant adrenaline rush ... I could feel the sound shuddering violently, jarring to the point of pain. I was thinking: *"Jason we have to get to Kendal, we have to hit that door, look up, don't look up, run, where is it, run, my children, door!"*

꙯ The roar. I am deaf to all things but the bone-shattering *roar*. I can hear the earth's shielding and the beloved atmosphere being shredded, ripped and torn apart. The door is close, maybe 12 feet, and I knew I could make it. It took all my courage, but I forced myself to look up ... and then I wished I hadn't.

꙯ Arcing down directly overhead was a huge reddish-orange, glowing and flaming, rounded monstrous rock. It was rough, pitted, dark-in-the-crevasses and glowing in the high points with flames torching out the sides. It was the size of a basketball at that distance.

꙯ I knew what was going to be the result of this, but had to try to escape the inevitable. I kept thinking, *We have to get to that door!* My son Jason and I were mirroring each other's movements. But, before I could lift my knee to even begin to run the agonizingly short distance to that door I was slammed flat to the ground on my stomach and bags flew from my grasp. Jason hit the ground just as I did. We had been thrown down by a solid wall of wind. The air being shoved out of the way by the meteor's entry caused the wind that took command of the situation. My mind was thrashing as I could see the door and my son in my peripheral vision, but I was flattened and held to the ground by the smothering weight of the unseen force.

꙯ All I could do was lie there and think of Kendal inside the house and that she didn't even know I was only feet away from her. Jason was within reach, but I couldn't move to make contact. I then prepared for the inevitable.

꙯ Suddenly and mercifully the premonition released its grip and I was extracted from the moment of the impact.

I convey this experience to you only to emphasize the level of emotion I was left to deal with. This vision was so absolutely real and so frightening to me that it activated in me the WILL that I have been speaking of. I know this was a real vision and one point that confirmed that in me was the wind that knocked me flat to the ground. I had never conceived that a flattening wind would hit me like that, and catch me completely off guard. Now I do know that there would be an enormous gust of air preceding an asteroid strike.

In addition, the evidence that cemented the truth of the vision was presented by my daughter Kendal. Before I had a chance to tell her about my experience, she came to me in a distressed manner and told me of her dream. She said she had been in a basement and there was a man with her, but she didn't know him. She told me she knew she was going to die and was afraid. She asked the man what it was going to feel like and was it going to hurt? Kendal said the stranger looked at her and said, *"It's going to feel like this"*... and he touched his finger to the center of her forehead. She said when he touched her everything went dark, she felt no pain, and she woke up. I was astonished, this was far beyond coincidence, and this was the confirmation I needed.

My entire life was changed at this point. All I could think of was how desperately I did not want this thing to happen and, to my thinking, there was nothing I could do. With all of my heart I didn't want this to happen, and it ceaselessly dominated my thoughts. I reacted as anyone would at this point...I started telling people. I did what other Visionaries have done, in my case on a much smaller scale as I don't interact with others much; but I did tell anyone that would listen of the approaching event, and though it was a real and viable premonition, it did not come to pass.

My son Jason and I have had many technical discussions in regards to the mechanics of all of these pertinent subjects. Not the Mysticism in these areas, but the physics of how it works. Clairvoyance, psychic abilities, life after death, telekinesis, alternate dimensions, extra-terrestrials, etc. ... basically we have covered from the last point of creation to the next point of creation.

We contemplate the mechanisms through how these things may actually work. On today's topic of empowerment as how the *seen* and *unseen* affect each other. Hyperdimensional physics touches on this arena. Hyperdimensional physics focuses on the equations of how all forces have direct effects on all other forces, no matter the distance involved. This is also where the universe made of matter and the unseen universes and dimensions meet, interact and create cause and effect.

For example, if you believe that life after death exists and an individual who has passed to the next plain has the WILL to cause any physical demonstration here... that would be in the category of Hyperdimensional Physics.

The summarization is that we are only limited because we *are told* that we have limits. It is said we could move mountains if we were empowered to believe that we could. Our family discussions have spanned years, so expanding much farther into our conclusions would take much more time than you or I have to focus on at this point.

One result we have reached is in the subject of Premonition and Vision and being able to change or adjust the future. We believe in the understanding that a single person could, through WILL alone, alter the outcome of certain premonitions. It was Jason who coined the term, *Adjustable Foresight*, in relation to this phenomenon. I believe that to be the perfect terminology and title for this manifestation.

In the end, if you are one of the Visionaries who have had such an experience, please know that you are not alone. If you don't yet see yourself as a Visionary, please try to do so because we all have the power. Try to realize that you were given the vision for a reason and the universe has chosen you to see the approaching future because it is you that through your WILL can change the experience, if need be. The God Energy also knows that you can bear the burden of walking the road alone and recognize that it was your WILL that faltered the plan in your vision. Don't question yourself in these things that you see. You are seeing the truth and you are changing the truth through the power of your WILL.

The purpose of my sharing is for me to reassure you with the trusting of your vision if you are a person experiencing the same as I. My hope is that upon reading my words you realize how powerful your mind truly is! This revelation in itself is very empowering! If you choose to exercise your mind, as I often do, try focusing on something or a question until the answer unfolds! There are times it takes days or even years to reveal itself to me. The more you allow yourself to practice, the more comfortable it becomes.

 My belief is; you are an ancient being and you walk
hand in hand Empowered with The God Energy.

Sighting: Gordon Michael Scallion www.matrixinstitute.com

Dedicated to my Granddaughter Harlo Monroe who rein-troduced me to the gravity of life. To my 2 tiny dogs, Bell my best friend and angel on Earth, and Bee, Bell's lively assistant. My Father Richard who passed years ago, but has stayed to watch over me.

Lisa Hardwick, Project Director at Visionary Insight Press, for giving me the opportunity to share my information. Without finding Lisa I may have lived my life without being able to complete my purpose for coming here. I want to thank my Mother Lilas Hardin and my Aunts, Joan Carnahan, Sugar Henry and Ginger Haney for their support. My Son Jason Vaughan and Daughter Kendal Vaughan for helping with this edition. Finally to Chelle Thompson, Visionary Insight Press' Editor-At-Large, for proof reading my work. Thank you Chelle. Thank you Lisa.

~ Catherine Madeira

Leena R. Haldar

LEENA R. HALDAR, is an International Transformational Workshop Leader and Life Coach (certified by Hay House USA) who has been steadily emboldening individuals to lead more fulfilling and prosperous lives. Today, Leena excels in teaching workshops and coaching people to live a well-balanced life. Furthermore, she is the Co-Founder of a company 'Rainbow Lightworkers,' A mother of two, Leena lives in Mumbai, India, with her family

www.leenarhaldar.com
www.rainbowlightworkers.com

❧ Can Cancer... Serve?

I have contemplated for many days as to what the purpose of writing this chapter is. Is it all about becoming a successful author, getting acknowledged and being praised for my journey?

Ultimately, it all boils down to inspiring someone out there to be courageous and stand firm in one's power. The lesson unveiled is ... that only by accepting a challenge, can you diffuse the energy of resistance and get onto a path of resolution.

"Oh, this is your number?" asked my gynecologist and I was a little taken aback! He'd called to give me a verbal report of the biopsy I'd done a couple of days ago. *"Beta ... it is malignant!"* he stated. *"We will know what stage the cancer has progressed to in a couple of days, but you will need to gear up to undergo surgery quickly."* Flustered and gathering my wits, I muttered a quick "OK" and hung up. Minutes ago, I'd imagined him saying that the lump is benign! I was all set to celebrate with a glass of wine.

I was uncertain, unsure of even how many more days I would live. At first, I was shocked. And then came the shame! Strong and shamelessly mounting. How could I ... I, who teach Louise Hay's work and pride myself on doing so many workshops annually ... land up with breast cancer?!! Something was drastically wrong ... this had to be somebody else's story. I am supposed to be this teacher who walks her talk. How will I face the world? I contemplated giving it all up. I feared people would laugh at me, point fingers and snigger behind my back!

Which toxic thought-pattern of mine had ended up causing this malignancy? These, and such other thoughts plagued me for about a week. I went from being a victim to frantically searching for some miraculous cure ... so that I could justify to the world what a hero I was!

More importantly, in the process, I realised that an illness like cancer is actually a journey of the whole family. My kids were already showing psychosomatic symptoms of being upset. I had to look at the bigger picture ... I made up my mind, to get operated, no matter what.

After the operation … came the chemos, six cycles, one every 21 days, health permitting. Dr. Sanjay Dudhat, my concerned onco-surgeon, recommended that I go bald! And use a wig to "escape" from the "social stigma" of having cancer. I was taken aback. If I wore a wig, I would feel guilty, as if I were hiding something from the world. At that moment, I decided that I would willingly go bald, rather than opt for a wig. I told my doctor, *"I will NOT wear a wig. I am willing to shave off my hair and walk around with a henna tattoo."*

And that is exactly what I did! My henna tattoo evolved to become a sacred geometry that had Warli tribesmen dancing around a central sun, dancing peacocks and blooming flowers. I dressed up nattily every single day, making sure that I was wearing chandelier earrings and ornate *bindis*. When I would step out, people would turn to look at me. Some even imagined that I was a *sadhu* of sorts and bowed down to me!

Nobody's life is free of challenges, only the type differs. I share my story with you, because, as Dr. Mitchell Gaynor M.D. says, *"Regardless of what someone is going through they can have inner peace!"*

The real meat of this experience that I'd like you to get is a three-pronged perspective; How I tackled my illness; what it taught me and what you can get from it …

1. How I Tackled My Illness:

൭ **At the hospital**: I made myself comfortable by dressing well with earrings, *bindi,* lipstick et al., so that I would walk into the hospital looking and feeling confident. And as I felt good inside, I started attracting a lot of compliments and admiring looks on the outside too. Every time I got myself weighed, I always made it a point to smile and speak to whoever was attending to me. I packed a lot of personal belongings that put me at ease … like my favourite blanket, my bathroom sandals, comfortable clothes, etc.

I took care to select my room (at Nanavati Hospital, Mumbai, India) and always asked for a room with a big window or balcony, so that I could look out. I began always by praying and clearing the energy of the room. I would light a diffuser and switch on chants invoking more divine energies into the room. I made sure I kept drinking water all the time, snacked on mini-meals every few hours and took frequent breaks to walk. I requested friends and relatives to come in at different time-slots to visit me. This ensured that I had enjoyable company and conversations that kept me joyful.

൭ **Food:** Consciously, I chose organic foods and food supplements. Since home-cooked food was becoming boring and monotonous, I asked my close friends and relatives to parcel me home-cooked savoury dishes, so that I could enjoy a variety of healthy cuisine.

- **An empowering process I did every time before a chemo:** This process can be modified and used by anybody going through surgery, chemotherapy, radiation or any sort of treatment. Before starting the process, get this clear—you are the boss of your body! And know that it is eagerly waiting to hear from you. As you give your body clear instructions ... your blood chemistry will change! You will become more relaxed, calmer and this mindset will empower you.

  Begin by taking a few deep breaths and relaxing your body. As you relax your body, connect with any Ascended Master that you believe in. Feel the presence within you and around you. Now, ask your higher self and your Guardian Angels to be present alongside, as you go through this process. Feel the divinity in and around you, connect to every cell of your body ... invoke the Violet Flame of St. Germaine and ask for it to blaze through every cell of your body, every hour of every day, till all the negative vibrations in your body are transmuted into the highest form of love!

  Now, speak to the cells of your body. Tell them how much you love and value them. Speak to the cancer cells ... tell them that you have learnt your karmic lesson. That you are thankful to them and you are now ready to let go of them. Speak to the healthy cells in your body too. Tell them that the chemotherapy is to be directed only to the malignant cells and then they can be flushed out of your body.

  Picture the chemo drugs coming in front of you. Speak to them, thank them for playing their role in your recovery. Tell them that they are a guest in your body and that their role is only to remove the malignancy from it. Direct them to the affected parts of the body, ask them to heal you swiftly and ... leave immediately.

  The affected cells are now being replaced by healthy ones. All your cells are now brimming with Golden Healing Light! Thank your body and the medication, for being in harmony with each other and working together for your Highest Good. Take a few deep breaths ... and whenever you are ready ... open your eyes.

- **Prayers were my mainstay:** If I was not reading prayers, I was listening to sacred chants or simply having a conversation with God!

- **Water**: I had two litres of water every day. But before, during and after the chemo, I upped it to four litres, in order to flush out the chemo swiftly from my system.

- **Alternate therapies:** Acupressure massages, aromatherapy, Reiki and Bach flower remedies, were some of the holistic approaches, among others, that I embraced. *'All Is Well'* by Louise Hay was my constant Bible, that superbly upped my "feel good" factor.
  Chants:
  I listened chants of every kind. Hindu mantras, gospel music, positive affirmations, Solfeggio vibrations, sounds of Nature … anything that made me feel at peace, every single day.
  Exercise:
  Whenever I felt like it, I would go for walks. My husband, Rohitesh would very sweetly take me to a club where I would walk in a secluded court.
  Resting:
  I made sure that I rested amply. Yes, I did do a few workshops, a lot of painting, art- craft and journaling. But I never pushed myself!

2. What It Taught Me:

- **Being courageous & facing up to my fears:** Fearful of the chemo, my body went into tremors during the very first cycle! The second time around, I decided to WILL my body to be calm, confident and not go into overdrive with tension. I took a few deep breaths and SPOKE to my body. I told my body that whatever is happening is happening for my Highest Good. And Boy … believe it or swoon … Nothing happened!
- **Reading:** I looked up a clutch of positive, uplifting and empowering books. Yes, I did have a very loving friend who sent me a gripping book … but, guess what … it was about the Taliban! And boy, was it brutal. Clearly, I remember being exceedingly depressed! *Moral: Go in for books with a high feel-good factor.*

3. What You Can Get From It:

- **Don't ever compare your journey:** Every journey is unique. Your experience may not be mine. This helped me not to panic or anticipate doom. It empowered me to chose how I could experience chemo in a different manner.
- **Find ways to keep yourself happy:** I always advocated taking complete responsibility, but cancer took it to another level. Yes, I did experience plenty of self-pity, fear, pain and frustration. I discovered my happiness striking a healthy balance between resting, meeting people, reading, watching funny videos and pampering myself with alternate therapies.

- **Don't surf the Internet ... it might scare you!** I surfed the Internet and it shocked the hell out of me! Many videos and write-ups of horrible things happening to people popped up. Surprisingly, very few motivational videos of cancer survivors emerged while I was surfing. Also, too much information confused me. What I found works best is to discuss YOUR CASE with YOUR DOCTOR. This sets matters into perspective and the discussion is customised to YOU.

- **Talk to people who encourage you:** This is not a time to be pitied. I remember a friend telling me "Be Strong." This was what I needed to hear and I clung on to these words as if my life depended on it!

- **Have the courage to speak the truth ... from a space of love:** Having practiced Louise Hay's work extensively, I knew that I could not afford to suppress my emotions anymore. I realized, *"I am precious, I matter, I deserve to be heard."* I started taking extra care to express myself and draw healthy boundaries. Today, I am not ashamed to bare my soul, if it helps someone.

- **There are 4 exit points in our body:** These are the excretory system, urinary system, respiratory system and the sweat glands in our skin. We need to throw stuff out from all of these, in order to maintain optimum health.

- **Become aware of your thoughts:** Yes, become mindful ... just now ... in this moment of time! Do not wait for your physical body to fall ill in order to transform and understand the power of your thoughts.

- **Have a doctor you can trust in blindly. Else don't hesitate to take a second opinion:** I still remember Dr. Dudhat greeting me with a smilingly face with a thumbs-up sign. This ushered me speedily into a comfort zone. And I braved this journey valiantly.

Dedicated to all my students who have attended my work-shops and coaching, who have asked questions, forced me to seek answers from the Divine and evolve. Also, to every cancer survivor who has learnt to face their challenges and rise above them.

Deep gratitude to my husband Rohitesh, for his unconditional love, my children Kaushek and Vishista for nurturing me. My brother Ajit (who also sub-edited this chapter) my brother-in-law Ritesh Haldar, My Uncles, aunts and cousins for their support and prayers. My friends especially Gauri, Sangita, Rinku and Depali, my partners and soul sisters Azeelia and Evelet, for their support. Aparna and Rukhmini for Reiki; Dr. Rahul Tambe; Dr. Sanjay Dudhat and all the wonderful staff of Nanavati Hospital, Mumbai, India, for their excellent contributions. 'The Rainbow Lightworkers' Community—for their love and prayers. Last but not the least to Visionary Insight Press for giving me this opportunity to share my story with the world.

~ Leena R. Haldar

Kimla Dodds

KIMLA DODDS is a Radio Host and has her degree in Metaphysical Counseling from the University of Sedona, AZ. She is certified in Astrology, (Western and Chinese) Mediumship, Tarot, Energy Resonance Healing® and is a Feng Shui Practitioner. Psychic from childhood, she has worked to accelerate balanced living through counseling services while sharing her acquired knowledge. Her passion and crusade is highlighting the awareness of unseen energy. She is currently residing in Chandler, Arizona, and travels the globe teaching, learning and experiencing this wonderful and challenging world called life.

Empowering Creative Chakra-Balancing Workshop

The energy that flows through the human body is called "Chi." The body has energy centers called "Chakras." Each center rules the essential organs and areas within the body to create a healthy vehicle in which to house the light of our soul. Learn as we balance these centers inside and out. Experience how to use the tools of breath, mind empowerment and creative writing to dive into the deeper levels and dissolve blocks, remove stubborn imprints and outdated beliefs. These techniques will be "life-changing" for everyone!

Your soul is an energy ball of light containing the essence of source. It is held into place within the physical body by a light network grid comprised of skin, bones, veins, arteries, organs and sophisticated systems like circulatory and digestive. The spine is the main line running throughout your skeletal system and there are energy fields containing specific frequencies called Chakras. These centers contract, expand, and swirl in a circle, sometimes clockwise and sometimes counter clockwise. It has been proven that sometimes they are even standing still. These energy centers take surrounding energies into the body, sometimes they leak energy outwards and sometimes they stand still, seemingly blocked from movement.

There are seven main Chakras, but many more located throughout your entire framework. We will work with the seven main Chakras, but will mention others as well. As our DNA is updated and re-connected, more Chakras will be awakened and become activated.

Why are these Chakras Important?

Chakras serve a very important purpose in our everyday life. They contain matching frequencies that relate or talk to our organs, glands and help contain and shape our emotional layer of beliefs, memory, values, and perception of our experiences. The Chi or breath of life filters through these centers and is responsible for our very vital life force that can lead to our joy, happiness and well-being or manage to produce unbalanced functioning that contributes to illness and depression.

These sacred Chakra centers contain ties to your physical, mental, emotional and spiritual and cosmic layers. We are about to see firsthand where they are located and how they correspond to your presence of attention. Let me introduce them to you. They are located straight through the front of the body to the back. (Please have your client lay down, face up, on a mat on the floor or bed. Have a pendulum in hand for locating the field of energy as a visual.)

༄ Chakra One — Root or Muldhara Chakra is located at the base of the spine.

The color is red and the musical note is C. This Chakra rules stability through your legs and feet. This is the grounding Chakra and is tied to your clan, tribe and validates you as self. Place the pendulum over this area. Holding your hand very still watch the energy field appear, as it will make the pendulum turn in a circular manner. If this circle is small, ask your client to visualize and breathe in an object made of the color red. I picture a red Ferrari, but red lipstick or a red rose will be just fine. Breathing in three times and mentally sending this color down to the base of the spine will automatically influence this energy circle of the Root Chakra. If this Chakra is turning counter clockwise and leaking energy, have the client picture an item made of the color black. This is a very effective color and tool for stopping the pendulum. Now, at a standstill, it is able to correct the spinning movement to a healthy clockwise direction. The crystal Obsidian can be placed here for support. The flower called Indian Paintbrush can be presented now, as well. The flower brings in a matching frequency to add as a needed resource for grounding and survival support.

If it still remains small and slow, there could be an emotional blockage in the Chakra itself. Ask the client to review their feelings regarding their family roots, clan or tribe. Have they trapped old beliefs, blame, pain, guilt or shame in this sacred center? Are they living caught between the options of fight or flight, trying to solve family situations? Do they feel ungrounded or not welcomed where they live? Once the attention has been focused, place the pendulum on the center again and see if the size of the energy field has expanded, denoting a dissolving of the blockage. Take note of the matter — the circumstance — and allow the client to write about it in detail afterwards. Grounding with a nature walk, gardening or hiking balances this Root Chakra.

∽ Chakra Two — Sacral or Svadhishthana Chakra is located two inches down from the navel.

The color is orange and the musical note is D. It rules sexuality and creativity through the reproductive organs. Place the pendulum two inches down from the navel and locate the energy center. Is it spinning clockwise at a larger span? Have your client visualize an orange fruit. Breathing it in and sending the color down to the sacred Sacral Chakra will enhance the energy at once. If it is spinning counterclockwise, please use the visualization of the color black to stop all movement. Then proceed again with the procedure. Placing a garnet or ruby here will support this Chakra. Also add the pomegranate flower for abundance. This will add to the understanding of why we pro-create through sexual experiences.

If this Chakra field is at a standstill or a very small energy circle, help support your client's emotional layer by placing attention on the level of comfortability of their trapped creativity, sexuality and even finances. After the awareness has been made, check the energy field once more and promote expression of their unique talents to enhance this energy center. Take note of the conversation and any difference in the energy field circumference to allow the client to write about it afterwards and release any fears surrounding their sexuality.

∽ Chakra Three — The Solar or Manipura Chakra is located three inches up from the navel at the bottom of the ribcage.

The color is yellow and the musical note is E. This sacred Chakra contains the Will and provides the emotional experience of self-esteem. It rules the intestines and stomach area. Placing the pendulum three inches above the navel, you will be able to pick up this sacred energy field. Observe the motion of the spinning field. Have your client visualize an object of the color yellow like a lemon. Breathing this in and sending it to the solar plexus area will support the expanding energy field here. Adding the Sunflower here at this location and the Tiger Eye or Yellow Calcite will also enhance the ability to use our thoughts, free will and reason with purpose and power.

Help support your client's emotional layer with attention to the subject of honoring and valuing thyself. Ask the client to be clear on what they will do or will not do. Also bring up the need for creating healthy boundaries and giving thyself permission to say *no*. Release the option of being overwhelmed with pleasing others for their approval. Take note of the replies from the client, so they can write about it in detail afterwards. Being outdoors in the sunshine and surrounding one with yellow paint color will help to bring this Chakra into balance.

❧ Chakra Four — Heart or Anahata Chakra is located in the center of the chest.

The color is green and the musical note is F. It rules the heart circulatory system through self love. Place the pendulum over the heart center and pick up the energy field here. There may be an emotional layer to break through if a wall has been created from heartbreak. Have the client visualize the color green, like the grass, and breath that color into the heart area three times. Observe the span of the field and if it is not expanding, add Malachite and rose quartz to the heart area. Also the wild rose matches the frequency here and does the managing job of balancing and enhancing this field of energy.

Observe your client and measure the "spirit" of the client. Do they seem to not engage? Do they appear frozen in this area? Do not be surprised when the color green starts to gain momentum in this area and the flood gates open emotionally. Your client may feel a "rushing" of an emotional experience. Either releasing with crying or a re-living of a heartbreak or an episode of needing forgiveness may come up now. This is a very tender and sacred Chakra center. Work slowly and concentrate on sending pure joy to your client. Self love is a divine component of life. Support them by suggesting a heartfelt story to be written afterwards. Making time for pampering self and a valuing of self keeps this Chakra in balance to remain open and thrive in well-being.

❧ Chakra Five — Throat or Vishuddha Chakra is located at the base of the throat.

The color is sky blue and the musical note is G. This sacred Chakra rules communication through the throat, lungs, sinuses and thyroid gland. Placing the pendulum at the base of the throat, you will be able to locate the circular energy field. Have the client visualize an object made of blue, as a body of water or a clear blue sky, and send that color to the throat area. Observe the spinning of the Chakra now and you can even play the musical note G. This will be felt as a vibration tuning the throat Chakra. Adding the flower called the Desert Larkspur will support this area. Also using the crystal sodalite, which matches this Chakra frequency, will help in enhancing the ability to speak up for oneself and take responsibility for the spoken word.

Evaluate the clarity of this Chakra by including more compassion in our thoughts and words. Have we spoken or judged others with fear? Have we blamed others for our actions? Are we responsible for our spoken word? Take note of the conversation with your client so they can write more about this in detail afterwards. Chanting or singing and being impeccable with our words are ways to enhance this sacred Chakra.

☯ Chakra Six — Third Eye or Ajna Chakra is located center of forehead above the eyebrows.

The color is indigo and the musical note is A. It rules intuition through the eyes and ears. Place the pendulum over the third eye area and detect the energy field and the span of the circle. If it is turning counterclockwise, the client may be feeling confused and suffer from a lack of direction. Breathing in the color of indigo, or sometimes I use the picture of an eggplant, will help the client with sending the color to the third eye area. After three breaths, observe the energy circumference. Is it is expanding? Sometimes the energy field may be very large and reach outside the body. It is all good and operating in a being of wellness and expansion. By placing the gemstone Azurite Lapis Lazuli here and adding the flower Aster, the client may awaken this area from this moment on.

Supporting the emotional layer by asking if the client believes in unseen energy is key. Are they open to new ideas and seeing others' points of view? Are they experiencing what they see through others' beliefs or their own truth? Observe their reactions so that they can write about these experiences afterwards. Allowing oneself to reach through barriers and release preconceived ideas is one way to enhance this energy field. Meditation is key to awakening this sacred Chakra.

☯ Chakra Seven — Crown or Saharan Chakra is located at the top of the head. It is where the spiral of the hairline is imprinted.

Ask your client to now bend at the waist and sit up comfortably. The color of this Chakra is violet and the musical note is B. This area rules the Divine Connection to Source through the brain. Place the pendulum over the top of their head and detect the circle of the energy field. Is it large and spinning at a fast rate? I have found this area to be the one with the largest traceable field of energy. If it is at a standstill or moving at a very small counterclockwise direction, the client may be using cynicism in some way. Stop and have the client picture a violet flower and then breathe that color in three times and send it to the top of the head area. Using the Amethyst crystal here will add support and also the Saguaro flower that matches the frequency and promotes cleansing throughout body. Supporting the emotional layer with questions that ask the client what is the Divine and what does spirituality mean to them, can bring about a clearer perspective of this powerful Chakra.

Observe the reactions to these questions so that the client can expand further by writing about it afterwards. This universal connection of Divine energy can enhance our experiences of synchronicity and spontaneity. Enhancing this Crown Chakra with attention and focus can open the energy circuits to channeling angels, guides and loved ones.

ᚼ **There are also two Major Chakras located above the Crown Chakra directly in a line to the Divine source.**
These are activated when an upgrade to the DNA takes place. Something to look forward to! The hands, arms, elbows, knees and feet house smaller Chakras, as well. These smaller Chakra are used for healing and balancing the body's coordination.

Thank you for allowing me to take you on this journey of introduction to your sacred Chakras. Once you know how to breathe the color into the location and place your intention, you can balance your Chakras anywhere at any time.

This is dedicated to my earth Mom Margaret, my heavenly Mother Mary and all of my Chinese Masters and World Teachers that have trusted me with their ways of wisdom. In honor and appreciation, I bow to all.

My loves, family and friends hold me in an inner circle of light that provides me with strength and a safe place to blossom and grow. I wish to thank them all for their inspiration and support. May a circle of love surround you, always.

~ Kimla Dodds

April L. Dodd

APRIL L. DODD, M.A.'s unshakeable passion to create possibilities has inspired two co-authored books, *"Awaken,"* and *"Living Your Purpose,"* and her first complete authorship of *"Holding Our Breath: A Family's Journey of Love, Faith, & Healing,"* detailing her personal journey as a mom with a son and a life-threatening illness.

April is an inspirational speaker, Executive Coach, compassionate Life Coach, award-winning actress, and author. With a master's in Spiritual Psychology, April is recognized as a trusted confidant, guide, and partner in co-creating transformational possibilities with thousands of children, professionals, and life enthusiasts. April resides in Chicago, IL, creating new possibilities every day with her husband and two children.

aprildodd.com

The Door of Possibilities

"*L*eave your shoes and your ideas about yourself at the door,*" the sign read at the entry to Bob's home. It was another Tuesday evening, and as usual, we all took off our shoes, believing that we were stepping out of ourselves and into the Oneness of which this week's *Satsang* and group meditation, held promise.

I walked in to secure a spot facing my spiritual teacher of four years, placing my cushion on the floor of his tiny minimalist apartment. I sat down in my usual position - Legs crossed, back supported against the wall, hands resting on my knees, eyes closed to the nonsense of the world. A minute later, I peeked my eyes open to see Bob quietly sit down across from me, wearing the same light blue Hawaiian shirt that always made his gray hair and kind blue eyes stand out. He crossed his elderly legs mindfully but easily, and lit a few sticks of *Nagchampa* incense, sticking each one in the tiny Zen garden next to him.

Someone asked him a question. I didn't hear it. I had already settled into my personal nirvana and was working to be still with my mind.

Suddenly his words ripped through my Zen and echoed within me for years to come." *You lean in meditation, you lean in life,*" he answered the questioner casually.

Yet when I opened my eyes I could see that he was looking straight at me. I bolted my back straight away from the wall. His eyes relaxed and returned to the incense, as if he'd never said a word.

I knew exactly why he had directed that statement to me. I was leaning. I was leaning on the wall just as much as I was leaning on my dysfunctional childhood, on other people to make decisions for me, on being right in order to hide from my own sense of unworthiness. I was even leaning on my spiritual practice to make me something I was afraid I was not - Perfect.

Since that day, I have used my cushion time to reflect on and reveal many answers to the question that left me sitting on the edge of my proverbial seat -*"How is this a reflection of how I lean in my life?"*

Years later, and many question and answer erect cushion sessions later, a new spiritual teacher came into my life. His version of leaning was not quite so subtle, and neither was he. *"You're obsessing,"* Richard pointed out, in his Yoda voice. *"It's time for you to take care of yourself. Stop waiting for the world to do it for you. It won't. Why is it that you think you need validation to be alive? There is no validation. What there is - is aliveness. You are alive because you are alive. Period."*

Pulling me out of my small and distracted world with stunning awareness, he went on: *"If you're not able to hold your own weight up, then something made your weight. Something else owns you. If you want to own yourself, you've got to practice, so you can at least own that you created yourself. Build your own self-worth."*

His statement left me unsettled and unleashed a new kind of mission, a personal journey to make my life unique, powerful, and alive. To make it mine. To not hand it over to the forces that challenged me. To make the simple Jedi move to leave my ideas about myself at the door and soar into the universe of aliveness that has always been waiting for me to lean upon.

Combining the core lessons from these two teachers brought about a deep and transformational fifteen-year journey. The twinning of their teachings served as an invitation to pay attention to when I was leaning, and accept the one question into my life that would empower my every choice: *"What am I leaning on that owns me right now?"*

Leaning in life helps us feel stronger in places we feel incapable. When we feel weak, we lean on someone, some thing, and even some time to help us feel strong. This kind of support usually isn't something healthy or even wise, so it doesn't always serve us - One wall behind me and my meditation cushion instantly made me feel like a "super spiritual meditator." In reality, I leaned because I didn't want to deal with the reasons I was slouching. The *"I'm not enough"* reason is often the first place I rest when life gets hard. It's like calling upon that old friend who always takes your side with you…they may not give the best advice, but it's validating and comfortable.

Our ability to empower ourselves is about ownership. I told myself that leaning was all right because my back hurt, instead of admitting that I was trying to take the easy way out of feeling inadequate. I could avoid the harder stuff, the darker stuff, the really ugly parts of me I didn't want to own. That's often what we divine beings having a human experience do. When being human gets too hard, we bypass it all with spiritual fodder. When we feel scared, we find someone else to feed us, or blame someone or something else for not giving us the soul food we need, or pretend we are beyond needing anything at all.

But this bypass only serves to leave us stuck, and we can only be stuck if we are attached. When we are still attached to the wall of life, we give up our power to the same issues, and after we follow its lead, we find it hard to stand on our own. We have essentially given over our power to something we believe will take over where we fall short. It means that we believe the extent of our possibilities lie outside us, not within us. We have effectively (or not so effectively) handed over authority of our lives.

But in my personal obsession and mission to help myself and others lead lives of possibilities, not perfection, I've learned a lot about taking a stand and championing the inner authority that resides within. For some, that is Spirit, for others it's simply an inner knowing, and still for some it is God, the Universe, Love Itself, or simply Empowerment.

In my fifteen years as a life and executive coach, I've spent time with my clients …from corporate CEO's to pre-teens… to strengthen their inner muscle to take back their power with this one critical authority - the signature of the One Inside. We work to carry our own weight and own our own creations and experiences. The good news is that we all can do this. We all have it coded within us to do so. We just have to use our spine and stop leaning on something outside ourselves long enough to know where we stand within ourselves.

In the dictionary, empowerment is defined as 'to give authorization'. Breaking it down further, we find that *"Em"* means "to cause to be in", and *"power"* is defined as the ability to do or act. Pulling it together, empowerment, then, is *"to cause to be in the ability to do or act."* Distilled to its essence, empowerment means *to cause possibilities!*

As a parent, I've come to learn all about causing possibilities. If I give my power to my child's tantrum, those are the possibilities I have to work with. If I give my authorization to my own tantrum, I have those possibilities. If I give clearance for my dysfunctional childhood to decide my life, then I hold only the possibilities a dysfunctional childhood can offer. And if I give my authorization to Spirit, I have the possibilities Spirit offers me.

Whether as a parent, a coach, or a spiritual warrior, the question is: To what person, place, thing, time, or space am I giving authority over my life? What owns me right now? Turns out, the answer is anything I am attached to, anything I give my authority to. And so it is for us all on the journey to get off the wall to have the courage to ask ourselves what we really want to cause to be in power. What possibilities do we want to own in our lives?

When we dare to ask this question, we can reckon with all the walls in our lives. We have to acknowledge them first, and then have the courage to give our authority to something else that holds us up for our highest good, but doesn't hold us back. Then we can stop seeking to lean against the destination of perfection, and play instead with the journey of possibilities within us.

I'll walk you through it. The next time you find yourself leaning on books, seminars, coaches, and trainings for validation outside yourself, or you're attached to something else creating your sense of aliveness – from a tantrum (yours or theirs) to a title at work – and you're overwhelmed with insecurity, dependency, or unmet expectations, commit instead to the art of practice.

Here are three truths I work with every day that you can begin to practice immediately:

1. Awareness is curative.

What we are not aware of runs us. What we are aware of allows us to own the moment. When we are attached to what we think, see, feel, or believe, we have created a barrier to possibilities. Awareness, then, is barrier removal. When we can turn our attention away from what our attachment says *"outta be,"* and toward how the present moment was created, we have essentially "cured" our dis-ease with our lives, *removing our shoes and our ideas about ourselves at the door of possibility.*

2. We only ever talk about ourselves.

It *seems* like we are talking about other people, places, or things. The reality is that everything we talk about is really a clue about our own conditioning, perceptions, and current realities. When we talk, we actually reveal what's going on inside ourselves more than we will ever say about what's going on with anybody else. Practicing owning that we are talking only about ourselves gives us authority over our own circumstances rather than blame our lives on someone or something else.

3. You are where you put yourself.

Building upon awareness, what we decide or define about who we are, or what situation we seem to be in, creates our reality. If that guy moving his car in front of ours leaves us at the red light, we decide we are *"stuck at the light because some jerk cut me off."* You decided that, framed it that way, and reacted from this place. You put yourself there. You can just as easily put yourself in gratitude for the extra time you got to enjoy the scenery on the way to work. Knowing that you are where you put yourself, calls for you to see something new. Yet, more than just seeing newly, it's about seeing the truth, being at ease with it, reining in all those parts of you that want to fight or disagree or hide, pull them into love and forgiveness, hold a new possibility, and take action from here.

If you'd like to experience this yourself, join me in something I call the *Empowerment Cleanse*. Remember, the word empower means to cause to be in the ability to do or act. To be the cause of your own power means to become the owner of where you put yourself so you can create the life of possibilities you want. Depart from your power in any way - and you no longer own your own life. You are owned. That's being imprisoned, not empowered. And imprisonment is the real enemy of possibilities.

Empowerment Cleanse:

- To start the Empowerment Cleanse, first ask yourself, "*What am I most triggered by?*" If you want to know what owns you, take a look at what you're really attached to - what scares you, pushes your buttons, what you feel most righteous about.
- Make a list of these "prison wardens." Once you have identified your captors, set yourself free. Ignite your awareness. Participate in a new way with what you are now aware of. Put yourself right here, and own this *now* moment. Notice and name something new. Act on it. Without excuses. Take a stand and act on the fact that there are no holidays for owning your life and creating possibilities. Remember, you are where you put yourself.
- Sound like a "sheer" slice? A risky shift? It is. Take back your power when someone else had it, and you're sure to be disapproved of, attacked, or booted out. Rosa Parks was jailed, yet was unmistakably the owner of where she put herself on that bus. Though your aftermath may be less traumatic, you may still feel wounded. You may even want to go back to leaning on someone else for validation. Stand tall. Keep your own balance. Hold steady. See it through. Know that you always have possibilities.

In my years as a life and executive coach, I've seen many people dive into the Empowerment Cleanse, only to find themselves cleansed of much more than they ever intended. It's often even uncomfortable. It can even feel like a death. And it is. A death to the jailer who held the keys to their freedom.

Despite all that seeks to own you, you will be the one with the keys, opening the door on all that seeks to emerge through you, leaving your shoes at the entry point of newness. And in this fierce light, you will see what my teachers have taught me: that we have faith in what we're attached to. If we are attached to other people creating our possibilities, then that's all that's possible for us.

But if, instead, we are connected to the center of our being, to our Spirit, to the expanse of what's possible, then those are the possibilities that await us. Let us sacrifice our way into the sacred and become what we are connected to, thus mastering the practice of empowering our life and living on the cushion of greatness.

To Mom2 (Mom, too), you are a beautiful reflection of what is possible in life and family when we stop leaning and start living. To Paul, you are a profound model of life's victories being won on the field of love.

To the USM Class of 2015, for seeing the loving essence, your eternal support, and unconditional love. You helped me redis-cover the immensity and freedom and gift that is each and every divine moment spent choosing this life.

~April L. Dodd, M.A.

Julie Blackwood

JULIE BLACKWOOD is an intuitive, clairvoyant, clairaudient and a medium—fifth generation, teaching others how to fish, rather just giving them the fish of this thing called life. She is a living spiritual guide, sometimes referred as a shaman. She helps people pray, meditate and come more into their own higher spiritual self, cleanse chakras and raise energy vibrations, while providing protection from negative energies inside and outside of time. We all have the gift of intuition and the ability to communicate with those in the afterlife.

She was raised in Cleveland, Ohio, then went off to Miami, Florida, for several years and now lives in Denver, Colorado, with her two dogs, Chewy and Lulu for over ten years. She works in small business development in the day and helps clients on nights and weekends.

She is driven by her passion to help others who seek more than what they can see with the naked eye to grow as an individual on their spiritual path. Her background includes the studies of Political Science (BA), a Sommelier certification, level one from the International Master Courts. A PHD in the school of life. Living each day with joy and love.

julsvern11@gmail.com
Facebook page and ghost name: Psychic-Medium-A-Cameille

✥ Afterlife

When I woke this morning, I didn't know today, July 10th, was going to change my life forever. The usual is wake-up, make coffee in my pajamas and go outside to the patio with coffee in hand and eyes almost open. Soaking up the morning warm sun, while feeling the cool breeze from the night before brush up onto me. These moments are the little pleasures of life. I then dash into the shower, dress and I'm off to the farmers market with my unborn son, Alex of seven months, for tonight's dinner. I didn't plan on being pregnant until later in life, but when things happen you roll with it. I felt like his mom since day one. I love him so much.

I jump into my `79 ragtop, yellow, classic super Beetle, sunglasses on and a handful of oversized bags. These are one of many family traditions I look forward to sharing with my son, as I did for so many years my dad, brothers and sisters growing up. There's the hunt for parking, then endless indoor/outdoor aisles of goodness. First is the fresh cut flowers, then coffee, donuts, smoked bacon, cured meats, fresh cheese to homemade breads to all the veggies this summer harvested. I think it's all staged in order for the *"smell o' vision,"* making everyone want to empty their pockets of cash by noon. I ended up with six bags of treasures. On tonight's dinner menu — sun tea, Italian warm/cold salad, grilled herb-crusted chicken breasts with fresh shaved parmesan cheese, grilled French green beans, and to finish it, pressed grilled watermelon, feta and mint. Food + Drink + Family equals the best of times. It's the balance of "our lives" during the busy weekdays of running around. I'm excited for this weekend's feast with my dad and stepmom.

I get this sharp pain in my stomach, so bad I can't even see where I am driving. I hope my son isn't coming today, we have two more months to go before the due date. The next thing I know, I drove myself to the E.R. I am so confused since time and chain of events don't match up. The pain is so bad I feel like I am going to pass out. I realize I am having contractions. I am rolled in by a wheelchair and the nurse asks me who we can call. *"My dad's phone number is 216-555-5555."* The nurse shoves me some paperwork for the insurance. I tell her I can't fill it out, wait for my dad. The pain and my son are the only things I can think of, as I go in and out of consciousness.

My parents arrive. My dad starts to fill out the paperwork and all of us are rushed up to the 4th floor. The nurse asks me if they have to choose who to save first, me or my son, who I choose. What kind of question is this? BOTH!! I shout out. I pass out again and when I wake up the nurse asks me to sign the power of attorney to my dad. So I scribble my name on the dotted line. My dad answers the nurse and says my daughter first, she can always have more kids. I can't even believe what I am hearing, let alone I feel like this is a bad dream. I start to pray in my head, this isn't real, oh, God, please help us all. My parents reassure me that everything is going to be OK. I am in so much pain like an electrical wave that runs up and down my body.

So more times passes and my dad realizes it's been ten hours and gets angry and runs out to the nurses' station and asks if anyone here? *"Did you forget about us? Do something now for my daughter and grandson! Nobody is going to die on my watch today!"* I am exhausted from the pain and start to feel like I am fading, my body doesn't want to fight anymore and I hope my son is OK inside of my belly. My dad sees that look in my eyes seconds before the nurses and doctors rush in and take me to yet another room.

I pass out again from the electrical waves of pain. My parents are praying next to me and the nurses try to remove them. My dad says, *NO WAY!!* The doctors say OK, then don't get in the way. I wake up to warm surgical lamps and the room being cooled down. The nurses and doctors are hooking up machines and IV's and moving and talking really fast.

I fade again and start to dream this time — a happy place, no more pain, but love, joy and a feeling of lightness. Is this how the other side feels, no pain and this overwhelming sense of love and joy? This is so amazing! I feel like I am outside of my body now. WHOA! I can hear my parents at the same time praying next to me, my dad saying, *"Please God don't let my daughter go before me, this isn't the way it's supposed to be. Please help my grandson I haven't even meet him yet"* My step mom is saying, *"Please lord, anyone up there? Keep my family safe."*

I can see the nurses and doctors doing all kinds of things to my body. One of the nurses says to the doctor, *"call it."* The doctor says no, *"I can sense something different about this one."* I then drift into the hallway, it's so bright and white, I get a sense of cold air and love. I see my dad's mom and all of my ancestors in some kind of European voyage boat from the 1889's. With no words they ask me if I want to stay or go with them. They say I have a choice. I say, *"NO! I want to stay, I have a lot of things to do still, and this isn't how I want to go."*

The next thing, I gasp for air like being underwater too long and say, *"I'm back!"* I open my eyes and try to sit up while the nurses try to help me lay back down. The doc says, *"I knew it! I could sense something different with this one."* Everyone in the room claps, laughs and hugs each other. You see I flat-lined and the doc was trying to revive me. It seems surreal, did I cross over? WHOA! I ask my dad about my son, Alex. He looks at my step mom and then back at me with eyes filled with tears, *"He didn't make it, I am sorry."* WHAT? I can't believe it, I start to panic in disbelief and get up and get dressed. I have to get out of here!! I can't stand it, how can they NOT save both of us, that's why we go to hospitals!! My dad says, *"I chose you first, it all happened so fast."* What happened, Dad? He says, *"Alex suffocated with some blockage in his throat. They tried everything."*

I tell my parents, "let's go" and we drove off home in silence. I crawl up the stairs into my bed with my clothes still on to wake up the next day to find them having coffee in the kitchen. They both get up and hug me real tight. I pour some coffee and the doorbell rings. My dad gets the door. It's a florist with about 25 to 35 bouquets of flowers with condolence cards. *"We are so sorry for your loss, no one should have to lose their son at such a young age."*

The postal man comes by shortly thereafter and drops off three letters from the hospital. First is my medical bill for twenty thousand, and Alex's is ten thousand, and the last one is from the hospital administrative department. It says, *"We are so sorry for your loss, we are offering to pay for both bills and burial fees for your son if you do not sue the hospital or staff."* I ask my dad what to do, he says I have two choices, go to court and relive this for about six years, hope they pay for the bills and compensation of loss OR you can accept this payoff of bills and move on and start to grieve and heal. I chose the latter. My dad hugs me while trying to be strong for both of us.

The next six months I live in shock, I can't feel any emotions and food doesn't taste like anything. I ask my dad when things are going to change inside of me. He explains the brain has a chemical reaction to trauma and death, it has a cycle. You will know the next stage of grief when it comes in. I read books of the stages of grief trauma. I decide to move back to Miami, Florida, had enough of Cleveland, Ohio. I went to stay with parents until the baby was born and figure out if I wanted to stay or go back to Miami. With the passing of my son, Alex, I could not have imagined *not* being with my parents while this all happened. I guess when you follow your intuition and spiritual guides, things fall into place and make sense later, like 20/20 vision.

I return to Miami with a grade school friend to be roommates, not wanting to live alone. I can't even think of dating, let alone getting back together with Alex's dad. Miami is like endless summers, the beach full of palm trees and tropical breezes; and the city life that never ends and all of those international places to eat. The grief and hopelessness start to come in. Alex's dad lives in Miami and I was in no way ready to deal with his mess and try to keep myself together. I see go and see a mental doctor—no help there after two months and medication.

I call my dad and ask for advice. He asked me what would make me happy and I replied, something small that needed me and vice versa. I'm not ready to have another child. It still pains me to see women with their kids. He says go and get a puppy at some puppy dog store and don't worry about the price, write a check and I will put money in your bank account later today. So I get into my new jeep and look for a puppy store. I walk in and see about forty dogs and I walk around I see this pug who keeps jumping up and down and looking at me! That's it, he is mine!

I take him to the vet's the next day and the vet tells me he is young and not ready to be weaned from his mommy, he has separation anxiety. He said I have some choices, return him, get another or make a bond with him using a human baby front-facing backpack and let him bond heart to heart. I chose the latter. This little guy needed me as much as I needed him!! We are a perfectly broken match. The healing process began, but not before anger and denial. The seven stages grief all have to play out before the healing starts, otherwise you stay stuck in the pain and can't move on with your life ...

I started slowly to feel some light at the end of the tunnel, renewal of self. I started to pray and meditate again. I started to read anything I could get my hands on how to connect to the other side. I know Alex has to be with my grandparents. I remember seeing my grandpa after he passed when I was nine. He came by to say goodbye and tell me he is ok and no crying. He will watch over me.

The meditation and prayers start to pay off—I sense my grandma and the smell of fresh lilacs. She says, *"You need to tell your dad to take care of his little brother, this was my final wish."* I call my dad and tell him this and he is not surprised, but relieved to hear she came by, and that I can connect with the other side. He started to look for my uncle and found him shortly thereafter. I am a 5th generation intuitive, clairvoyant, clairaudient and medium, but was blocked by the pain. I then asked my grandma about my son, Alex, and the energy faded.

The next several weeks all kinds of spirits start to come in like never before. I felt like my life had a new purpose, helping people with loss of loved ones and teaching them it's not *goodbye,* but rather *see you later.* I continue to learn about clearing your chakras, raising your vibrations and protection of negative energies, and how to connect to the other side and be grounded at the same time. I was studying all kinds of religions and metaphysical practices, like Kabbalah for the Jewish faith and the saints with Catholicism, in order to become a professional guide and help those who need the help, heal faster and know that the other side is real. Not to just give messages, but to help heal, grow and walk away with a skill set of being able to take care of self, others and reconnect yourself with loved ones from the afterlife. Since the Egyptian times people have tried all kinds of mantras, prayers and symbols to connect to the afterlife.

I have two dogs and will always have them around me, with a total of five dogs since that day so many years ago, and the one and only son, Alex, who watches over me and helps guide me with my spiritual guides, angels and ancestors. I help people over the phone and in person. I am humbled, blessed and a peaceful warrior of life on this side. I live in the space of eternal love, joy and gratitude in every moment knowing tomorrow is another day.

Dedicated to all the people, animals and travels that have made this journey what it is. Would not have it any other way. I stand free of all life experiences and rejoice and bask in the love of all those who I love near and far.

I am blessed to have my spirit guides, guardian angels and loved ones, who have crossed over into the afterlife, watching down on me. I continue to grow and help others. I wish special thanks to my dad Ray and my step mom Louella for always being there and being the loves of my life. I couldn't be who I am without them.

To some of my dearest friends/sisters Katina, Jennetta, Shelly and Lill, you are like the glue in this thing called life — without you all I couldn't find courage in darkness and light. But most of all, you all know the song in my heart and sing it back to me when I've have forgotten how it goes.

Thank you for the opportunity to share a slice of my life with you all. Here is to many more years of fun and learning. CHEERS TO LIFE AND THE AFTERLIFE.

~ Julie Blackwood

Hope Lamb

HOPE LAMB is Founder and CFO of Lambs' Nursery, Inc., Flowerscape Solutions Inc., and The Institute of Positive Living.

She resides in Clermont, Florida, with her husband Tom Lamb and their Australian Terrier, Eddie Bear.

HopeLamb@aol.com

The Journey

The "possibility" of triumph over adversity exists within the human spirit. We feel empowered when we cultivate a mindset of possibilities and opportunities. Intellectually, we know that the thoughts that occupy our minds determine the starting point from which our dreams are chiseled into reality. Our words, our thoughts and our actions directly and powerfully impact our destiny. So, we carefully monitor our speech and consciousness, while mentally rehearsing only the best outcome possible, right? Wrong! It should be true, but it isn't always.

Too often, we feel blindsided by an illness, personal loss, economic setback, or a troubled relationship. Suddenly, we slip into an abyss of self-indulgence in the form of disappointment, discouragement, pity and blame. We begin to feel powerless as negative thoughts clutter our thinking, obscuring our focus and resiliency. Language filled with bitterness and anger becomes the norm, anxiety replaces clarity, and energy is depleted. This is often followed with the words, *"I feel depressed."* It's when we reach this point of anguish and desolation that the journey towards empowerment may seem out of reach.

The good news is that empowerment *is* within reach. It may start with the stripped-down version of believing in yourself—called hope. By removing the current mental canvas painted with self-destructive shapes of doubt and images of pessimism, we make room for a new positive picture to emerge. Starting with a clean canvas, we can reclaim our thoughts and visualize the affirmative mental picture we want for our life.

Songs, people, places, books and even movies can jumpstart the human spirit toward empowerment. In the 1976 award-winning movie *Rocky*, the fictional character Rocky Balboa inspired thousands. In that rousing scene, etched in the minds of generations of viewers, the underdog boxer Rocky sprints up the stone steps of the Philadelphia Museum of Art to the song "Gonna Fly Now" which became known as "The Rocky Theme." It was an iconic moment for the disempowered to feel empowered. The character, the song, and the place continue to empower even today, as visitors make their way to Philadelphia to tackle the famous steps.

The path to empowerment is a personal journey of choices. Each step requires a conscious decision to develop a new awareness of our thoughts and actions.

So if you're ready, come with me, and let the adventure on the road to empowerment begin:

∽ **What is your passion? What makes your heart race with excitement?** Are you driven to explore the world, write a book, or launch your own cooking blog? Maybe it's changing government policy through the political process, or learning a new sport or activity. Maybe it's building a robust relationship with a spouse, a family member, co-workers, or friends. Our dreams and desires come alive with passion.

∽ **For some, following their *passion* means a neatly-outlined future filled with goals and objectives.** For others, passion is ignited by affirmations and visualizations leading the way to life's purpose. Some find passion through a freestyle, spontaneous approach to life. And of course there are many hybrids of the above, all leading to the self-discovery of passion. Passion will quiet fears and push through obstacles, overcoming adversities to complete the chosen journey. So whatever path you choose, empower it with passion and enthusiasm.

∽ **Music is empowering and can define a culture or inspire a heart.** It can initiate the pulsing vibration of hope and nourish the spirit. Music can evoke an emotional response that can be transformed into positive action or soothe the soul. Regardless of the desire, music is a power we often ignore or underestimate. Life's rewards for choosing a theme song, or a selection of songs to start your day, are immeasurable. Our music can serve as a prelude to our goals, the symphony for our work, the fight song for our crusades, the crescendo for our triumphs, and an encore to a dream realized. It's the quickest, easiest, and most enjoyable way to empower your life. So *zippity doo dah!* What are you waiting for? Let's hear your song!

∽ **Now let's add a little dance to our song to offset the "sitting disease."** It's time to empower our life by movement. Rapid advancements in technology have changed the way we communicate, enter personal relationships and spend our free time. Through computers and phones we have reconnected with friends, created and sustained social networks, all while growing businesses through the click of a mouse. The drawback of all this amusement is the proliferation of a sedentary lifestyle which can contribute to ill health and even death. There are physical activities available for every shape, size, age, and skill level—whether it's biking, swimming, Tai chi, yoga, or a walk in the park. Every activity is a movement in the right direction.

☙ **While we are singing and dancing our way to empowerment, we must take care to be *deliberately aware.*** We eat food we don't taste. We suddenly realize we've arrived some place other than our planned destination (and don't remember how we got there). We left our keys, purse, phone, and missed an appointment. We stumbled, we fell, and even broke a toe. What were we thinking, or were we even thinking at all? Chances are your mind checked out, or at least took a leave of absence. So before you find your keys locked in your car again, maybe it's time to check-in and become aware of the only time you really have, and that's ***this*** moment. There are many ways to be mindful, aware and present.

The empowering moment starts by developing mindful skills like savoring our food, slowly, and deliberately. It can be built by simply taking deep breaths, while being aware of each inhale and exhale. We can enhance our personal inter- actions by really listening to what others are saying to us, truly being engaged in the conversation. By committing to being mindful, we can learn to be present in our life. The practice of being present, this mindfulness, is an integral component of the Buddhist tradition and is taught through meditation. Mindfulness has become the subject of books, been accepted by mainstream psychologists and even been included in corporate retreats. Whether you create a daily habit of awareness, or commit to a lifelong study of mindfulness, you will feel distractions melt away and be empowered in the moment.

☙ **Remember the first time you stuck your toes in beach sand or used a walking stick to climb a hill?** When was the last time you picked a wildflower, planted a tree or hiked through a forest? Have you seen a dolphin leap, a leopard give chase, an eagle take flight, or deer graze in a field? It's time. Somewhere near you there's a local, state or national park. Opportunities await you to stroll along a seashore or saunter through the wilderness, to fall in love with the smallest of creatures, and the most fierce. Nature is an awesome gift of life, embrace it. Don't wait, the time is now!

So next time you wish you had said *no* instead of *yes*; when you yell, *"Help! I'm stressed out! What to do, what to do,"* while running your fingers through your hair (most of us have been there a time or two); when the *shoulda, woulda, coulda's* take over and you feel confused, boxed in, and frightened, choose to focus on a person, place, experience, or thing that brings you joy and happiness. Turn on or mentally tune into your favorite song, and feel the music as you sway or dance around the room. Think only of this moment, your breath, the movement, the music, and the love you feel inside for being alive. Remember your path is forever changing and you're changing with each step. How you go down that path is your choice — choose hope, awareness, enthusiasm, and joy as the companions for your life's journey.

Along the way you may stumble and fall, but the wisdom and knowledge you have accumulated through living a positive, empowered life will support you throughout your journey of personal growth. Hallelujah!

Dedicated in love and gratitude to Tom Lamb, Gloria and Ed Wildes, Buzz Lamb, Tina Gaudio, Nicole Martin, and Hal Turville

Thanks to my sister Cathy Mayberry for her support, encouragement, feedback, proofreading skills and for enthusiastically supporting my journey into the world of writing.

~ Hope Lamb

Bibliography

Andrews, Ted. (2012) Animal Speak: The Spiritual and Magical Powers of Creatures Great and Small. Woodbury, MN: Llwellyn Publications.

Beckwith, Michael Bernard. Life Visioning Process"

Benson, Herbert. (1975). Relaxation Response. New York, NY. Harper Torch

Bloomfield, Harold. 1985 Making Peace With Your Parents. New York: Ballantine Books.

Braden G. The Divine Matrix: Bridging Time, Space, Miracles, and Belief. Hay House Inc, 2008

Braschi, Gianluigi (Producer), and Benigni, Robert (Director). (20 Dec. 1997). *Life is Beautiful* [Motion Picture]. Italy: Miramax Films.

Byrne R. The Secret. Atria: Beyond Words Publishing, 2006

Carroll L. Alice's Adventures in Wonderland. Macmillan, London, 1865

Chopra, Deepak, M.D. (1990.)
Success Principles: How to Get from Where You Are to Where You Want to Be.
New York, NY: Collins

Choquette, Sonia.
Answer Is Simple… Love yourself, Live your Spirit
Hay House

Cohen, Alan.
"Create A Masterpiece; When mistakes turn into miracles."
healyourlife.com. N.p., 31 Dec. 2010. Web. 13 Mar. 2011.

Covey, Stephen R. (1989).
The Seven Habits of Highly Effective People. New York: Simon & Schuster.

Crane, Patricia J. (2002.)
Ordering From the Cosmic Kitchen:
Essential Guide to Powerful, Nourishing Affirmations.
Bonsall, CA. Crane's Nest.

Dalconzo, Joseph Hu (2002)
Self-mastery: A journey home to your… Self!
Forked River, NJ. Holistic Learning Centers

Dyer W Dr. The Power of Intention. Hay House Inc, 2005

Emote, Masaru. 2004. The Hidden Messages in Water. Oregon: Beyond Words
Publishing

Foundation for Inner Peace. A Course in Miracles. 2008

Fox, Emmet — "The Mental Equivalent: The Secret of Demonstration"
Publisher: Merchant Books

Frankl, Viktor E. (1959). Man's Search for Meaning. Cutchogue, NY: Buccaneer
Books, Inc.

Franklin, Benjamin. (1996). Philip Smith (Ed.) The Autobiography of Benjamin
Franklin. Mineola, NY: Dover Publications, Inc.

Frederickson, Barbara L. "The Role of Positive Emotions in Positive Psychology: The
broaden-and-build theory of positive emotions". American Psychologist, vol. 56(3),
March 2001, p. 218-226.

Gaiwan, Shakti. Creative Visualization.
New World Library, Nataraj; 25th anniversary edition, September 19, 2002

Gilbert, Daniel. (2005).
Stumbling on Happiness.
New York, NY. Vintage

Gilligan, Stephen. (1997).
Courage to Love: Principles and
Practices of Self-Relations Psychotherapy.
New York, NY. W.W. Norton &Company

Goleman, Daniel. (1995).
Emotional Intelligence: Why it can matter more than IQ. New York,
NY: Bantam Dell

Grant, Dr. Toni — Being a Woman: Fulfilling Your Femininity and Finding Love
Publisher: Random House; 1st edition (February 12, 1988)

Hay, Louise L.
All is Well By Louise Hay with Mona Lisa Schulz.
(1982.) Heal Your Body. Carlsbad, CA. Hay House, Inc.
(1984.) You Can Heal Your Life. Carlsbad, CA. Hay House, Inc.
(2002.) You Can Heal Your Life Companion Book. Carlsbad, CA. Hay
House, Inc.
(1991.) Power Is Within You. Carlsbad, CA. Hay House, Inc.

Hay L. Official Website. http://www.hayhouse.com and http://www.louisehay.
com/about/
Hay House Wisdom Community. http://www.hayhouse.co.uk/wisdom/
HYL Training. http://www.healyourlifetraining.com/teacher-training/

Heer D. Access Consciousness. http://www.accessconsciousness.com

Hicks E & J. Ask and It Is Given: Learning to Manifest Your Desires. Hay
House Inc, 2004

"Holiday Stress." *The National Child Traumatic Stress Network*. Center for
Mental Health Services. 12/2014. NCTSN jointly coordinated by UCLA and
Duke University.19August2015. http://nctsnet.org/resources/public-awareness/
holiday-stress.html>

Holmes, Ernest — "The Science of Mind: The Complete Edition"
Publisher: Tarcher; Box Leather Deluxe edition

I Can Conference. http://www.hayhouse.co.uk/lectures-events/event-tours

"Inspirational Quotations by Alan Cohen."
alancohen.com. N.p., n.d. Web. 13 Mar. 2011.

"It's The Most Wonderful Time of The Year." *MetroLyrics*. 2015. CBS Interactive, Inc. 19 August 2015. <http://metrolyrics.com/its-the-most-wonderful-time-of-the-year-lyrics-andy-williams.html>

Jeffers, Susan — Feel the Fear and Do It Anyway
Publisher: Ballantine Books

Kagan A. The Afterlife of Billy Fingers. Hampton Roads Inc, 2013

King, Serge Kahili. (2008) Huna: Ancient Hawaiian Secrets for Modern Living. New York, NY. Atria Books, A Division of Simon & Schuster, Inc.

King, Serge Kahili. (1985) Mastering Your Hidden Self: A Guide to the Huna Way. Wheaton, IL. Quest Books, Theosophical Publishing House.

Kyron. Kryon Book VII: Letters from Home. Kyron Writings, 2013

Landrum, Gene. (2005).
Superman Syndrome: You Are What You Believe.
Lincoln, NE. iUniverse

Leaf, Caroline. 2007. Who Switched Off My Brain? South Africa: Switch On Your Brain Organization (Ltd).

Lesser, Elizabeth.
Broken Open.
N.p.: Random House, 2005. Print

Linn D. The Secret Language of Signs: How to Interpret the Coincidences and Symbols of Life. Ballantine Book Publishing, NY, 1996

Lipton, Bruce H., Ph.D. (2005.)
Biology of Belief: Unleashing the Power of Consciousness,
Matter & Miracles. Carlsbad, CA.
Hay House, Inc.194

Mandino, Og. (1977)
The Greatest Miracle in the World.
New York,NY: Bantam Books.

Millman, Dan.
Life You Were Born To Live. Tiburon, CA:
HJ Kramer Inc, 1993. Print.

Moat, Richard. Moativational Medicine ™

Morain , Padraig O
Mindfulness on the Go

Morrissey, Mary. N.p.: n.p., 2009
Life Solutions at Work, LLC. Print.

Neill, Michael. (2006).
You Can Have What You Want:
Proven Strategies for Inner and Outer Success.
Hay House

Ozwald, Jafree. (2013) Affirmations to Manifest an Awakened, Empowered and
Abundant Life! Enlightened Beings International

Patanjali. (1953). How To Know God: The Yoga Aphorisms of Patanjali. Trans. Swami
Prabhavanand with Christopher Isherwood. Hollywood: Vedanta Press.

Pennabaker, James W. (1997). Opening Up: The Healing Power of Expressing
Emotions. New York, NY: The Guilford Press.

Pert, Candace B. 1997. Molecules of Emotion New York: Scribner.
Schucman, Helen—A Course in Miracles: Only Complete Edition
Publisher: Foundation for Inner Peace

Redfield J. The Celestine Vision. Warner Books, 1998

Reivich, Karen and Andrew Shatte. (2002). The Resilience Factor: 7 Keys to Finding Your Inner Strength and Overcoming Life's Hurdles. New York: Broadway Books.

Scovel Shinn, Florence
The Game of Life

Storlie, Jean. "Rocks, Pebbles, Sand: A Story-bite About the Important Things in Life." *Storlietelling*. 7 August 2013. 23 August 2015. <http://storlietelling.com/2013/08/07/rocks-pebbles-sand-a-story-bite-about-the-important-things-in-life.html>

Tolle, Eckhart. (1999.)
Power of Now: A Guide to Spiritual Enlightenment. Novato, CA.
New World Library.
A New Earth: awakening to Your Life's Purpose.
N.p.: Plume, 2008. Print.

Trismegistus, Hermes— "The Kybalion: A Study of The Hermetic Philosophy of Ancient Egypt and Greece by Three Initiates"
Publisher: The Yogi Publication Society Masonic Temple— An unabridged edition of the 1908 printing

Truman, Karol.
Feelings Buried Alive Never Die. Las Vegas, NV:
Olympus Distributing, 1991. Print.

Twyman J. Emissary of Light. Findhorn Press, Scotland, 2007

Virtue, Doreen
Assertiveness for Earth Angels: How to Be
Loving Instead of "Too Nice"
Hay House, Inc., November 4, 2014

Virtue D PH.D, The Lightworker's Way. Hay House Inc, 1997

Vitale J & Ihaleakala Hew Len. Zero Limits: The Secret Hawaiian System for Wealth, Health, Peace, and More. John Wiley & Sons, Inc, Hoboken, New Jersey, 2007

Weiss B Dr. Many Lives, Many Masters. Piatkus, GB, 1994

Williamson, Marianne. (2009).
Age of Miracles: Embracing the New Midlife.
Carlsbad, CA. Hay House

Williamson, Marianne. (1993) A Return to Love: Reflections on the Principles of A Course in Miracles. New York, NY. Harper Collins.

Wolinsky, Stephen. (1991).
Trances People Live:
Healing Approaches In Quantum Psychology.
Falls Village, CT. Bramble Company

Yogananda, Paramahansa
Autobiography of a Yogi

A Call For Authors

Most people have a story that needs to be shared. Could you be one of the contributing authors to be featured in an upcoming compilation book? As a result of becoming a Published Author, some of the Visionary Insight Press contributors are now writing and speaking around the world.

Visionary Insight Press is leading the industry in compilation book publishing and represent some of today's most inspirational teachers, healers and spiritual leaders.

Their commitment is to assist this planet we call "home" to be a place of kindness, peace and love. One of the ways they fulfill this promise is by assisting others with the sharing of their inspiring stories and words of wisdom.

They look forward to hearing from you.

Please visit

www.visionaryinsightpress.com

CPSIA information can be obtained at www.ICGtesting.com
Printed in the USA
LVOW11s0100271015

459848LV00002B/36/P